DREAM

DESTINATIONS OF EUROPE

ABOUT THIS BOOK

Spectacular volcano landscapes, the longest and deepest fjords in the world, pristine national parks, mysterious monuments from the Stone Age, windswept coastlines, formidable cathedrals, splendid castles and palaces, serene monasteries, gentle lakes and rivers, cosmopolitan cities, romantic vineyard towns, the largest and most exciting museums in the world, medieval hamlets, dark forests and rugged mountains, idyllic fishing villages, ancient temples, island paradises in the Mediterranean…Europe!

This book presents the most fascinating destinations on the "old" continent, many of which are protected UNESCO World Heritage Sites. Breathtaking images take you to paradisical locations that everyone should have the pleasure of seeing at least once. In addition to the absolute must-see sights such as Venice, London or Paris, you will see landscapes and places that are simply begging to be discovered in person. The Island of Skye in Scotland, the romantic Duero Valley in Spain… these are both dream destinations that are all worth a visit.

Read, look, dream…travel.

We wish you an exciting journey…

The Publisher

Contents

Preceding pages: The photographs on the preceding pages show a typical scene from Tuscany – "the quintessence" according to Pope Boniface VIII – as well as an aerial photograph of Vatnajökull, Iceland's largest glacier.

Contents

Tower Bridge, built between 1886 and 1894, is one of London's most distinctive landmarks. It links the City of London on the Thames north bank with the London Borough of Southwark on the south bank. The two towers are 65 m (213 ft) tall, and opening the bascule bridge takes a mere one and a half minutes.

Contents

Contents

Contents

Santorini, the southernmost of the Cyclades group, is the dream of Greek island life per se. The waves of the Aegean Sea wash the shores of the island, born from fire and ash and clinging to the rim of a volcanic crater. At night, it is spanned by an breathtakingly beautiful starry sky.

Contents

Iceland

GEYSIR

Location: South-west Iceland
Best time to travel: mid-April to September
www.visiticeland.com

Iceland was formed by dramatic changes in the Earth's crust: as the Eurasian and North American continental plates drifted apart, magma rose up and cooled to create an island whose landscape is rich in glaciers, volcanoes, geysirs and mighty fields of lava, sand, and gravel. Geysir is the first geyser known to scholarship and the earliest geyser known to Europeans.

Every five to ten minutes, Strokkur ("Butter barrel"), a hot-water spring in the Geysir area of thermal activity (after which all other geo-thermal springs are named), ejects a boiling column of water up to 25 m (80 feet) into the air.

GULLFOSS

Location: South-west Iceland
Best time to travel: mid-April to September
www.world-of-waterfalls.com
www.visiticeland.com

Over the course of the last 10,000 years, the Hvítá, a glacial river, has carved out a canyon 35 m (115 ft) deep and some 2.5 km (1.5 mi) long. The flow rate of the river averages 109 cu m/s (3,850 cu ft/s) but after the spring thaw this can rise to 2,000 cu m/s (70,600 cu ft/s). At Gullfoss, the Hvítá river, which rises beneath the Langjökull glacier, plunges into a crevice 32 m (105 ft) deep. As one first approaches the falls, the crevice is obscured from view, so that it appears that a mighty river simply vanishes into the earth.

The "Golden Waterfall" is one of Iceland's most beautiful.

HRAUNFOSSAR

Location: West Iceland
Best time to travel: mid-April to September
www.goiceland.org
www.visiticeland.com

Despite its name, only ten percent of this volcanic island in the North Sea is actually covered in ice, although Vatnajökull is the largest

glacier in Europe. Besides the glaciers, the island has more than 200 volcanoes, a multitude of geysirs and mighty fields of lava, sand, and gravel, making up a vast and sparse landscape of which more than two-thirds is uninhabitable. Some 700 hot springs make it possible for the entire population to be supplied with geo-thermal heating. Another

common feature consists of the many waterfalls. The Hvitá, a glacial river rising in Vatnajökull, sinks away in part into a lava field before continuing its course underwater as it reaches impervious rock strata. The river has eroded away the lava field near Húsafell, uncovering the layer of rock which halts the water's

progress, and the water which has permeated its way upstream reappears as if from nowhere to form hundreds of waterfalls.

The waterfalls on the Hvitá River near Húsafell are called "Hraunfossar" as they seem to spring directly from the lava (Icelandic: *hraun*).

Iceland

THINGVELLIR

Location: South-west Iceland
Best time to travel: mid-April to September
www.thingvellir.is

The Germanic tribes called the designated place in the open air where freemen assembled to debate the "Thing". The Thingvellir (literally, the "valley of the Thing") is the official place where Iceland's freemen have assembled and read out law since 930, the time when land grabs ceased in Iceland and the Icelandic state was established. The Althing, which sat for two weeks, is the oldest democratic body in the world. Each current law was read out by a "law speaker" and improvements or additions affecting the entire population were discussed; one of the most important was the adoption of Christianity in the year 1000. All major events in the history of Iceland have taken place at Thingvellir. From the 17th century onwards, Iceland experienced a series of plagues and natural catastrophes which hastened its decline and made it completely dependent on Denmark. The last Althing was held in 1798. Thingvellir nonetheless retained its almost mythical importance, and in 1944 the republic was declared here, signalling Iceland's complete independence. Thingvellir, which was declared a national park in 1928, is located on Iceland's expansion zone, directly above a geological rift valley. The Althing was held in the valley of Almannagjá ("Everyman's Valley") about 5 km (3 mi) to the west, whose steep walls amplified speeches without producing an intrusive echo.

The Thingvellir widens in places to form a valley covered with Arctic tundra. The Öxará river, which rises at the Botnssúlur volcano, flows through the national park.

KRAFLA

Location: North Iceland
Best time to travel: May to
mid-September
www.goiceland.org
www.visiticeland.com

Krafla is the name given to an area
of volcanic activity near Myvatn
which lies right on the junction
of the slowly diverging Eurasian and
North American continental plates.
The gap created by this continental
drift is continually being filled with
lava, which bubbles up and causes
the region's great variety of volcanic
activity. Such activity is still centered
on Krafla's main crater even though
the name, which once included only
the volcanic mountain, is now ap-
plied to the entire region.

Believed for almost 2,000 years
to be extinct, Krafla suddenly ex-
ploded to life at the beginning of the
18th century, smothering the region
under a thick layer of lava and ash.
What remained was a sparkling,
emerald-green crater lake measuring
320 m (1,050 ft) across at its widest
point. Krafla erupted again in 1975,
this time continuing for almost a
decade. Its sulfur mud pots, which
have been bubbling and steaming
ever since, are now a popular tourist
attraction, as well as the most visible
icon of Iceland's continuing volcanic
activity known as the famous "Krafla
fires".

Situated just to the
north-east of Myvatn, the
countryside around Krafla, an
active, 818-m (2,684-ft) volcano,
is tectonically one of the least
stable regions in Iceland.
Instead of the usual conical
form, the main crater is a
flattened depression riven
with fissures aligned along a
north–south axis, beneath
which a giant magma
chamber lurks.

Iceland

GODAFOSS

Location: North Iceland
Best time to travel: May to September
www.world-of-waterfalls.com

Godafoss owes its name ("Waterfall of the Gods") to Thorgeir, the speaker of the Althing (Iceland's parliament) who converted to Christianity in the year 1000 (along with the rest of the island) and is said to have thrown the statues of the former pagan gods into the river. The Icelanders' decision was also a pragmatic one: King Olaf of Norway had threatened to cut off their supplies of timber, a move that would have meant the end of Iceland's vital shipbuilding industry.

Despite its modest height, the width and volume of the Godafoss make it one of the most impressive waterfalls in Iceland.

DETTIFOSS

Location: North Iceland
Best time to travel: May to September
www.dettifoss.is

Dettifoss is by some margin the most powerful waterfall in Europe. This exceptional status is due neither to its height of 44 m (144 ft) nor its width of 100 m (328 ft); it is because of the sheer volume of water which plunges into the depths below. At its greatest, the flow approaches 1,500 cu m/s (53,000 cu ft/s) and the average flow is still an impressive 193 cu m/s (6,800 cu ft/s).

A path connecting all three waterfalls offers fantastic views of the 10-m (33-ft) high Selfoss, which lies to one side of the Dettifoss, and the approximately 27-m (89-ft) high Hafragilsfoss, which lies to the other.

MYVATN

Location: North Iceland
Best time to travel: May to
September
www.myv.is
www.myvatn.is

"Mosquito Lake", which lies roughly 30 km (17 mi) east of Godafoss,
was formed by the escaping lava
from two volcanic eruptions about

2,000 and 3,500 years ago respectively. The lake, which today covers
an overall area of 37 sq km (14 sq
mi), is only 4 to 5 m (13 to 16 ft)
deep and is constantly fed by hot
springs. A great variety of moss,
grasses, ferns, herbs, and birches
grow along the lakeshore and on its
numerous islands. Huge clouds of
mosquitoes gather over the rapidly

warming waters during the summer
months, and along with the insect
larvae in the water, these provide
nutrition for bountiful fish stocks as
well as the countless waterfowl
which nest in the network of bays.
Myvatn is considered to be one of
Iceland's most spectacular landscapes because of its location in a
zone of extreme volcanic activity.

Strolling along the well-marked
footpaths you will see an array of
unusual lava formations.

**The best view of the
pseudocraters in and around
Mývatn is to be had from the
circular wall of the Hverfjall
eruption crater, an ash cone
about 170 m (560 ft) high.**

Iceland

VATNAJÖKULL

Location: South-east Iceland
Best time to travel: June–August
www.vatnajökull.is

Covering a vast area of roughly 12,000 sq km (4,632 sq mi), this national park has a variety of attractions: moors, swamps, birch groves, scree fields, and sandy terrain. The park is set against the magnificent backdrop of Vatnajökull ("water glacier"), which contains a larger volume of ice than all the glaciers in the Alps combined. The integration of the Skaftafell and Jökulsárgljúfur National Parks into the protected area in June 2008, made this the largest national park in Europe.

The mighty ice sheet of Vatnajökull, a giant among Europe's glaciers, can reach a thickness of up to 1,000 m (3,280 ft). It is the largest glacier mass in Europe.

VÍK I MYRDAL

Location: South-east Iceland
Best time to travel: mid-April to September
www.goiceland.org
www.visiticeland.com

Vík I Myrdal is the southernmost settlement on the island and the only coastal town to have no port. The ring road which encircles the entire country leads from here to Dyrhólaey, a promontory forming the southernmost point of the island. Many common species of North Atlantic waterfowl occupy different levels of the cliffs: at the top there are puffins, which dig burrows in the turf, and kittiwakes and fulmars inhabit the rocky ledges below.

Legend has it that the rock formations on the beautiful lava beaches of Vík I Myrdal are petrified trolls.

Iceland

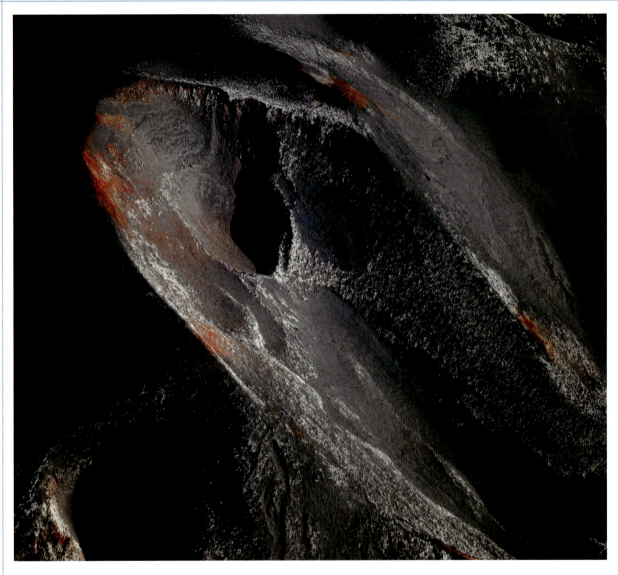

HEKLA

Location: South Iceland
Best time to visit: June–August
www.volcano.si.edu
www.visiticeland.com

Hekla rises to 1,491 m (4,892 ft) high and is certainly Iceland's most famous volcano. It is part of the Heklugjá system of fissures, which stretches for some 40 km (25 mi) on a north-east to south-west axis. Over the millennia, a 7-km (4-mi) long volcanic fissure has grown into a majestic central volcanic cone. To be more precise, Hekla represents a transitional form between a fissure and a stratovolcano (from the Latin *stratum*, "layer"). The information center at Leirubakki has all kinds of fascinating information about the volcanic ridge, which was considered a symbol of evil in the Middle Ages and to some seemed reminiscent of a dragon's back. Old travelogues often describe the Hekla volcano as the "gates to hell", behind which the screams of lost souls could be heard. In more recent times scientific dating of the ash layers (tephrochronology) has established that the Hekla volcano has erupted more than a hundred times in five great cycles.

Hekla's cycles of volcanic activity were punctuated with peaceful periods lasting centuries, after which there was an especially violent eruption.

SKÓGAFOSS

Location: South Iceland
Best time to travel:
April–September
www.skogasafn.is
www.goiceland.org
www.visiticeland.com

The basin of the Skógar river, which crosses the island's ring road south-east of majestic Mydalsjökull, is worth seeing for two reasons: Skógafoss, the 63-m (207-ft) high and 25-m (82-ft) wide waterfall surrounded by meadows, and the folklore museum in Skógar. Unlike many other waterfalls, it is possible to view Skógafoss both from the bottom and the lip.

The first settlers at Skógar are said to have hidden a treasure chest behind the waterfall; to this day, there are said to be glimmers of gold behind the water when the sun shines.

SELJALANDS-FOSS

Location: South Iceland
Best time to travel:
April–September
www.goiceland.org
www.visiticeland.com

Located on the island's ring road between Hvolsvöllur and Skógar, the Seljalandsfoss waterfall is one of the most picturesque in Iceland. Just before its confluence with the Markarfljót, the Seljalandsá river plunges into a chasm some 66 m (217 ft) deep. The waterfall is located in the south-western corner of Eyjafjallajökull, Iceland's sixth-largest glacier; the volcano of the same name which lies beneath it hit the headlines in March 2010.

Standing behind Seljalandsfloss's tumbling masses of water is a unique experience.

Norway

STAVANGER

Location: South Norway
Best time to travel: April–October
www.regionstavanger.com
www.visitnorway.com

Stavanger, on the Boknafjord, is the capital of the county of Rogaland. Around the year 872, King Harald Fairhair united the still disparate parts of the Norwegian realm here, an event commemorated by Viking sword sculptures in the Hafrsfjord. Begun in 1125, the Romanesque cathedral is the best-preserved religious stone building from the Middle Ages in Norway. Stavanger is now a center for the oil and natural gas industries.

Stavanger's Old Town is one of the world's largest districts to consist entirely of wooden buildings (far right; right, a view of Stavanger's marina).

LYSEFJORD

Location: South Norway
Best time to travel: April–October
www.lysefjordeninfo.no

East of Stavanger, the Lysefjord cuts through roughly 40 km (25 mi) of the vast Ryfylkeheiene mountain region. Thrills are guaranteed, from the famous boulder wedged into a crevasse at Kjerag to the sheer cliffs of the Prekestolen ("Preacher's Pulpit"). If, however, you prefer to admire the scenery from sea level, take the car ferry through the Lysefjord.

Right: The cliffs at Kjerag offer a sheer drop of 1,000 m (3,280 ft) to the Lysefjord below. The rocky plateau of the Prekestolen is only 25 m (82 ft) square, but its walls drop away vertically for 600m (1,970 ft) on three sides; the view across the Lysefjord to the mountains of Ryfylke is magnificent.

Norway

HARDANGER-FJORD

Location: South-west Norway
Best time to travel: April–October
www.hardangerfjord.com

A grand 150 km (93 mi) in length, Hardangerfjord is considered to be the king of the fjords. Breaking up into a network of tributary fjords, it stretches from the islands of the south-west to the foot of the Hardangervidda, the largest mountain plateau in northern Europe, and a national park. The north-eastern arms of the fjord surround the Folgefonna Peninsula, whose glaciated reaches have also been protected as a national park.

Glaciers on the upper slopes, Riviera sun-traps below (right: island homes in the fjord): Hardanger boasts some of the most picturesque scenery to be found in Norway.

ÅLESUND

Location: West Norway
Best time to travel: April–October
www.visitalesund-geiranger.com
www.alesund.kommune.no

Ålesund, the largest town in the Sunnmøre region and Norway's largest fishing port, lies among the islands at the entrance to Storfjord. The unbroken art nouveau skyline of its Old Town is unique in Norway. The Ålesund Maritime Museum offers a good overview of the seafaring history of this coastal town, which burnt down in 1904 but was rebuilt within three years. The town's speciality, which has been exported for hundreds of years, is *klippfisk*: cod salted and left to dry by the fishermen on the rocks (*klippe*) near the coast, hence the name. The smaller islands just off the coast protect the town and port

HARDANGER-VIDDA

Location: West Norway
Best time to travel: April–October
www.hardangervidda.org

Hardangervidda is the largest mountain plateau in northern Europe, and 3,422 sq km (1,321 sq mi) of its area have been a national park since 1981. To the west, the uplands halt at a 1,000-m (3,280-ft) cliff which descends to the Sørfjord, but to the east they ease into the Østlandet valleys. The moors of this gneiss and granite plateau are home to some of the largest herds of wild reindeer in Europe. The ice and snow does not melt until the summer, although Sandfloeggi, the highest mountain, which is partially glaciated, is only 1,719 m (5,640 ft) high.

The view from the cliffs at Trolltunga across Ringedalsvatnet Lake is not for vertigo sufferers.

from the open sea. The most famous island in the Sørøyane Archipelago is the Runde, with its fascinating bird sanctuary (accessible by boat from Åndalsnes).

Every year, some 500,00 to 700,000 sea birds jostle for nesting space on its 250-m (820-ft) cliffs, including the 5,000 breeding pairs making up Norway's largest colony of fulmars. Puffins, kittiwakes, and northern gannets also find this an ideal place to mate. There is ample opportunity to discover and learn about the life and the fragile habitats of sea birds if you take a boat trip alongside the cliffs.

The best panoramic view of the Norwegian municipality of Ålesund, which is located between Bergen and Trondheim, is to be had from the town's Aksla mountain. This can be reached up a flight of 418 steps from the municipal park.

Norway

BERGEN

Location: West Norway
Best time to travel: April–October
www.visitbergen.com
www.bergen-guide.com

The narrow alleys between the merchants' homes and warehouses still reek of tar and wood, and hatches open to reveal the pulleys which 500 years ago were used to load salt cod, fish oil, furs, beer, wine, salt, swords, and textiles. Even today a cog, the boat used to take these wares to the towns of the Hanseatic League, is moored in the historic port. From the 14th to the 16th centuries, it was mostly German merchants who controlled business dealings in the trading and port town of Bergen. The Germans ran the salt trade, an important ingredient needed to conserve the fish catches from the Norwegian Sea. In those days, salt fish was sold as far away as the Mediterranean and, thanks to its extensive commercial ties, Bergen eventually became one of the most important towns in the Hanseatic League. On the Tyske Bryggen Quay – which means German Bridge and is a clear reminder of its use by Hanseatic merchants – gabled warehouses bear witness to the former prosperity of this once mighty trading port. However, the 58 wooden houses that have been carefully preserved in the historic district do not actually date back to the Middle Ages; they were rebuilt in their original style after a fire in 1702. Fires have continued to cause damage in Bergen, which is still a major Norwegian port, with the most recent occurring in 1955.

The main attractions of Bergen, the second largest city in Norway, are the picturesque yacht marina on the Byfjord and the unique Old Town.

Norway

SOGNEFJORD

Location: West Norway
Best time to travel: April–October
www.sognefjord.no
www.visitnorway.com

The Sognefjord is not only Europe's longest fjord at 204 km (127 mi), but also the world's deepest at 1,308 m (4,292 ft). The cruise ships and the Hurtigruten passenger boats which come here in summer are headed for the Nærøyfjord tributary fjord in Aurland; in places it is only 250 m (820 ft) wide. Both Nærøyfjord, flanked on both sides by rock cliffs up to 1,800 m (5,906 ft) high, and Aurlandfjord are arms at the southeastern end of Sognefjord. The local stave churches in their romantic settings are also worth a visit.

The waters of the Sognefjord reflect the clouds and mountains in the atmospheric light of dusk.

URNES

Location: West Norway
Best time to travel: April–October
www.stavechurch.com
www.visitnorway.com

Norway's stave churches are unique among religious Christian buildings: the framework of the medieval wooden structures comprises staves reminiscent of ships' masts, which is why they are also known as "mast churches". The magnificent Viking wood carvings both inside and out depict animals, dragon's heads, closely entwined animal and serpentine forms. Other typical features include the steep tiered roofs, open balconies, and porches.

Dragons, lions, and snakes adorn the northern portal of the Urnes stave church (the oldest remaining) – the interior is equally impressive.

BORGUND

Location: South Norway
Best time to travel: April–October
www.stavechurch.com
www.visitnorway.com

Norway's most important cultural legacy from its centuries-long period of Christianization are its wooden stave churches. While stone churches were built in big cities, hundreds of stave churches were built in rural areas from the time of King Olaf II († 1028). Most were demolished after the Reformation, although some were transported to other locations and erected again there. The name of these single- to triple-naved ecclesiastical buildings derives from the vertical posts ("staves") supporting the roof. The exterior walls are formed by wooden planks set into a frame. The "staves" are often compared to ships' masts, but it is still disputed whether their design has been adopted from shipbuilding or the architecture of Nordic royal halls. A further characteristic of the churches are their steep, multistorey roofs. Borgund, probably the best-preserved stave church in Norway, was built in 1150 and is famed for its wealth of carvings. The pagoda-like bell tower is to be found near the church. It can be visited by making a short detour inland along the E16 after the long Lærdal Tunnel.

Borgund stave church is located near Borlaug in inner Lærdal county.

HEDDAL

Location: South Norway
Best time to travel: April–October
www.stavechurch.com
www.visitnorway.com

Just a short distance from the "blues" town of Notodden you will find the Telemark village of Heddal and the largest surviving stave church in the world. Owing to its picturesque exterior, with a triple-layer roof and a tower, it is also considered one of the most beautiful. This triple-naved "cathedral" among the stave churches was built in the 12th and 13th centuries and was restored to its original state in the 1950s with the removal of post-Reformation additions. The structure is now more or less in the same state as when it was completed and dedicated to the Virgin Mary in 1242 (a runic inscription near the southern portal suggests it was on 25 October). According to legend, the master builder was a troll named Finne; as he was unable to stand the sound of the bells, he eventually fled from the town. The verandah surrounding the church (beneath the lowest layer of the roof) was where the congregation would deposit their weapons before entering the nave.

Like all other stave churches, Heddal was not built in a town but in a remote location amongst romantic and atmospheric scenery.

Norway

GEIRANGER-FJORD AND NÆRØYFJORD

Location: West Norway
Best time to travel: April–October
www.geirangerfjorden.net

"Fjord" is a Norwegian word for valleys initially formed by rivers and then shaped by glaciers during the Ice Age. If statistics are anything to go by, the Geirangerfjord is one of the most impressive landscapes worldwide. The inner arm of Storfjord is roughly 120 km (75 mi) long and visited by more than 150 international cruise ships from around the world each year. Along this popular route there are a multitude of views, including three famous waterfalls: Seven Sisters, the Suitor, and the Bridal Veil. During the summer months, the Hurtigruten passenger ships dock in Geiranger, a small village of about 250 people at the end of the fjord.

The Ørneveien pass (or Eagle Road), from the Geirangerfjord to the Norddalsfjord further north, featuring hairpin turns and stunning vistas, is one of the most breathtaking roads in all of Scandinavia. The best viewpoint, however, the nearly vertical Flydalshornet, 1,112 m (3,648 ft) above the fjord, can only be reached on foot. The rivers originating in the surrounding mountains often form waterfalls as they flow into the fjord, although this is yet to be exploited for hydroelectric power in Geiranger or Nærøyfjord. Both fjords run parallel to the coast before merging with another fjord system.

Geiranger, a town of only 250 inhabitants, is located at the end of Geirangerfjord. A pleasure trip on the fjord will take you to the "Seven Sisters" waterfall, which drops 300 m (990 ft, far right). In places, Nærøyfjord narrows to only 250 m (820 ft) wide.

JOSTEDALSBREEN

Location: West Norway
Best time to travel: June–August
www.jostedalsbre.no
www.jostedal.com

Jostedalsbreen is the largest glacier in mainland Europe. From the interior arms of the Sognefjord, this plateau glacier stretches about 100 km (328 mi) to the north-east, reaching widths of up to 15 km (9 mi). The ice is 500 m (1,640 ft) thick in places. In the middle of the glacier stands the Høgste Breakulen, a 1,957-m (6,421-ft) glacial cone covered in ice. Only a few rocky islands break through the ice cover, the highest of these being the Lodalskåpa at an impressive 2,083 m (6,834 ft). The best approach is to take Route 604 to the Jostedalen Valley, which runs for 50 km (31 mi) and contains a network of valleys with glacial fingers stretching toward the east. Brigsdalsbreen is the best-known glacier arm on the sunnier north-west side. The glacier has been in continual retreat for the last 200 years, although its arms have recently begun to grow again.

The Melkevollbreen, an arm of the largest glacier in continental Europe, flows into a valley above Oldevatnet, a lake in the Jostedalsbreen National Park.

JOTUNHEIMEN

Location: Central Norway
Best time to travel: June–August
www.visitnorway.com

Jotunheimen National Park, home to northern Europe's highest summits, is the most easily accessible hiking and mountain sports region in all of Norway. At 2,469 m (8,101 ft), Gald-høpiggen is the highest peak in Scandinavia, although more than two hundred further summits surpass the 2,000 m (6,562 ft) mark in this glacial mountain range. The landscape on the Vestland side is characterized by Alpine ruggedness while the Østland side features far gentler, undulating terrain. The name Jotunheimen ("Home of the Giants"), which derives from Old Norse literature, was given to the many peaks in the area by the poet Aasmund Olavsson Vinje in the 19th century. Approximately 1,151 sq km (444 sq mi) of these central highlands are protected within the national park. The eastern edge of the park contains the best-known hiking trail in Norway: the Grat Besseggen above the emerald-green waters of Gjende lake.

The mountainous Jotunheimen National Park is a Mecca for nature lovers, but you are more likely to meet sheep than giants.

Norway

DOVREFJELL-SUNNDALS-FJELLA

Location: Central Norway
Best time to travel: June–August
www.dovrefjellradet.no

It was once thought that the trim peak of Snøhetta 2,286 m (7,500 ft) was the highest point in Norway, but this is now known to be Galdhøppigen 2,469 m (8,100 ft). In the steep tributary valleys of the Sunndalsfjord, the Vidda plateau descends to the valley as a unique and very impressive series of 100-m-high (328-ft) rock formations. The animal world is as diverse as the truly spectacular landscape here – at a latitude of 13 degrees south, it is hardly distinguishable from that of Central Europe, while the mountain plateaus and the northern reaches have a more Arctic feel. Some of the plant life predates the last ice age. The musk ox, the iconic animal of the Arctic, has been reintroduced all the way from Greenland to the tundra of Dovrefjell. The area protected within the national park includes Hardangervidda and Rondane, and is one of the largest areas of wilderness in Norway. The actual number of specimens of many of the species can only be guessed at.

Dovrefjell-Sunndalsfjella National Park is a mixture of expansive Vidda plateaus (far left) and the glacial high mountain range of the Snøhetta. Moose, reindeer and musk ox (left, from top) are just some of the species that roam the tundra of the national park. The ox, a recent arrival from Greenland, seems a clumsy herd animal, but when threatened it can run at high speeds and gore its attackers.

Norway

LOFOTEN

Location: Northern Norway
Best time to travel:
May–September
www.lofoten.com

The Lofoten chain of islands, part of the county of Nordland and separated from the mainland by the Vestfjord, is actually a submerged mountain range. The islands have been popular with visitors to Norway since the 19th century: the majestic contrast of mountains and sea views, the archipelago with the islands of Austvågøy, Vestvågøy, Moskenesøy, Flakstadøy, Værøy,

Gimsøy, and Røst, and the attractive little towns scattered across the landscape make the scenery spectacular even by Norwegian standards. Austvågøy is the largest island and also has the highest peak in the Higravtinden (1,161 m/3,809 ft). The island chain protrudes out into the North Sea for 250 km (155 mi) like a jagged wall of rock topped with snow-covered peaks. Despite their lush green valleys, the islands' steep cliffs mean that usually only the coastal areas are inhabited. A typical feature of these towns are rorbuer, brightly painted wooden houses that

jut out over the water on stilts. The bays and fjords also conceal remote but enchanting beaches of white sand, such as those found on the coast of Austvågøy. The bird life on the islands is impressive, with waterfowl and migratory birds living alongside sea eagles. Once forested, the islands' flora is now rather diminished, but different species of Alpines, beach plants, and meadow flowers grow in abundance. The balancing temperate influence of the Gulf Stream seldom allows the temperature to drop beneath freezing even in winter, and these warm cur-

rents have made the Vestfjord a popular breeding ground for cod and herring, and encouraged the breeding of trout and salmon in the bays and fjords. Dried cod is considered a delicacy, and between March and June hundreds can be seen twisting in the wind as they hang from wooden frames. The combination of midnight sun and mountain panorama is best viewed between the end of May and mid-June!

Moskenesøy Island is known for the village of Sakrisøy, with its houses built on stilts.

ALTA

Location: Northern Norway
Best time to travel:
May–September
www.alta.kommune.no

The Alta region is located north of the Arctic Circle, at the sheltered end of a fjord. Thanks to the North Atlantic Current, it is not glaciated and therefore habitable. In 1973, no fewer than 3,000 rock drawings were discovered in an area covering more than 40 sites. The images are considered to be crucial evidence of the human settlement of northern Europe at the end of the last great Ice Age. The images were most probably drawn between about 4200 and 500 B.C. Chiseled deep into the stone, the well-preserved pictures portray moose, reindeer, and bears as well as vivid scenes from everyday life: people fishing or navigating boats, hunting, and performing religious rituals and ceremonies. They also portray the prehistoric people's relationship with nature and spirituality. More recent excavations near these sites have now unearthed settlements that were inhabited at around the same time as the rock drawings were made, thus helping us to understand the lifestyle and habits of people from that time.

The carvings are an impressive record of the way of life and level of development of the settlers, who clearly knew how to make snowshoes or skis.

NORTH CAPE

Location: Northern Norway
Best time to travel: June–August
www.nordkapp.no

The rocky promontory to the north of Magerøya Island, also known as North Cape, has for centuries wrongly been regarded as mainland Europe's northernmost point. Admittedly, the actual northernmost point is not far away: the next rocky spit of land, Knivskjellodden (above). Jutting about 1.5 km (0.9 mi) further northward into the sea, it is comparatively flat and not quite as spectacular as its more famous neighbor, a tall headland protruding 307 m (1,000 ft) into the Norwegian Sea. It was an Englishman named Richard Chancellor, the chief navigator of a fleet of seven ships undertaking the first journey in search of the North-East Passage between 1553 and 1554, who first spotted this impressive rocky bluff and, believing it to be the northern tip of the continent, named it the "North Cape".

Tens of thousands of people come to the North Cape plateau on Magerøya island to experience the midnight sun at midsummer.

VESTERÅLEN

Location: Northern Norway
Best time to travel:
May–September
www.visitvesteralen.com

The Vesterålen archipelago off the coast of Troms extends for 150 km (93 mi), and in the south merges al-most seamlessly with the Lofoten archipelago. The Raftsund strait and the Trollfjord on the Lofoten side are considered the dividing line. The overall landscape resembles that of Lofoten: fjords, straits, bays, sker-ries, rivers, lakes, moors, valleys, plains, almost Alpine summits, and sandy beaches like those in the south. The main islands are Hin-nøya, the largest island in Norway covering 2,205 sq km (851 sq mi), Langøya and Andøya. In 2003, the lakes and highlands on Hinnøya island were protected as the Møysalen National Park. The 51-sq-km (20-sq-mi) area extends from Indrefjord to glaciated Møysalen (1,266 m/4,154 ft), the highest peak on the Vesterålen.

Blooming fireweed transforms the moors of the Vesterålen island of Hinnøya into a sea of pink.

SVALBARD (SPITSBERGEN)

Location: Northern Norway
Best time to travel: June–August
www.sysselmannen.no
www.svalbard.com

In 1194, the Vikings landed on an archipelago that they subsequently named Svalbard ("Cold Coast"). This name was later extended to the Norwegian administrative district comprising ten larger and countless smaller islands located about 600 km (373 mi) north of the mainland. Some 36,502 sq km (14,090 sq mi) of the archipelago, which covers roughly 61,022 sq km (23,554 sq mi), are glaciated. The main town and seat of government is Longyearbyen on Spitsbergen, the largest of the islands and the only one inhabited year round. *Nomen est omen*; having set out in 1594 from Amsterdam with two ships to find the north-eastern passage to Asia, the Dutch seafarer Willem Barents was inspired by the island's mountain peaks and in 1597 named this major Arctic Ocean island "Spitsbergen". The narrow Liefdefjord (shown above with the Monaco Glacier) northwest of Svalbard is a must-see for visitors. Large quantities of ice from the Monaco Glacier regularly break off into the sea, and the surrounding tundra is frequently roamed by polar bears.

In geological terms, the polar bear, which is closely related to the brown bear, has adapted to life on the coast at the North Pole and the edge of the pack ice only relatively recently – within the last 50,000 years or so. The almost white coloration of its extremely thick coat, from which water runs off effortlessly, enables this excellent swimmer and diver to blend in with the landscape.

Sweden

STOCKHOLM

Location: South-east Sweden
Best time to travel:
throughout the year
www.stockholm.se
www.visit-stockholm.com

Founded in 1252, Stockholm has been the Swedish capital since 1634 and has a long history as a dynamic and international city. Its wonderful mix of grandiose buildings, parks, waterways, and bridges give the vibrant metropolis a unique ambience. All of the major sights can easily be visited on foot during a stroll through the Old Town (Gamla Stan), and there are roughly one hundred museums. In addition to the Nationalmuseet, which houses the country's most important art collection, and the Moderna Museet, focusing on contemporary art, there are also Skansen, the world's oldest open-air museum, and the Vasamuseet. The latter exhibits the Vasa, King Gustav Adolphus II's flagship. Construction began in 1626, after a thousand oaks had been felled to build the ship, and was completed two years later. On 10 August 1628 the majestic craft was launched; after travelling only 1,300 m (three-quarters of a mile), the crew and spectators gasped in horror as the ship, which was under full sail, pitched over and sank, dragging dozens to a watery death. The Vasa was raised in 1961 after 300 years at the bottom, and now has a whole museum dedicated to her. At the northern end of Stockholm's maze of streets you will find the tower of the Church of St Nicholas, also known as Storkyrkran, first documented in 1279 and the city's oldest church. St Gertrude's, or Tyska kyrkan ("German church") is a converted guild house. The mighty royal palace in the north-eastern corner of the Old Town looks almost out of place among the squat buildings sur-

rounding it. The various parts of this baroque building, which dates from the late 17th-century, surround a square courtyard and the whole complex is large enough to accommodate several museums, including the treasury house. The changing of the guard in front of the castle gates is spectacular and attracts crowds of camera-toting tourists. The king has long since been relieved of the day-to-day running the country, and the impressive parliament building takes up about half of the little island of Helgeandsholmen immediately to the north of the Old Town. The other politically important building is the town hall, which attracts international interest once a year when an official dinner to honor the various recipients of the annual Nobel Prize is held here. Cruise visitors approaching Stockholm from the Baltic Sea will pass the Skärgård, an archipelago of more than 20,000 islands and islets poking out of the water; the smaller ones are uninhabited but the larger ones are very popular holiday resorts. The islands and their landscapes were all created at the same time, being worn smooth by the glaciers that rolled over them during the last Ice Age. The land rose as the ice melted about 10,000 years ago and now the islands are above sea level. The people of Stockholm love to sail from island to island, and the Skärgård is also a great place for tourist to visit.

Top: The photograph shows Riddarholmen Island with the steeple of Riddarholmskyrka church. This ceremonial place of worship is now a museum and the last resting place of the Swedish kings. Bottom: Royal Stockholm. The first Swedish regent to use the castle (Kungliga Slottet) was King Adolph Frederick in 1754. With 600 rooms, it is one of the world's largest royal residences.

Sweden

TANUM

Location: South-east Sweden
Best time to travel: May–October
www.tanum.se

Located in Bohuslän Province in Jutland, the fascinating rock carvings at Tanum are one of the most important prehistoric sites in all of Scandinavia. A Bronze Age village has also been reconstructed in the town. The carvings are included in the World Heritage List because of their unique artistic quality, the depiction of aspects of life in the European Bronze Age and the continuity of local rural life they represent. The millennia-old rock carvings at Tanum, the most extensive finds in Scandinavia, give a fascinating insight into life during the Bronze Age in northern Europe. They were probably made at the end of the second millennium BC at what, at that time, was the sea shore, and are a precious record of a long-lost culture. Preserved in scenes of great artistic quality, the objects and people show the social life of Bronze Age Scandinavia, as well as its religious and ritual practices. The rock carvings, which have been painstakingly scratched into granite boulders, represent various hunting and battle scenes, people dancing, fertility rituals, as well as horse, bears, weapons, tools, cult figures, and jewellery. There are also a striking number of ship pictures. A few remaining scraps of evidence suggest that the original drawings were probably brightly painted. Excavations nearby have also unearthed rune stones and Neolithic grave chambers.

Battle scenes make up a considerable proportion of the almost 10,000 rock carvings at Tanum. The motifs include humans, weapons, boats, fishing nets, the sun, bulls, horses, deer, birds, and other scenes of daily life.

Sweden

DROTTNINGHOLM

Location: South-east Sweden
Best time to travel:
throughout the year
www.sfv.se
www.visitsweden.com

Completed in around 1700, Drottning-holm Palace (or Queen Island) is majestically located on Lovön Island in Lake Mälar. It was constructed on the site of an earlier building dating back to the 16th century. Commissioned in 1662, by Hedwig Eleonora, wife of the late King Charles X Gustav, it is the largest baroque palace in Sweden and widely regarded as the architect Nicodemus Tessin's masterpiece. The main façade of the rectangular structure faces the water, and is the finest example of an 18th-century northern European royal residence inspired by the Palace of Versailles. The palace was enlarged after 1750, and numerous rooms were furnished in the lavish style of the rococo. When the palace was increasingly used for state visits, starting in 1777, some of the important rooms were remodeled in an elegant neoclassical design. King Gustav III (1771–92) had the gardens laid out in English landscape fashion. In addition to the splendid rooms from a range of periods, the China Pavilion and the Drottningholm Theater, one of very few rococo theaters still in use, are a great draw for modern visitors.

Set beside Lake Mälar, Drottning-holm Castle is a perfect mix of culture and natural beauty, and is still used as a summer residence by the Swedish royal family. It is Sweden's best preserved palace constructed in the 17th century.

GRIPSHOLM

Location: South-east Sweden
Best time to travel:
throughout the year
www.sfv.se
www.visitsweden.com

One of the best sights just 60 km (37 mi) to the west of Stockholm, is Castle Gripsholm in the little town of Mariefred on an island in Lake Mälar. It is one of ten Royal castles in Sweden. Mariefred cemetery, which is named after a medieval Carthusian monastery, is the last resting place of Kurt Tucholsky, who immortalized the location in his novel *Castle Gripsholm, a Summer Story*. Bo Jonnson Grip, an imperial administrator, built the first castle on the site in 1380, and after this burned down, King Gustav Vasa I began construction of the current water château in 1537. The castle was remodeled under Gustav III in the late 18th century and in 1864 Charles XV became the last monarch to live in the castle, which had been extended several times by this stage. Gripsholm is now a museum with many picturesque rooms, including Gustav III's bedroom and the Astrak Hall with its coffered ceiling which dates from 1570. This fascinating castle contains furniture and interiors from four centuries, and today is also the home of Sweden's National Portrait Gallery, Sweden's most significant collection of portraits of important personalities from the last 500 years.

At Gripsholm you can take a royal stroll around the romantic castle grounds or meet the royal deer at the Hjorthagen nature reserve.

Sweden

ÖLAND

Location: South Sweden
Best time to travel:
April–October
www.olandsturist.se

Öland, the second-largest island in Sweden after Gotland, has a unique geological composition that limits agricultural activities. To the east, the land slopes down gently to the sea, but only the south-eastern end with its moraine soil can be cultivated. Elsewhere sandstone, slate, and limestone dominate the island's southern plateau of windswept landscapes. The now protected Stora Alvet, a 40-km (25-mi) long limestone heath entirely devoid of trees, has been over-grazed and deforested for centuriesso that the bare limestone is now visible in places. Many species of orchid and rare herbs nonetheless flourish in this bizarre wilderness. Despite the obvious geographical and climatic challenges of the region – low rainfall in summer can cause droughts – humans have lived in southern Öland for at least 5,000 years. Numerous Iron Age burial grounds, the Bronze Age passage grave at Mysinge Hög, and several ringforts from the Migration Period even indicate permanent settlement. Eketorp Castle, now an open-air museum, offered shelter and protection to people here between AD 400 and 1300. The 5-km (3-mi) long wall built right across the island by King Charles X Gustav in 1653 is especially striking. Wind turbines now stand shoulder-to-shoulder with the 400 remaining historic windmills (there were once 2,000) which are now protected monuments.

These gigantic stones, possibly marking graves, are signs of prehistoric settlement.

VISBY (GOTLAND)

Location: South-east Sweden
Best time to travel:
April–October
www.gotland.info

Evidence suggests that this town on the north-western coast of Gotland Island was settled as early as the Stone Age. In the 12th century, German merchants visited Visby, initially using it as a stopover for the extremely lucrative trade with Novgorod in the Russian interior, and soon after as a base for the expansion of the mighty Hanseatic League into the east. The Baltic cities of Riga, Reval, Gdansk and Dorpat were ultimately assimilated from here. In the 13th century, Visby was probably the only town to vie with Lübeck for the title of most important trading town in northern Europe. The town even minted its own money and became a legislative center for international marine law that held sway across the entire Baltic Sea. Visby's relatively short heyday ended in 1361, however, when Danish King Valdemar IV conquered Gotland. Nonetheless, the powerful town walls, 3.4 km (2 mi) long and in places up to 9 m (30 ft) high, still testify to the city's former prosperity. All told, 38 historic watchtowers still stand guard over the town. The numerous 12th- and 13th-century merchant houses lining its narrow medieval lanes reinforce Visby's reputation as one of the best-preserved Hanseatic towns in Europe. Some affectionately call Visby the "city of roses and ruins".

Visby's city walls are especially impressive; they total 3.4 km (2 mi) in length and are topped with 38 well-preserved medieval watchtowers.

Sweden

HIGH COAST (HÖGA KUSTEN)

Location: East Sweden
Best time to travel:
April–October
www.hogakusten.com
www.highcoast.net

These island chains in the Gulf of Bothnia were shaped by the last Ice Age, which began about 80,000 years ago and ended in Scandinavia about 9,600 years ago. The giant ice sheets covering the land on the coast were more than 3,000 m (9,800 ft) thick during this period, and when they melted, sea levels rose by some 115 m (380 ft). As a result, vast tracts of land were left underwater. Freed from the weight of the glaciers bearing down upon it, the land gradually rose, and skerries (rock islands) emerged from the sea. To date, the region has risen by 285 m (935 ft), and the process is still in motion. In fact, the ground is rising at a rate of around 93 cm (37 in) every century. The charming hills making up the remote landscape of the hinterland are now up to 350 m (1,150 ft) high. The Ice Age has left a legacy of rich, chalky soil and many lakes. With these freshwater lakes, the brackish water of the shallow coastal sounds with their off-shore islands, and the open waters of the Baltic, the small High Coast region boasts three water systems of geological and biological significance. The Skuleskogen National Park is located in the middle of the protected area and boasts 130 km (81 mi) of coastal paths that offer stunning views for walkers.

Stones that have been worn smooth and round by glaciation and water action are typical finds on the skerries (rock islands).

ABISKO

Location: North Sweden
Best time to travel: October–June (for skiing)
www.abisko.nu

Lapland, the northernmost third of the country, is an almost deserted expanse of somewhat melancholy beauty. Only the reindeer herds of the Sami people are able to find enough to eat in the barren empire of the midnight sun. The Sami or Samek ("swamp people"), as the local people call themselves, have lived in the northern reaches of Scandinavia for millennia. They have traditionally accompanied their giant herds of reindeer across this thinly populated country, covering enormous distances every year in the process. "Laponia", which includes the national parks of Padjelanta, Sarek, Muddus, and Stora Sjöfallet, is one of only four UNESCO World Heritage Sites still inhabited by the original population. Abisko National Park, which lies on the Swedish-Norwegian border about 200 km (125 mi) north of the Arctic Circle, is known for the diversity of its mountain plants and its charming *fjäll* (fell, hill) scenery and was one of the nine national parks established by Sweden in 1909, the first of their kind in Europe. This small "Arctic Herb Garden" of only 77 sq km (30 sq mi) marks the beginning of the 440-km (275-mi) long Kungsleden ("Royal Way"), which makes its way south through the beautiful landscape.

Ancient legends used to describe the Northern Lights or *aurora borealis* (seen here in Abisko National Park) as "fairy veils". It is most visible closer to the poles due to the longer periods of darkness and the magnetic field.

Sweden

SAREK

Location: North Sweden (Lapland)
Best time to travel: June–August
www.naturvardsverket.se

The Alpine scenery of the Sarek National Park was long considered "Europe's last wilderness". Anyone venturing here should be properly prepared: this area of 1,970 sq km (760 sq mi) is one of the least accessible regions of Europe. The park has no marked trails, no accommodation, and only two bridges, and was only properly mapped by the Swedish geographer Axel Hamberg at the turn of the 20th century.

Almost all the steep cliffs, glaciers, and tumbling waterfalls in the Sarek National Park lie above the coniferous tree line and are a habitat for many rare European animals.

PADJELANTA

Location: North Sweden (Lapland)
Best time to travel: June–August
www.padjelanta.com

"I was indeed in the mountains of Lapland for the first time" wrote the Swedish naturalist Carl Linnaeus, whose treatise entitled *Systema natura*, published in 1735, provided the basis for modern biological taxonomy. In July 1732, he had traveled to the west of Sweden near Norway to visit the Padjelanta region of Lapland, 1,984 sq km (766 sq mi) of which are now protected as Sweden's largest national park. Here, Linnaeus was amazed to discover "more than I had ever dreamed of".

The park is primarily comprised of a vast plateau around two unusually large lakes, but the diversity of the flora is extremely high. The fauna is rich as well.

STORA SJÖFALLET

Location: North Sweden (Lapland)
Best time to travel: June–August
www.turism.jokkmokk.se

There is plenty of evidence in the Stora Sjöfallet National Park that the Sami people have lived here since prehistoric times. In fact, the oldest Sami settlement has been discovered on Lake Gårtjejávvre. The southern section of this national park of 1,278 sq km (493 sq mi) is composed of highlands covered in coniferous forests, while to the west there are glaciated mountain peaks, such as Akka (2,015 m/6,611 ft), after which Selma Lagerlöf named the leader of the wild geese in her famous Nils Holgersson novel, *Akka of Kebnekaise*.

Mount Slugga in the national park forms an almost perfect pyramid.

MUDDUS

Location: North Sweden (Lapland)
Best time to travel: June–August
www.naturvardsverket.se

At only 500 sq km (193 sq mi), Muddus National Park is the smallest of the nature reserves which were combined in 1996 to form the UNESCO World Heritage Site of Laponia (approx. 9,400 sq km/3,630 sq mi). About half of it is covered with ancient coniferous, mixed, and birch forests containing pines that are up to 600 years old and spruces which can reach 300 years old. Reindeer, bears, lynxes, and wolverines have found a habitat here amongst the primeval forest, large boggy grounds, and deep ravines.

The extensive swamps and lakes at the heart of the Muddus National Park are closed to the public to protect the precious habitats.

Denmark

COPENHAGEN

Location: East Denmark
Best time to travel:
throughout the year
www.visitcopenhagen.com
www.kk.dk

It has become even easier to travel between the two "united kingdoms" since Denmark and Sweden have been connected by the ambitious Öresund Bridge. The much-loved and down-to-earth Queen Margrethe II formulated probably the most accurate travel recommendations for Denmark: "No country is as much like Denmark as Denmark itself". It is certainly an ideal destination for people who love the sea – where else can you find 7,400 km (4,598 mi) of mostly undeveloped and freely accessible coastline, with a choice of the blue, shimmering Kattegat, the mild Baltic, the rough waters of Jutland, or the tidal North Sea?

In Copenhagen, which has been the capital of Denmark since 1443, visitors will find history and tradition around virtually every corner. The ambience is at once cosmopolitan and pleasantly tranquil, and most of the sights can be comfortably visited on foot. The city on the Öresund experienced its first period of economic prosperity as a trading port back in the late Middle Ages, but a renewed golden age came about in the 16th and 17th centuries, in particular under King Christian IV, who did much to extend and improve the capital. The Nyhavn Canal district is particularly charming with its old wooden sailboats and a slew of cafés.

The famous statue of the Little Mermaid (Lille Havfrue) in Copenhagen bay was created by the sculptor Edvard Eriksen. She is based on the main character in the eponymous fairytale by Danish poet and author Hans Christian Andersen.

Denmark

EGESKOV

Location: Fünen (island)
Best time to travel:
May–September
www.egeskov.dk

Egeskov means "oak wood" and the name is a reminder of the entire oak forest that was felled to provide hundreds of wooden piles for the foundations of Castle Egeskov, which is located in the middle of a small lake on the island of Fünen and was completed between 1524 and 1554. With its two enormous round towers, a moat, and a drawbridge, this three-storey, red and pink brick building is without doubt one of the most beautiful water castles in Europe.

Castle Egeskov has some 15 ha (37 acres) of grounds. An old stable block by the lake shore is now used to house a vintage car exhibition.

FREDERIKSBORG

Location: Seeland (island)
Best time to travel:
throughout the year
www.frederiksborgmuseet.dk

Like many of Denmark's finest buildings, this Renaissance castle, built near Hillerød to the north of Copenhagen between 1602 and 1620, was commissioned by Christian IV. Unfortunately, a fire in December 1859 destroyed the majority of the castle buildings, which stood on three little islands in the lake surrounding the complex. Later financial help from the industrialist Christian Jacobsen meant that these could be completely restored. Castle Frederiksborg now houses the National Historical Museum.

The Treaty of Frederiksborg between Denmark and Sweden was signed in the Knights' Hall here in 1720.

Denmark

KRONBORG

Location: Seeland (island)
Best time to travel:
throughout the year
www.ses.dk

The location of the Danish royal palace on the Öresund, the narrowest part of the sound separating Denmark and Sweden, was of great strategic importance. The Feste Krogen had controlled the entire sound from this point since the early Middle Ages, ensuring that import duty was paid. Kroneborg even has some literary fame – built in the 16th century and restored in the 17th after a fire, the castle is the backdrop for *Hamlet*, Shakespeare's famous tragedy.

In 1425, the Danish King Eric of Pomerania decreed that every ship passing through the sound had to pay a tax.

ROSKILDE

Location: Seeland (island)
Best time to travel:
throughout the year
www.visitroskilde.com
www.roskilde-info.dk

Until the Reformation in the 16th century, Roskilde, a city on the island of Sjælland, some 30 km (19 mi) west of Copenhagen, was Denmark's ecclesiastical center. As the royal seat, Roskilde was also the capital of Denmark until 1443. Roskilde was founded by Bishop Absalonthe, architect of the first Romano-Gothic brick church in Scandinavia, who erected his church on the foundations of two former smaller churches in 1170, in order to give the royal residence a dignified place of worship.

Many Danish kings have been buried in Roskilde Cathedral since the 15th century.

Denmark

JELLING

Location: Central Denmark (Jutland)
Best time to travel: throughout the year
www.kongernesjelling.dk
http://jelling.natmus.dk

Located in front of Jelling church is Denmark's most impressive royal tomb. The grave artifacts found here are testimony to the great power of the Vikings, who gained control of the northern seaways in the early Middle Ages. The entire complex – two massive grave mounds with diameters of 60 and 77 m (197 and 253 ft) respectively, with a church and two rune stones between them – is also an historic symbol of the Christianization of Denmark, which saw the country become a fully European state. The still heathen King Gorm (c. 860 to 940) and his wife Tyra were originally entombed in the northern part of both grave mounds. The remains of the couple's son, the first Christian Danish King, Harald Blåtand (c. 940 to 986, baptized 960), were later moved into the newly-built church. The inscription on the older of the two rune stones was a dedication by King Gorm to his wife Tyra. The larger rune stone from approximately 980 is the location of Scandinavia's oldest depiction of Christ.

The rune stones at Jelling, a town near Vejle in East Jutland, are among the finest of their kind.

BORNHOLM

Location: South-east Denmark
Best time to travel:
throughout the year
www.bornholm.net
www.brk.dk

The island of Bornholm lies about 40 km (25 mi) off the southern Swedish coast – a great distance from Denmark. The island, whose climate had earned it the nickname "the Pearl of the Baltic", has ferry connections to Copenhagen and Ystad, a Swedish town which has gained fame through Henning Mankell's Wallander crime novels. Bornholm tends to attract nature lovers – the island is 600 sq km (230 sq mi) of Scandinavia in miniature, with extensive beaches, lakes and moors, deciduous and coniferous forests, stretches of heath, sand dunes, and an underlying geology that is unique in Denmark. There have been plenty of prehistoric finds on Bornholm. The island's biggest settlement is Rønne, where many of the old buildings, including a number of half-timbered houses, have been preserved. White-painted herring smokers are a typical feature of this charming and picturesque coastal village.

Lying far from Denmark, the "Pearl of the Baltic" features almost every kind of scenery found in Scandinavia and has plenty of tourist attractions, including its thatched, half-timbered houses and old windmills.

Finland

HELSINKI

Location: South Finland
Best time to travel:
throughout the year
www.visithelsinki.fi
www.hel.fi

Roughly 500,000 people live in Finland's compact capital, a city originally founded by King Gustav I of Sweden in 1550. After a series of fires, Czar Alexander II commissioned the Berlin architect Carl Ludwig Engel with the reconstruction of Helsinki in a neoclassical style. Twenty of the monumental edifices from the period between 1820 and 1850 still remain today and combine with other famous buildings, in architectural styles that range from art nouveau to modern, to form the unique cityscape of this impressive capital on the Gulf of Finland. Engel's Senate Square, with the cathedral and the statue of Czar Alexander II, the Government Palace, the main university building, and the university library are all worth a visit, as is the impressive Orthodox Uspenski Cathedral, built in 1868, which boasts a lavish interior. Other attractions include the historic market place and buildings on the south side where the ferries dock that take visitors to the island fortress of Suomenlinna and the skerries. Numerous art nouveau buildings line Luotsikatu, one of Helsinki's most elegant streets, and the esplanade, the capital's pedestrian zone, is bordered by parks. Here you will also find Stockmann's flagship department store, the largest of its kind in Scandinavia. The best panoramic view across Helsinki can be enjoyed from the Katajanokka Peninsula.

The 150-year-old cathedral and the statue of Czar Alexander II on Helsinki's Senate Square. A mighty flight of steps leads up to the cathedral, which contains monuments to Agricola, the reformer of Finland, amongst others.

Finland

OULANKA, URHO KEKKONEN

Location: North-east Finland
Best time to travel: throughout the year
www.ruka.fi

Located to the north of the city of Kuusamo near the Arctic Circle,

Oulanka National Park covers an area of some 270 sq km (104 sq mi) and protects a diverse region surrounding the river landscape of the Ouloankajoki and its many tributaries. It is very rich in animal and plant species, even endangered ones.

The region had long been settled by the Sami before the first Finns arrived toward the end of the 17th century. The park is a popular place for hikers, particularly in the fall when the leaves take on astonishing hues. Urho Kekkonen (1900–1986), was

the Prime Minister of Finland in the years 1950–3 and 1954–6 and the country's President in 1956–81. As the longest-serving president he maintained good relations with the neighboring USSR without allowing his alliance with the western

democracies to deteriorate. As a result, it is fitting that this second national park, which covers approximately 2,550 sq km (984 sq mi) of land in Finland's extreme north-west near the Russian border, should bear his name. Originally the home of the semi-nomadic Sami people, this fascinating woodland with its rich flora and fauna is another popular destination for hikers and trekkers. Reindeer keeping is still a common livelihood in the area. There are more reindeers in the north of Finland than people.

Animal life, including the golden eagle (opposite), seen here descending on its prey, has adapted to the harshest of conditions in the northern reaches of Finland. These proud hunters are dark brown, with lighter golden-brown plumage on their heads and necks. Their wingspan averages over 2 m (7 ft) and they eat small to medium-sized mammals – anything from a gopher to a goat kid. This page, clockwise: a brown bear, a reindeer, a throated diver, and two great gray owls.

Finland

KOLI

Location: East Finland
Best time to travel:
throughout the year
www.outdoors.fi

The Koli mountains are the remains of a prehistoric mountain range which was worn away so completely during the Ice Age that only the hardest strata of quartzite were left. These now tower over the surrounding lakes. In addition to Ukko-Koli, there are two other mountain peaks, Akka-Koli (339 m/1,112 ft) and Paha-Koli (334 m/1,096 ft). These mountains were a site of pagan worship in the pre-Christian era and about 30 sq km (12 sq mi) of the region have been conserved as a national park.

There are superb views of Lake Pielinen from the modest summit of Ukko Koli, a 347-m (1,139-ft) granite rise in Karelia.

SAIMAA

Location: South-east Finland
Best time to travel:
throughout the year
http://gosaimaa.fi
www.visitsaimaa.fi

Lying about 250 km (155 mi) north-east of Helsinki, Lake Saimaa stretches almost to the Russian border and contains nearly 14,000 islands. Up to 90 m (295 ft) deep in parts, it has a coastline of about 14,000 km (8,700 mi). This body of water covers a vast area of about 1,460 sq km (564 sq mi), not including the islands, and was created when an ice age glacier thawed to form the largest connected lake district in Finland.

The southern half of Finland is made up of a network of between 50,000 and 60,000 lakes and pools. Some 12 percent of the country's total area is composed of lakes.

SAVONLINNA

Location: East Finland
Best time to travel: April–October
www.savonlinna.travel

Savonlinna is located at the heart of the labyrinthine network of the Saimaa lakes. The sights of this lovely little town include the provincial museum, which is located in a former grain storehouse on Riihisaari Island in front of the gates of the castle; the converted museum ships Mikko, Savonlinna, and Salama; the market square with its docks for boat excursions into the Saimaa lake district; and the 100-year-old wooden villa Rauhalinna a short way outside of town.

Olavinlinna, an impressive fortress accessible via a pontoon bridge, dates from the year 1475. It has hosted the Savonlinna Opera Festival for more than 30 years.

Estonia

TALLINN

Location: North Estonia
Best time to travel:
throughout the year
www.tourism.tallinn.ee
www.visitestonia.com

Tallinn is the capital and largest city of Estonia. It is situated on the northern coast of the country, on the shores of the Gulf of Finland, 80 km (50 mi) south of Helsinki. After being severely damaged in World War II, the historic center of the Estonian capital was rebuilt in an 18th-century style. Originally called Reval by the Swedish, Danish, and Germans (a Latin reference to the surrounding area), since 1920 the city has been known as Tallinn, a name whose meaning is still disputed. The Old Town is clustered around Cathedral Hill. Sights worth seeing include St Mary's Cathedral (begun 1230), the Church of the Holy Spirit (12th/13th centuries), St Nicholas' Church (13th to 14th centuries), and St Olaf's Church (13th century) with its 123-m (404-ft) tall steeple which for many years served as a lighthouse. St Mary's Chapel was built between 1512 and 1523. The trade guilds here also commissioned grand buildings for themselves as symbols of civic pride. The Great Guild, for example, which provided the membership of the municipal council, moved into its hall in 1410. The two-storey town hall, built in the early 15th century, is surrounded by well-preserved medieval houses. The baroque Kadriorg Palace was built as a royal summer residence between 1717 and 1725.

There are a multitude of merchants' houses and churches throughout the city to remind visitors of Tallin's heyday. Right: St Olaf's Church with its distinctive steeple (seen here from the cathedral with the city walls in the foreground).

Latvia

RIGA

Location: Central Lithuania
Best time to travel:
throughout the year
www.rigatourism.lv
www.latviatourism.lv

Riga is situated on the Baltic Sea at the mouth of the Daugava River. Of the many important churches in the city, the cathedral, which was begun in the year 1211 but only completed in its present form in 1775, is of particular interest. Another sight worth mentioning is the octagonal wooden steeple of the Lutheran Jesus Church (1819–22). Of the once mighty fortifications, only the 14th-century Powder Tower and the 13th-century Ramer Tower have survived unscathed. The Citadel was begun in 1760, while the area was under Swedish rule, and the Swedish Gate also dates back to this period. The Guildhall is the only remaining medieval administrative building in Riga. The "Small Guild", built around the middle of the 14th century and remodeled in 1866, is one of the most prestigious buildings in the city. The Latvian Stock Exchange was built between 1852 and 1855 in the style of a Venetian palazzo with a witty façade. Other architectural delights include splendid patrician houses such as the Reutern House, begun in the year 1683, and some outstanding art nouveau buildings by Mikhail Eisenstein.

The magnificent Blackhead's House stands on Riga's town square. The façade, which has been preserved in a 16th-century Dutch Renaissance style, is beautifully illuminated at night. The unmarried foreign merchants who would congregate here were once known as "blackheads" after St Maurice, their patron saint, who was often depicted as coming from Mauretania.

Lithuania

VILNIUS

Location: South-east Lithuania
Best time to travel:
throughout the year
www.vilnius.lt
www.visitlithuania.net

As with many medieval cities, the Old Town of this former trading settlement on the left bank of the Neris River spreads out from the base of its castle. The city experienced its heyday in the 15th and 16th centuries as a link between the cities of the Russian czardom and what were then the strongholds of the Hanseatic League. As a result of its location, the Lithuanian capital features remarkable urban architecture that mirrors the turbulent history of this small nation. Among the older buildings, a number of late-Gothic churches such as St Anne's Church, St Nicholas' Church, and St Bernard's Church, as well as some baroque-era noblemen's palaces, are of particular historical interest. The 17th-century Church of Saints Peter and Paul is also baroque in style. The heart of the Old Town is dominated by St Stanislaus' Cathedral, whose current appearance dates back to construction undertaken between 1783 and 1801. Neoclassical in style, it resembles a Greek temple. The cathedral's bell tower was originally the defensive tower of the Lower Castle, which was built in the 13th century. During the Soviet period, the church was used as a large exhibition space. Vilnius Town Hall was also later remodeled in a neo-classical style. The Gates of Dawn, one of Vilnius' city portals, features a Renaissance gate capital and a chapel housing a revered icon of the merciful Mother of God. Consecrated in 1901, the Orthodox Church of the Holy Mother is evidence of Vilnius' Russian connections.

Vilnius' cathedral was consecrated in 1801, and its separate bell tower is a typical feature of churches in the Baltic.

LONDON

Location: South-east England
Best time to travel: throughout the year
www.visitlondon.com

The whole world in one city – not just a great advertising slogan but a reality. London is a truly global metropolis, created and defined by people from every country, bringing with them their different cultures to form the unique urban melting pot that is the British capital. A major settlement for two millennia, its history goes back to its founding by the Romans, who called it Londinium. The Thames is the city's lifeblood, combining old and new, and linking modern buildings with traditional icons such as the Palace of Westminster (better known as the Houses of Parliament) and Big Ben with the London Eye and the Royal Festival Hall. Construction of both the Palace of Westminster and Westminster Abbey was begun by Edward the Confessor (1003–1066), although the abbey was replaced in

the 13th century with a Gothic cathedral where, until 1760, every monarch was buried. William the Conqueror built the Tower of London as a fortified residence and an observation post for shipping. The castle's current appearance dates back to the 13th century. Buckingham Palace, which had been built in 1703 by John Sheffield, Duke of Buckingham and Normandy, was acquired for the royal family by George III in 1761 and it has been the monarch's official residence since 1837. Buckingham Palace, Westminster Abbey, and the Palace of Westminster are just a few of the United Kingdom's most historic and iconic buildings. The political heart of the country beats here in the historic center of the City of Westminster.

A view across the Thames taking in the city skyline, with St Paul's Cathedral to the left and the 180-m (591-ft) high Swiss Re Tower (popularly known as the Gherkin), designed by architect Norman Foster, in the middle.

United Kingdom

HAMPTON COURT PALACE

Location: South-west of London
Best time to travel:
throughout the year
www.londonpass.com

Hampton Court Palace is one of the most attractive of the English royal palaces. The 14th-century central structure was enlarged as a Tudor palace between 1514 and 1520 by Cardinal Thomas Wolsey (1475–1530), archbishop of York and Lord Chancellor under Henry VIII. When Wolsey refused to approve the annulment of the king's marriage with Catherine of Aragón, he fell into disfavor and was stripped of both office and property. Hampton Court was used as a royal residence until the reign of George II (1727-60).

Legend has it that the Palace is haunted by the ghosts of two of Henry VIII's wives.

WINDSOR CASTLE

Location: South-west of London
Best time to travel:
throughout the year
www.thamesweb.co.uk
www.windsor.gov.uk

The coronation of Elizabeth II in Westminster Abbey on 2 June 1953 was the first global media event. It lasted for 11 hours and was watched by millions of television viewers around the world. The British royal family continues to attract the interest of the world as the stories and scandals of its members are splashed across the gutter press. This may have shaken the self-confidence of the "Firm", as the royals refer to themselves, but the media is unlikely to bring down the house of Windsor. Windsor Castle, from which the family takes its name, is not only the largest in Great Britain, it has also

ROYAL BOTANIC GARDENS

Location: West of London
Best time to travel: June–August
www.kew.org

The history of the present-day Royal Botanic Gardens in Kew, to the south-west of London, began with a herb garden laid out in 1759. Before that, a complex of gardens and parks with many buildings had existed on the site, including Kew Palace (1631), which was built in the Dutch style. The gardens were not converted into a scientific institution until 1773, when the famous botanist Sir Joseph Banks, who had sailed around the world with Captain Cook, became its director.

The best-known landmark in the gardens is the 20-m (66-ft) high PalmHouse, which was completed in 1848.

been occupied for the longest continuous period. A castle has stood here in the Thames Valley to the west of London for almost 1,000 years, since William the Conqueror first built a fort here. The building was changed and expanded several times, serving alternatively as a garrison, a fortress, or a prison, depending on the particular politics of the day. The current structure largely dates back to the 14th century, when Edward III added the State Apartments, the Round Tower, and the Norman Gate. The last major alterations were undertaken at the beginning of the 19th century under George IV. Windsor Castle has remained Elizabeth II's favourite residence to this day.

Windsor Castle is one of the principal royal residences of the British royal family, along with Buckingham Palace in London and Holyrood Palace in Edinburgh.

LEEDS CASTLE

Location: South-east England (Kent)
Best time to travel: throughout the year
www.leeds-castle.com
www.visitkent.co.uk

Lying in the heart of the county of Kent, moated Leeds Castle stands on two islands in the river Len surrounded by an extensive park. Leeds is for many the epitome of a medieval castle, and yet it owes its present appearance largely to the 19th century Tudor-style additions. The gatehouse, at least, is a relic from the 13th century, when Edward I had the former manor house enlarged as a royal palace. Many queens and widows of kings made this their home and thus provided the epithet "Lady's Castle".

The Banqueting Hall is a reminder of the castle's former glory.

BODIAM CASTLE

Location: South-east England (East Sussex)
Best time to travel: throughout the year
www.nationaltrust.org.uk
www.visitsussex.org

Built in 1385 Bodiam Castle is one of the most romantic castles in England. The castle did not see combat until the English Civil War, which was fought between followers of King Charles I and Parliament between 1642 and 1649. In order to prevent the king, who was later to be beheaded in London, from using the fortress as a stronghold, parliamentary troops destroyed the roof and parts of the castle's interior. Bodiam Castle has since remained unoccupied.

Surrounded by its moat, the eight towers of Bodiam Castle resemble a fortress in a fairytale.

SISSINGHURST, HEVER, STOURHEAD GARDEN

Location: Southern England
Best time to travel:
May–September
www.nationaltrust.org.uk
www.hevercastle.co.uk

Those unaware of the British reputation for being passionate gardeners should visit Sissinghurst Castle in Kent. Created by Vita Sackville-West and her husband, who lived there from 1930, the gardens feature beautiful wide open spaces and attractions such as the geometrically shaped hedges or enchanting corners that seem like miniature biospheres. Divided into ten "garden rooms" there are such delights as the White Garden, which is planted only with white and silver blooms, and the herb garden, where aromas of saffron and thyme delight the senses. The parks of Hever Castle, also in Kent, welcome visitors with the artful topiary of their hedges, lavish flowerbeds and a maze made of yew hedges. Here too, the basic principles of English garden design – that a beautiful garden should never stray too far from nature and should not be too symmetrical – are clearly apparent. "Nature abhors a straight line", proclaimed English landscape gardener William Kent, in an elegant summary of the approach. This is exemplified at Stourhead Garden farther west in Wiltshire, a unique "landscape painting" created between 1741 and 1780 with lakes, streams, woods, and small temples all harmoniously set in a truly breathtaking setting.

English gardening at its finest: Stourhead Garden, Hever Castle, and Sissinghurst Castle (left, top to bottom).

United Kingdom

SALISBURY

Location: Southern England (Wiltshire)
Best time to travel:
throughout the year
www.wiltshire.gov.uk
www.visitsalisburyuk.com

Lying close to Stonehenge at the confluence of the Rivers Avon and Wylye, Salisbury's Old Town with its medieval gabled houses and historic inns is best explored on foot. The city's magnificent early Gothic cathedral was largely built between 1220 and 1258. With its tall arched windows, the church is an outstanding and very rare example of an English Gothic style, characterized by its minimalism, which is known as "Early English".

At an impressive 123 m (404 ft), Salisbury's spire is the highest church steeple in England.

EXETER

Location: South-west England (Devon)
Best time to travel:
throughout the year
www.exeter.gov.uk

Dominating the skyline of Exeter, St Peter's Cathedral, which was built in the "Decorated Style" between the 11th and the 14th centuries, was constructed on the foundations of an earlier Norman church. There is nothing understated about this building; the west façade is a riot of decoration, but even this cannot compare with the stunning, breathtaking interior of the building – the noble vaulting of the 90-m (295-ft) long nave resembles a petrified forest.

The lavish interior of St Peter's Cathedral is topped with an impressive stone vault.

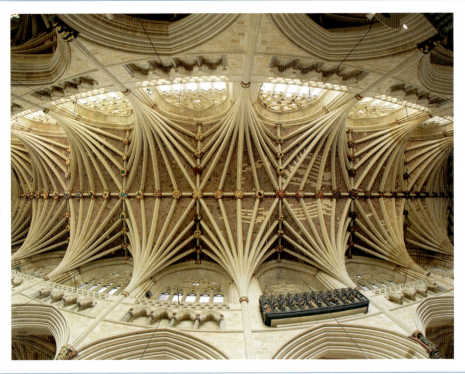

CANTERBURY

Location: South-east England (Kent)
Best time to travel:
throughout the year
www.canterbury.ac.uk

Begun as a Norman structure in the year 1070, Canterbury Cathedral, the mother church of the Anglican Communion, was to achieve infamy a mere 100 years later, in 1170, when Archbishop Thomas Becket was assassinated there by followers of the king. The archbishop was buried in the cathedral and beatified just three years later; the church became a popular destination for a steady stream of pilgrims. After almost completely burning down in 1174, it was rebuilt by the architect William of Sens.

The beautiful cloisters of Canterbury Cathedral were built between 1396 and 1420.

WINCHESTER

Location: Southern England (Hampshire)
Best time to travel:
throughout the year
www.visitwinchester.co.uk
www.winchester.gov.uk

Winchester of is of huge importance to the British Isles. This settlement on the banks of the River Itchen was the first capital of this Anglo-Saxon island kingdom; political interest shifted to London only after the Norman Conquest. The city is now the county town of Hampshire but the cathedral, which was begun in 1079, with parts still dating back to the 12th and 13th centuries, remains its icon. It is a stunning city.

Winchester Cathedral is the longest medieval church building in Europe, with a nave of 170 m (558 ft).

THE JURASSIC COAST

Location: South-east England (Dorset and Devon)
Best time to travel: March–October
www.jurassiccoast.com
www.southwestcoastpath.com

The Jurassic Coast is a World Heritage Site on the English Channel coast of southern England. The site stretches from Orcombe Point near Exmouth in East Devon to Old Harry Rocks near Swanage in East Dorset, a distance of 153 km (95 mi). This part of the coastline is like an open history book of the Mesozoic period. Strata dating back to the Triassic, Jurassic, and Cretaceous periods allow an uninterrupted view of the three layers of the Earth's middle geological period. The coastline first came to the attention of geomorphologists,

EASTBOURNE

Location: South-east England (East Sussex)
Best time to travel: March–October
www.visiteastbourne.com
www.eastbourne.org

Originally built east of a small stream called the Bourne, Eastbourne declared itself the "Sunshine Coast" and began attracting visitors with a promise of more hours of sunshine than anywhere else in England. It wasn't long before grand hotels shot up along the elegant beach promenade to serve holidaymakers from the cities. The best view of the coastline is probably to be had from Eastbourne Pier, preferably on a sunny day.

Many resorts along the English coast have Victorian pier pavilions; built in the 1870s, Eastbourne's is one of the most beautiful.

scientists who research the formation of the Earth's surface, in the year 1810, when Mary Anning, an 11-year-old girl, discovered a "dragon" in the rocks near the fishing village of Lyme Regis. In fact, it was the first complete fossil imprint of an ichthyosaurus, a name meaning "fish lizard", as the fossil seemed to be a cross between a giant fish and a reptile. It was the first of many finds along the coast of Dorset and East Devon. The rocky scenery here is changing at a breathtaking pace due to constant erosion, and a stroll on the beach is a beautiful journey of discovery though the various stages of evolution and geology.

The path along the south-west coast has some fantastic views of Dorset and East Devon. The fossil remains here offer a fascinating insight into 185 million years of the Earth's geological history.

BRIGHTON

Location: South-east England (East Sussex)
Best time to travel: March–October
www.tourism.brighton.co.uk

In the middle of the 18th century, a doctor named Richard Russell wrote a treatise describing the effectiveness of seawater – and in particular the water off the coast of Brighton – in curing certain diseases. His endorsement sparked off a period of unexpected popularity for the fishing village. In 1786, when the Prince of Wales, later George IV, built the faux-Oriental Royal Pavilion, the crowds of visitors turned into hordes. Brighton is still a popular destination for daytrippers, thanks to its proximity to London.

Enlarged by John Nash in 1815, the Royal Pavilion is decorated in a style any Indian Moghul would recognize.

United Kingdom

ST. MICHAEL'S MOUNT

Location: South-west England (Cornwall)
Best time to travel: April–October
www.stmichaelsmount.co.uk

St Michael's Mount is located in Penzance Bay on the south-western tip of Cornwall. According to legend, a fisherman saw the Archangel Michael appear on the island in the year 495 and since then, it has been known as "Michael's Mount"; a church was built here in the 15th century. A monastery was also built on the island, although this was transformed into a country mansion by subsequent owners.

At low tide the island can be reached on foot via a causeway. Historians assume St Michael's Mount to be the historical island of Ictis, an important center for local trade in tin during the Iron Age.

LAND'S END

Location: South-west England (Cornwall)
Best time to travel: April–October
www.visitcornwall.com
www.cornishlight.co.uk

The westernmost point in England features a number of archeological sites. These include tombs from the Iron and Bronze Ages, stone circles, Celtic crosses, and entire villages from the time before the birth of Christ; all of which are witness to thousands of years of settlement. The overland journey from Land's End to John O'Groats in northern Scotland is 1,406 km (900 mi) – the furthest distance between any two points in the United Kingdom.

The waves of the Atlantic crash incessantly against the peninsula. The Romans named it "Belerion", or "sea of storms".

ISLES OF SCILLY

Location: South-west England (Cornwall)
Best time to travel: March–October
www.scillyonline.co.uk
www.simplyscilly.co.uk

The 140 Isles of Scilly which lie about 40 km (25 mi) off the coast of south-west Cornwall, can easily be reached by ferry from Penzance. Some 2,000 people, who live mostly from tourism and exporting flowers, are spread out over five inhabited islands consisting of steep granite cliffs, white sand beaches and turquoise bays. The mild climate allows palm trees and exotic plants to flourish here. A collection of the exotic plants indigenous to the islands can be seen at the Abbey Garden in Tresco.

The best way to explore the islands is on foot or by bike.

ST. IVES

Location: South-west England (Cornwall)
Best time to travel: March–October
www.stives-cornwall.co.uk
www.stives.co.uk

St Ives has a history of attracting painters and sculptors, who find inspiration in the enchanting light and landscapes here. The typical little grey granite houses of this former fishing village line the edges of one of Cornwall's most attractive beaches. The Tate Gallery has opened a museum that towers above Porthmeor Beach to the north and features the works of local St Ives artists. These include paintings by Patrick Heron and Ben Nicholson, who lived here with his wife, the artist Barbara Hepworth.

In former times St Ives was commercially dependent on fishing.

United Kingdom

DARTMOOR

Location: South-west England (Devon)
Best time to travel: March–October
www.dartmoor-npa.gov.uk
www.discoverdartmoor.co.uk

Dartmoor is famous for being where Sir Arthur Conan Doyle's Sherlock Holmes encounters the Hound of the Baskervilles. The landscape is virtually untouched and can be very romantic as well as a bit spooky, especially when it is cloaked in the typically dense fog. The Dartmoor National Park, founded in 1951, covers more than 950 sq km (367 sq mi) and is noted for its vast meadow and moor landscapes. Much of the land belongs to the Duchy of Cornwall, currently run by Prince Charles' estate.

Grantie "tors" (towers) that have managed to withstand the forces of erosion, are typical of the area.

STONEHENGE

Location: Southern England (Wiltshire)
Best time to travel: March–October
www.stonehenge.co.uk

Stonehenge, an inspiring arrangement of megaliths dating back to around 2000 BC, is still a mystery. How were these stones transported hundreds of miles from their origin, and what was the true purpose of the site? The stones each weigh in at several tons and tower to heights of up to 7 m (23 ft) while an impressive trench 114 m (374 ft) wide surrounds the entire complex. The stones were apparently oriented toward certain heavenly bodies, giving rise to the theory that the complex may have served both religious and astronomical purposes.

The megaliths are arranged as a circle of pillars supporting horizontal capstones.

United Kingdom

AVEBURY

Location: Southern England (Wiltshire)
Best time to travel: March–October
www.avebury-web.co.uk

Avebury, to the east of Bath, is the site of an ancient monument consisting of a large henge, several stone circles, stone avenues, and barrows. It is one of the finest and largest Neolithic monuments in Europe. It has the same orientation as Stonehenge and was built between 2600 and 2500 BC. According to an 18th-century British scholar, this Neolithic sanctuary and druid temple was destroyed during the 1300s on orders from the Church.

Only 36 of the original 154 stones remain at Avebury. Of these, 27 are part of the large outer circle of stones (left). Each stone has been dug into the earth to a depth of 15–60 cm (6–24 in).

United Kingdom

BATH

Location: South-west England (Somerset)
Best time to travel: throughout the year
visitbath.co.uk

Located not far from Bristol in the county of Somerset, Bath is England's most important spa town. The Romans established spa facilities and baths near the thermal springs, but the curative waters here are said to have been discovered much earlier, by the Celts. According to legend, Bladud, a Celtic king who suffered from leprosy, was healed by the hot mud from the springs. The Romans eventually built a bath complex and an accompanying temple in 100 AD. The greenish water typical of these springs still gurgles its way to the surface at around 46 °C (115 °F). Bath Abbey, which was once part of a monastery, was completed in 1156. Badly damaged in the 13th century, it was restored to its present appearance in the 1700s. Having been a bishop's seat since the 10th century and the center of the textiles trade during the Middle Ages, Bath became England's most popular spa resort in the 17th century and indeed the most important social center beyond London. The town owes its largely Georgian cityscape primarily to the late-18th-century projects of the architects John Wood and Son. The elegant streets lead to neo-classical masterpieces such as the Assembly Rooms, the Royal Crescent, a crescent-shaped terrace of houses in a late Georgian style, and Pulteney Bridge, which was designed in the year 1770.

Pulteney Bridge across the River Avon is reminiscent of the architecture of Palladio. Designed by Robert Adam and completed in 1773, it is one of the few bridges in the world to have stores on both sides.

United Kingdom

OXFORD

Location: Southern England (Oxfordshire)
Best time to travel: throughout the year
www.visitoxford.org
www.oxfordcity.co.uk
www.visitbritain.com

Oxford, a city dominated by student life, is home to the oldest university in the United Kingdom, dating back to the 12th century. Buildings in Oxford demonstrate an example of every British architectural period since the arrival of the Saxons, including the iconic, mid-18th century Radcliffe Camera. Oxford is known as the "city of dreaming spires", a term coined by poet Matthew Arnold in reference to the harmonious architecture of Oxford's university buildings. The Bodleian Library houses one of the most important collections of literature in the world with some 4.5 million volumes.

Hertford Bridge is known as the "Bridge of Sighs" because it resembles the bridge in Venice.

CAMBRIDGE

Location: South-east England (Cambridgeshire)
Best time to travel: throughout the year
www.visitcambridge.org
www.visitbritain.com
www.visitcambridge.co.uk

Cambridge has become a center for modern technology and science. Its rich history began in 1220, when a group of scholars unaccountably defected from Oxford. Peterhouse, the oldest college, was founded in 1284. No less than nine Nobel Prize-winners studied at St John's College. Margaret Beaufort, the mother of Henry VII, was an avid supporter of the institutions here during her lifetime and it was the executors of her estate who established St John's as a college in 1511; among its graduates are the writers William Wordsworth and Douglas Adams as well as Maurice Wilkes, a pioneer in the field of information technology.

Countless treasures to be found on the shelves of Trinity Hall's library

BLENHEIM PALACE

Location: Southern England (Oxfordshire)
Best time to travel: February–December (closed in January)
www.blenheimpalace.com

Blenheim Palace near Woodstock in Oxfordshire is one of the most beautiful and compelling jewels of baroque architecture in Britain. A grateful nation bestowed this superb residence upon John Churchill, the first Duke of Marlborough, in a gesture of gratitude for his successful campaign against French and Bavarian troops in the Battle of Blenheim in 1704. The palace was built between 1705 and 1722 under the supervision of Sir John Vanbrugh, one of England's most highly regarded architects. The three wings of the two-storey baroque palace feature towers and arcades arranged around a massive courtyard. The extensive gardens have been remodeled several times over the years. Initially designed by Henry Wise and based on the model of Versailles, the park was returned to a more naturalistic state by landscape gardener Lancelot "Capability" Brown, who transformed it into a more romantic environment through the addition of a number of waterfalls and a lake, both of which were popular features at the time. The ensemble of palace and park reflects some of the primary concerns of Romanticism: a return both to nature and to the nation's roots.

The Duchess of Marlborough tried in vain to persuade the architect Sir John Vanbrugh to make Blenheim Palace a bit more homely as it was being built. The Great Hall (opposite, top) is the modern visitor's first intimation of the opulence which awaits. Winston Churchill was born here in 1874.

United Kingdom

CHESTER

Location: Western England (Cheshire)
Best time to travel: throughout the year
www.visitchester.com

Chester, known in ancient times as "Castra Cevana", was founded in the year 79 AD by the Romans and remained a vital outpost in Britain until well into the 4th century. Today, Chester is one of the most beautiful cities in the United Kingdom.

Chester Cathedral (right) was a Benedictine abbey church until 1540. The city is famed for its "rows", half-timbered arcades and the 1897 clock tower.

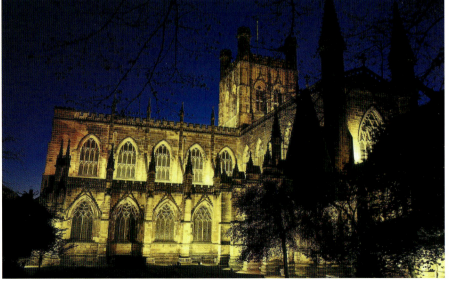

YORK

Location: Northern England (Yorkshire)
Best time to travel: throughout the year
www.visityork.org
www.york.gov.uk

York is one of the most beautiful English cathedral cities and York Minster, the seat of the Archbishop of York, is the largest Gothic cathedral on the island. This 158-m (518-ft) long building was constructed between the 11th and 15th centuries.

York Minster (top) is the largest Gothic church north of the Alps and also has the largest array of medieval stained glass windows.

United Kingdom

YORKSHIRE COAST

Location: Northern England (Yorkshire)
Best time to travel: March–October
www.yorkshire-coast.com
www.discoveryorkshirecoast.com

One of Yorkshire's greatest attractions is its natural beauty, which can be enjoyed along the coast in a variety of forms, whether in villages such as Staithes or picturesque coves like Saltwick Bay and Robin Hood's Bay. There is also a magnificent view from Sutton Bank. The best way to explore this beautiful coastline is to walk the North Yorkshire Coast Path (86 km, 53 mi).

Quite why Robin Hood's Bay on the Yorkshire coast between Whitby and Scarborough was named after the hero of Sherwood Forest has never been made clear.

DURHAM

Location: North-east England
Best time to travel: throughout the year
www.thisisdurham.com
www.durham.gov.uk

Durham is well known for its Norman Cathedral and 11th-century castle, and is home to Durham University. The historical city centre of Durham has changed little over the past 200 years. Built on a cliff in the county of Durham in a Romano-Norman and Early Gothic style, Durham Cathedral is one of the most important ecclesiastical buildings in England. Its romantic location high over the River Wear has inspired a number of artists to take up their brushes. A Norman keep was built here in 1072 as a bulwark against the Scots, and this grew to include a Benedictine monastery and the seat of a bishop

who was also the local ruler until 1536. Construction of the cathedral was begun in 1093 and the building was intended to hold the relics of the Venerable Bede and of St Cuthbert, whose tomb was once a majestic monument of green marble and gold. Since the memorial's destruction in 1538, only a simple stone grave remains. The church is considered to be one of the finest architectural achievements of the conquering Normans. The long and low nave is a peculiarity of English Gothic and the fan vaulting over the choir stalls is the oldest of its kind to have survived, ensuring the cathedral an important place in the architectural history of Europe.

The fortress-like palace of the Bishop of Durham dominates the River Wear. Several of the Cathedral's stained glass windows recount episodes from the life of St Cuthbert and Bible stories.

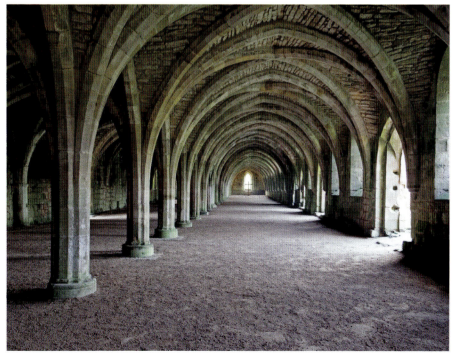

FOUNTAINS ABBEY

Location: Northern England (North Yorkshire)
Best time to travel: throughout the year
www.fountainsabbey.org.uk

The Cistercian monastery at Fountains Abbey was founded by monks from York. Until its dissolution in 1539 as a result of the schism between the English church and Rome, the abbey enjoyed a period of enormous prosperity. The 123-m (404-ft) long church, 55-m (180-ft) high tower above the north transept, and the monastery buildings are all well preserved.

Fountains Abbey was ransacked in the wake of Henry VIII's dissolution of all the monasteries in the country. It is now a romantic feature in the grounds of Studley Royal Park.

United Kingdom

NORTH YORK MOORS

Location: Northern England
Best time to travel: April–October
www.northyorkmoors.org.uk
www.yorkshiremoors.co.uk

Founded in 1951, the North York Moors National Park covers an area of 1,300 ha (3,200 acres) and protects England's largest continuous stretch of moorland. Visitors can explore the undulating hills, lush green valleys, and many wild flowers of the park, which extends as far as the Yorkshire coast, along more than 2,300 km (1,430 miles) of tracks and paths.

A hike along the Cleveland Way National Trail or a bike tour through the spectacular scenery of Dalby Forest are just some of the delights the national park has to offer.

YORKSHIRE DALES

Location: Northern England
Best time to travel: April–October
www.yorkshiredales.org.uk

The Yorkshire Dales, which lie to the west of York between the Lake District and the North York Moors National Park, are a Mecca for hikers. A "dale" is a valley, and there are at least 18 of these, running down from the Pennine hills, with unique limestone formations, stone walls, caverns, and intervening hills and moors. This thrilling scenery was formed by Ice Age glaciers, and it is recognised that there were settlements here even in prehistoric times.

Romans, Vikings, and Danes have all left their mark here. The Yorkshire Dales National Park was founded in 1954.

HADRIAN'S WALL

Location: Northern England
Best time to travel: March–October
www.hadrians-wall.org

Upon entering the port of Newcastle you will be able to see the very eastern end of Hadrian's Wall. The Wall runs parallel to the border between England and Scotland from Carlisle to the Solway Firth at Bowness on the the Irish Sea, 120 km (75 mi) away. The structure was originally built as part stone wall, part earth mound. Aside from the actual wall, which was built along an ancient military route, the complex also features military camps, milecastles (fortified structures), larger fortresses, turrets, and gates. The wall, which was about 5 m (18 ft) tall and almost 3 m (10 ft) thick, was built by the emperor Hadrian between 122 and 132, to stave off the threat of fierce Scottish tribes, especially the Picts, who continually invaded Roman territories. After the withdrawal of the Roman army in about 410, the wall quickly fell into disrepair.

Parts of the stonework of Hadrian's Wall, the largest structure in Great Britain, have been preserved and wind their impressive way through the landscape of northern England.

LAKE DISTRICT

Location: North-west England (Cumbria)
Best time to travel: March–October
www.lakedistrict.gov.uk
www.lake-district.com

The Lake District, one of the most popular tourist destinations in Great Britain, has been run as a national park since 1951, but it was more than 200 years ago that the "Lake Poets", part of the Romantic movement whose greatest exponent was Wordsworth, began extolling the beauty of this stunning landscape. Great Langdale valley is one of the most beautiful dales in the area, and the summits of the two Langdale Pikes, the higher of which rises to 730 m (2,395 ft), can be reached on a trail that is just under 10 km (6 mi) long. A road will take you to the remains of a Roman fort at the Hardknott Pass, from which there are superb views of the Eskdale Valley.

Hiking, climbing, sailing, or wind-surfing enthusiasts are well served in this varied park comprising twelve large lakes and numerous small ones such as Lake Buttermere (above), or you may just prefer to enjoy the beautiful scenery.

DUNSTANBURGH CASTLE

Location: North-east England (Northumberland)
Best time to travel: throughout the year
www.nationaltrust.org.uk
www.visitnorthumberland.com

The land around the Scottish border has long been the subject of bitter conflict, as can be seen from the series of mighty castles that line the Northumberland coast. Dunstanburgh Castle was built in 1313 for Thomas Plantagenet, (1278–1322), the second Earl of Leicester, who led a legendary uprising against King Edward II.

Protected on one side by the sea and on the other by steep cliffs, Dunstanburgh Castle was once one of the largest and most beautiful castle complexes in the country but now only a ruin remains.

LINDISFARNE CASTLE

Location: North-east England (Northumberland)
Best time to travel: Mid-February until late October
www.nationaltrust.org.uk
www.visitnorthumberland.com

The lonely ruins of Lindisfarne Castle stand on an island off the north-east coast of Northumberland which can be reached along a 4.8 km (3 mi) causeway uncovered only at low tide. It is also known as the "Holy Island". Stones from a Celtic monastery which was abandoned in 875 after numerous Viking raids were used to build the castle in 1540.

Those wishing to keep their feet dry should visit Lindisfarne Castle at low tide. This originally Tudor fortress came into private hands in 1903.

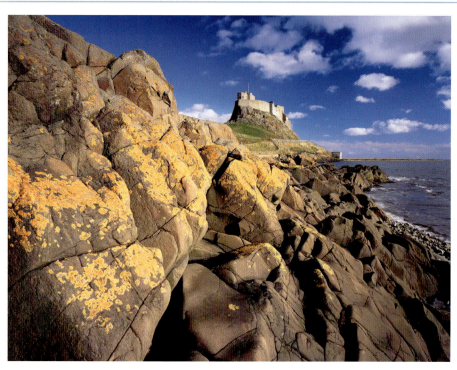

WARKWORTH CASTLE

Location: North-east England (Northumberland)
Best time to travel: throughout the year
www.english-heritage.org.uk
www.visitnorthumberland.com

On the banks of the River Coquet, which flows the entire length of Northumberland, there stands a stunning fortress which has been immortalized in literature. Scenes in Shakespeare's *Henry IV Part 2* where the Earl of Northumberland confers with his son, Harry Hotspur, all take place in this castle, which was built in the 14th century and extended in the 15th. The gatehouse and 15th-century keep are particularly well preserved.

Warkworth Castle lies on a picturesque bend in the river about 3 km (2 mi) north of Amble.

BAMBURGH CASTLE

Location: North-east England (Northumberland)
Best time to travel: March–October
www.bamburghcastle.com
www.visitnorthumberland.com

Local red sandstone has been crafted to make the royal residence of Bamburgh a typical coastal fortress. The first attempts to fortify this area seem to have been made in prehistoric times, and the kings of Northumbria were crowned here during this imposing castle's heyday between 1095 and 1464.

Bamburgh stands proudly on a dolerite cliff right next to the sea. Its keep and parts of the curtain wall date back to the Norman period, but the living quarters were built in the 19th century for Lord Armstrong.

PEMBROKE

Location: West Wales
(Pembrokeshire)
Best time to travel:
throughout the year
www.pembroke-castle.co.uk
www.castlewales.com

Pembroke has traditionally been regarded as the county town of Pembrokeshire, even though the actual administrative center is Haverfordwest. This little town and the nearby community of Pembroke Dock are great places from which to explore the local highlights, such as the Pembrokeshire Coast Path, a hiking trail divided into twelve stages, each representing a day's walk.

Pembroke Castle was built by Roger of Montgomery in 1093. Protected by water on three sides, it resisted all attempts by the Welsh to overcome it.

PEMBROKESHIRE COAST

Location: West Wales
(Pembrokeshire)
Best time to travel: March–October
www.pcnpa.org.uk
www.visitpembrokeshire.com

Pembroke is also the gateway to the Pembrokeshire National Park, which encloses the coastal area of the peninsula between Tenby to the south and Fishguard to the north. The area is the site of a number of important prehistoric finds, such as the Neolithic barrow grave at Pentre Ifan. The national park's coastal scenery is wild and fascinating.

The grave chamber of the megalithic tomb at Pentre Ifan has been formed with mighty stone boulders for 6,000 years. The capstone is more than 5 m (16 ft) long.

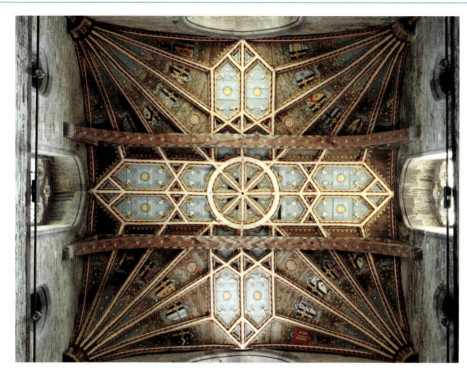

ST DAVID'S

Location: North Wales (Pembrokeshire)
Best time to travel: throughout the year
www.stdavids.gov.uk

Wales' westernmost city is located on the northern shores of St Bride's Bay. Although it might seem surprising that such a small town should be described as a city, it is due to the cathedral here: a church of such a size may stand only in a "city", no matter how few inhabitants live there.

St David's Cathedral was a pilgrimage site in the Middle Ages, and St David (c. 512–587) the patron saint of Wales, became the abbot here as he went about his missionary work. The building dates back to the 12th century, although the imposing carved ceiling was completed in the 16th century.

United Kingdom

SNOWDONIA

Location: North Wales
Best time to travel: April–October
www.eryri-npa.gov.uk
www.snowdonia-society.org.uk

Densely wooded valleys, mountain lakes, expansive moors and picturesque ocean inlets, all juxtaposed with a fascinating succession of ragged peaks – just some of the delights of the Snowdonia National Park. Founded in 1951, it was the first Welsh national park and is still the largest of three (the Pembrokeshire Coast National Park was founded a year later, and the Brecon Beacons National Park in 1957). Snowdonia extends from Conwy in the north to the peaks of Machynlleth in the south. Its highest point is Mount Snowdon at 1,085 m (3,560 ft), which is also the highest mountain in Wales. The Park's entire coastline is a Special Area of Conservation, which runs from the Llyn Peninsula down the mid-Wales coast, the latter containing valuable sand dune systems. The many hills and mountains in the national park are often draped in clouds and mist, lending the scenery an almost mystic air. It is a paradise for ramblers and rock climbers, and there are any number of rare plants and animals to discover in this excitingly diverse area, including the golden eagle and the merlin. A pleasantly nostalgic way to explore the park is to take a trip on one of the narrow-gauge railways. From Caernarfon it is also possible to take a ferry to the island of Anglesey off the north-western coast of Wales.

The dramatic scenery of the Snowdonia National Park (2,180 sq km/840 sq mi) is the result of millions of years of erosion. The valleys, moraines, and corries were created during the Pleistocene period more than 10,000 years ago.

CONWY, HARLECH, CAERNARFON

Location: North Wales
Best time to travel:
throughout the year
www.visitconwytown.co.uk
www.harlech.com
www.caernarfon.com

Gwynnedd, a rugged region of north wales, was ruled for centuries by the minor aristocracy until being conquered by Edward I (1239–1307). After his victorious campaign in Wales in the year 1284, Edward secured his position in the area with the construction of three strongholds on the English border. Conwy Castle was intended as a monument to English rule and a staging post in the systematic settlement of Wales by the English. Begun in 1283 and completed in the incredibly short time of just four and a half years, the castle is considered a masterpiece of medieval military architecture. It was built by James of St George, a leading fortifications architect who also supervised work on the castles at Harlech and Caernarfon, both of which were started in the same year. Together with the later castles of Aberystwith, Beaumaris and Flint, they formed a chain of fortresses along the coast of North Wales.

King Edward I built nine castles in Wales in the space of nine years after his victorious campaign in the 13th century: Caernarfon Castle (top) was built at the mouth of the River Seiont in 1283. Harlech Castle (bottom) was captured by the Welsh rebel Owain Glyndwr in 1404. The walls of Conwy Castle with its eight round towers (opposite) are up to 4.5 m (15 ft) thick.

United Kingdom

EDINBURGH

Location: South-east Scotland
Best time to travel:
throughout the year
www.edinburgh.org
www.edinburgh-inspiring
capital.com

Edinburgh, the capital of Scotland, features a fascinating architectural contrast between the sprawling medieval Old Town and the carefully planned Georgian New Town. Dominating the Old Town, the fortifications of Edinburgh Castle date back to the 11th century. The Royal Mile, which is formed by Lawnmarket, Canongate, and the High Street, is the main thoroughfare of the Old Town and descends from Castle Rock to the numerous lanes and inner courtyards surrounding such elegant mansions as Gladstone's Land, and a host of religious buildings such as the late-Gothic St Giles' Cathedral. At the eastern end of the Royal Mile there is the Palace of Holyrood House, built in 1128 as an Augustinian monastery and later used as the residence of the Scottish kings. Opposite the Palace is the modern building of the new Scottish Parliament. Despite its declining political importance after Scotland's union with England in 1707, Edinburgh remained an important cultural center. The Georgian New Town, with its disciplined grid of streets, was laid out at the end of the 18th century. The annual Edinburgh Festival, which takes places in August, is a one-of-a-kind experience where almost every street is taken over by performers. Theater troupes and musicians take the stage, and there is a host of cabaret, circus, opera, comedy, film, and ballet to be watched; the background music is provided by bagpipes, of course.

Towering over the whole city the bell towers of the Balmoral Hotel and Edinburgh Castle are the high points of the Edinburgh skyline.

DUNNOTTAR, SLAINS, CRATHES

Location: East Scotland
Best time to travel: throughout the year
www.dunnottarcastle.co.uk
www.scottish-castles.de
www.nts.org.uk

A trip through Scotland is also a journey through history. The earliest evidence of hunter-gatherers in the far north dates back to about 7000 BC. Later, when the clan system had taken hold, Scottish chiefs continued their struggle to control this rugged, expansive landscape. In the Highlands alone there were roughly 180 clans. They allowed farmers to cultivate the land, made pacts with royal houses – while simultaneously conspiring against them – and built castles and palaces as a symbol of their power. As a result of all this success they were able to erect these impressive structures in the heart of breathtaking scenery; the castles are inextricably interwoven into local culture and have become icons of of Scotland. Dunnottar Castle, for example, near the small port of Stonehaven, enjoys a panoramic backdrop of majestic rocky cliffs and is so impossibly picturesque that it could be the creation of an inspired set designer. Slaines Castle, on the coast north of Aberdeen, is the property of the 19th Earl of Errol and inspired Bram Stoker to pen his world famous novel *Dracula* in 1895. Crathes Castle, situated to the east of Banchory just beyond Aberdeen, is famous for its beautiful gardens.

Scotland combines the most dramatic history with the most beautiful scenery, as is amply proven by the castles at Slains (top right), Crathes, and Dunnottar (opposite).

HIGHLANDS

Location: West Scotland
Best time to travel: Mid-May
to mid-September
www.visithighlands.com
www.visitscotland.org

There is no more iconic landscape in Scotland that the Highlands. Largely escaping English influence, this area of astounding natural beauty was ruled by the Scottish clans for centuries. Scenery comprising majestic mountains, glens, and lakes with breathtaking sea views is a paradise both for hikers and for those wishing to explore the local animal and plant life. Before the 19th century the Highlands was home to a much larger population, but due to a combination of factors including the outlawing of the traditional Highland way of life following the Jacobite Rising of 1745, the infamous Highland Clearances, and migration to urban areas during the Industrial Revolution, the area is now one of the most sparsely populated in Europe. A tectonic fault known as the Great Glen or *Gleann Mór* divides the North-West Highlands to the north from the Grampian Mountains to the south. Ben Nevis, the highest mountain in the British Isles, rises majestically from the Grampian Mountains to a height of 1,344 m (4,410 ft). It is one of 284 "munros", a name given in Scotland to mountains of more than 915 m (3,000 ft) whose summits stand out noticeably from others. While the mountain's north-west slopes are relatively easy for hikers to climb, the 460-m (1,509-ft) rock face of the steeper north-east approach is a challenge even for experienced climbers. Glencoe is a beautiful and wildly romantic valley. Rannoch Moor is the largest expanse of moorland in Great Britain and one of the last virtually untouched natural habitats in Europe.

Storm clouds gather round Ben Nevis and Loch Eil at dusk.

LOCH NESS

Location: Northern Scotland
Best time to travel: April–October
www.lochness.com
www.loch-ness.org

With a length of roughly 36 km (22 mi), this forbidding body of water would be an ideal home for the monster we have come to know as Nessie. Loch Ness is on average 1 km (0.6 mi) wide, up to 230 m (755 ft) deep, and never gets warmer than 7°C (45°F). Nessie is said to have emerged for the first time in 556, only to be chased back into the depths by the Irish missionary St Columba with the words: "go thou no further, nor touch the man; go back with all speed!" The monster kept out of sight for some 1,000 years thereafter, supposedly re-emerging in the 16th century to devour three men before disappearing again until 1933. "Sightings" have been continually reported since then, and scientists have attempted to prove Nessie's existence. In 1976, a research team from the USA reached the conclusion that something indeed lives in Loch Ness: a roughly 15-m long (50-ft) vertebrate that breathes with gills. Theoretically, however, some thirty to fifty specimens would need to live in the lake to have ensured the survival of the species since the first sighting. Those feeling the urge to watch the water in the hope of sighting this mysterious creature should visit Urquhart, a castle built around 1230 near the town of Drumnadrochit on the west bank of the loch, which has the best view.

Cataloguing the unknown: Nessie has been a protected species since 1934, and anyone catching this famous saurian will be required to return her to the loch immediately. A visit to Urquhart Castle, which stands on a spit of land in Loch Ness, is a more realistic ambition for tourists.

EILEAN DONAN CASTLE

Location: North-west Scotland
Best time to travel: April–October
www.eileandonancastle.com

Standing on an island set against the majestic mountains of Glen Shiel, the fairytale castle of Eilean Donan is surrounded by the waters of Loch Duich. The castle's name is a clue to its location – *eilean* means "island" in Scots Gaelic. The fortress is connected to the mainland by a causeway and a stone pedestrian bridge. It is thought that the site where the castle now stands was first settled in the 6th century, but the earliest fortifications were built in the 13th century by Alexander II of Scotland to guard the lands of Kintail. The clan Mackenzie, who later became the Earls of Seaforth, took over the house, leaving its running to their factors, the Macreas. In April 1719 the castle was occupied by Spanish troops attempting to start another Jacobite Rising. The castle was recaptured, and then demolished, by three Royal Navy frigates on 10–13 May 1719. The Spanish troops were defeated a month later at the Battle of Glen Shiel. The castle was restored in the years between 1919 and 1932 by Lt. Col. John MacRae-Gilstrap. The restoration included the construction of an arched bridge to give easier access to the castle. A curious distinction is that it has one of only two left-handed spiral staircases in a castle in Great Britain, as the reigning king at the time of building held a sword with his left hand. The museum here recounts the turbulent history of this unique building.

The picturesque location of Eilan Donan Castle on Loch Duich in Glen Shiel. Internationally acclaimed films such as *Highlander, Braveheart,* and *The World Is Not Enough* were shot against the backdrop of its stunning scenery.

HEBRIDES

Location: North-west Scotland
Best time to travel: May–September
www.isle-of-lewis.com
www.explore-isle-of-mull.co.uk
www.isle-of-iona.com
http://guide.visitscotland.com

Wind, clouds, and a mild Atlantic climate: the roughly 500 islands of the Inner and Outer Hebrides off the north-west coast of Scotland are a geological mixture of volcanic rock, slate, and gneiss, creating a rugged, unspoilt landscape of wide, grassy moorland with more than 100 lakes. Barely 80 of the islands are inhabited by roughly 60,000 people, who make their living from cattle-farming, fishing, and tourism. The Hebrides were settled during the Mesolithic era around 6500 BC, after the climatic conditions improved enough to sustain human settlement. Little and North Minch and the Barra Sound divide the archipelago into the Inner and Outer Hebrides (the "Western Isles"). Connected by an isthmus, the two islands of Lewis and Harris together form the largest land mass in the Outer Hebrides, known as "Long Island". The scenery of the island of Mull in the Inner Hebrides is a mixture of rolling hills and mountainous *karst* peaks. The druid island of Iona at its southern tip is considered the birthplace of Scottish Christianity: St Columba, a Celtic monk and missionary, landed here in 563 and founded the first monastery. Staffa can be reached by boat from Mull and Iona only in good weather; legend has it that this tiny island, only 600 m by 200 m (1,970 ft by 660 ft), represents the Scottish end of the Giant's Causeway in Northern Ireland.

Islands of light: the Isle of Mull (top), and the Isle of Staffa (bottom). Opposite: Iona Abbey was built on the island of the same name around 1200.

STANDING STONES OF CALLANISH

Location: Isle of Lewis,
North-west Scotland
Best time to travel: May–September
www.callanishvisitorcentre.co.uk
www.isle-of-lewis.com

The area around Calanais is home to over 20 monuments erected between 3000 and 4000 years ago. The rock monoliths of Callanish on the Isle of Lewis form what is probably the most beautiful stone circle in Scotland. Exactly 47 of the upright prehistoric megaliths (*menhirs*) can still be seen today, and were presumably erected by hand at various stages between the years 3000 and 1500 BC. The menhirs are made of Lewisian gneiss, a type of stone typical of these islands. The northern avenue of the complex is particularly impressive and is made up of two almost parallel rows of stones stretching roughly 82 m (270 ft) with the stones 8.2 m (27 ft) apart. In the center, there is a circle comprising 13 menhirs; the large central stone in the middle is 4.75 m (16 ft) high, weighs around five tonnes (5.5 short tons) and forms the western edge of a small chamber housing a communal Neolithic grave. The circle is surrounded by 13 more monoliths forming a ring 11 to 13 m (36 to 43 ft) in diameter. The Callanish megalithic site is certainly compara- ble to Stonehenge in southern England, and has become the symbol of the Western Isles. It is thought that the alignments of the various stones were used to mark significant points in the lunar cycle. The overall layout of the monument recalls a distorted Celtic cross.

Prehistoric evidence of a mysterious culture: the circles and radii formed by the 47 Standing Stones of Callanish make up a "sun cross".

INNER HEBRIDES

Location: Western Scotland
Best time to travel: May–September
www.skye.co.uk
www.isleofskye.com

Although the Outer Hebrides form a separate administrative district, the Inner Hebrides are part of the Highland Region, falling under the jurisdiction of Argyll and Bute. Traditionally, the Inner Hebrides have been subdivided into two groups (northern and southern). Combined, the islands cover an area of 4,158 sq km (2,583 sq mi). The Isle of Skye is the largest island and its unique character is shaped by peaks such as Cuillin Hills (1,009 m/3,310 ft) and the Quiraings, not to mention bizarre geological formations like the Old Man of Storr. Fog and brief rainstorms followed by rainbows will transform any trip along the remote coastal paths into an unforgettable adventure. Since the construction of the bridge connecting the Kyle of Lochalsh on the Scottish mainland directly to Skye, the largest island of the Inner Hebrides has become more popular than ever. With a total surface area of 1,735 sq km (670 sq mi), Skye has plenty of excellent routes for hikers. Approximately 8,000 people live here, most working in the tourist industry. The Vikings called the island *Skúyo*, the "Island of Clouds". In Scots Gaelic it is known as *Eilean Sgiathanach*, the "winged isle", because of its jagged coast, or *Eilean a Cheo*, "mist island", in reference to the usual weather conditions. There is a center here where you can learn Scots Gaelic, and some 60% of the islanders still speak the language. The fugitive Bonnie Prince Charlie took his leave of Flora MacDonald, who is still revered as a heroine even now, in the Royal Hotel at Portree in 1746.

Benin Edra on Skye's Trotternish Peninsula reaches a height of 611 m (2,005 ft).

ORKNEY

Location: Northern Scotland
Best time to travel: May–September
www.orkneyjar.com
www.visitorkney.com

Only 18 of the Orkney Islands lying about 30 km (19 mi) off Scotland's north-eastern coast are inhabited, and these are best reached from the John O'Groats and Thurso ferry ports. Agriculture is most important sector of the economy and the significant wind and marine energy resources are of growing importance. The local people are known as Orcadians and have a distinctive dialect and a rich inheritance of folklore. The major islands in the archipelago are Mainland, Hoy and South Ronaldsay, whose rolling scenery was formed by glaciers during the last Ice Age. Despite their location in the far north, the Orkneys enjoy a relatively mild climate thanks to the warm Gulf Stream. A number of stunning monuments from the Neolithic Age – shining examples of the cultural achievements of northern European civilizations between 3,000 and 2,000 BC – have been unearthed on Mainland, the main island of the Orkney Islands. The most fascinating of these include the large passage grave of Maes Howe, dating back to 2,500 BC, which has a diameter of more than 30 m (98 ft). The remnants of the stone cross at Stenness can also be traced back to prehistoric times, and the famous Ring of Brodgar is not far away. The stones here measure up to 4 m (15 ft) in height and form a circle approximately 100 m (328 ft) in diameter. The Stone Age settlement of Skara Brae was exposed by accident in a storm 150 years ago and is the best-preserved Neolithic structure of its kind in Europe.

The Standing Stones of Stenness date back to the 3rd century BC and once formed a stone circle with a diameter of about 30 m (100 ft).

DUNLUCE CASTLE

Location: North Northern Ireland (Antrim)
Best time to travel: April–October
www.northantrim.com
www.ni-environment.gov.uk

Built in the 16th century on an imposing basalt cliff, Dunluce was the base of the formidable Sorley Boy MacDonnell, a descendant of the Scottish clan MacDonald who had been intent on conquering Ireland. Sorley Boy's son was the first to make efforts at reconciliation with the English crown.

Spectacular location, dramatic history: Dunluce Castle, built high above the sea, has lain abandoned since 1839. The fortress was once defended against the English with cannons from a beached Spanish galleon.

GIANT'S CAUSEWAY

Location: North Northern Ireland (Antrim)
Best time to travel: April–October
www.giantscausewayofficial guide.com

Some 40,000 mostly hexagonal basalt columns rise spectacularly out of the sea near the fishing town of Ballycastle. Forming a complete headland, they are estimated to be around sixty million years old and were created as streams of lava cooled in the sea to form crystals. This natural phenomenon became known as the "Giant's Causeway" because of a legend in which the Irish giant Finn was challenged by a rival and built a stone path across the sea to Scotland.

The Giant's Causeway resembles a huge staircase built by a giant.

Ireland

DUBLIN

Location: East of Ireland
Best time to travel:
throughout the year
www.visitdublin.com

The first to settle here were the Vikings, who named the area "Dyfflin", meaning "Black Puddle". A bad omen, perhaps, and more than 1,000 years of Dublin's history have largely been shaped by external powers, primarily the English, who took Ireland as their first "colony". Dublin eventually became the flagship of the Anglo-Irish administration and yet, at heart, it was never really British at all. Gaelic traditions, music, poetry, storytelling, and playful banter were nurtured throughout the occupation until the battle for Irish independence began with the Easter Uprising in Dublin in 1916. Dublin experienced a dramatic boom in the 1990s, with the Irish economy growing more quickly than any other in the European Union, and the old charm of the city, such as the the beautiful 18th-century Georgian architecture, was enriched

with some new features. Distinctly modern urban lifestyles and attitudes are particularly apparent in Temple Bar, with its up-market galleries, lively bars, and fancy restaurants. Some of the main sights include St Patrick's Cathedral, built in the Early English style, and Trinity College with its Old Library. The city has a world-famous literary history, having produced many prominent literary figures, including William Butler Yeats, George Bernard Shaw, Samuel Beckett, Oscar Wilde, Jonathan Swift and the creator of Dracula, Bram Stoker. It is arguably most famous, however, as the location of the greatest works of James Joyce. His most celebrated work, *Ulysses*, is set in Dublin and full of topical detail, which brings history alive.

The pedestrian bridge connecting Temple Bar with Liffey Street was built in 1816 and is officially called Wellington Bridge; users were required to pay a halfpenny toll and it soon became known as the Halfpenny Bridge.

DONEGAL

Location: North Ireland
Best time to travel: April–October
www.donegal.ie
www.visitireland.com

The town of Donegal, which achieved renown as the family seat of the mighty O'Donnell clan, also gave its name to Ireland's northernmost county. The Irish name *Dún na nGall* means "Strangers' Fort" and refers to a 9th century Viking stronghold. The north coast of Donegal is a sparsely populated, lonely stretch of land. The cliffs of Slieve League, which fall a dramatic 601 m (1,972 ft) into the sea, are among Europe's highest. The Fanad Peninsula offers visitors a variety of scenery, featuring a coast-line with beautiful sandy beaches, wooded areas and truly amazing rock formations. In 1607, an event took place in the nearby Carmelite Friary at Rathmullan that was to be a turning point in Irish history: the flight of the Earls O'Neill and O'Donnel in the face of the superior numbers of the English Army cleared the way for Northern Ireland to be settled by Scottish Protestants. The broad expanse of Lough Beagh lies at the heart of the Glenveagh National Park. At some point in the 19th century, a speculator named John George Adair bought this piece of land and evicted the peasants who lived there; breeding sheep, he had figured out, was more profitable than rental income. Henry P McIlhenny, an American of Irish descent, bought the land in the 20th century and donated it to the state; it is now a national park once again open to the public. At its heart is Glenveagh Castle, a beautiful late Victorian 'folly' that was originally built as a summer residence.

The spectacular lighthouse at the tip of the Fanad Peninsula was built after the frigate Saldana foundered near the previously unmarked rocks in 1812.

Ireland

CONNEMARA

Location: West of Ireland (Galway)
Best time to travel: April–October
www.connemara.ie
**www.connemaranationalpark.
com, www.clifdenchamber.ie**
www.galway.net

Connemara, in the western part of County Galway, is a mountainous region of lakes and moors possessed of an almost mythical beauty. Peat bogs extending between two mountain ranges, the Twelve Bens and the Maumturks, are surrounded on three sides by a coastline of tiny bays dotted with countless little islands. A region of approximately 20 sq km (8 sq mi) on the north-western slopes of the Twelve Bens was declared a nature reserve, and Connemara National Park, which is open all year round, can be explored on two signposted tracks starting from the visitors center. The inhabitants of Connemara have traditionally been quite poor. After the Famine of the 1840s, when the potato blight deprived almost the entire population of its staple food, many gave up the battle to make a living from the poor soil here and emigrated to the United States. Fresh Atlantic air, a magnificent location above the mouth of the river Owenglin, and the nearby Twelve Bens Mountains combine to make the city of Clifden the most popular place on the west coast of Connemara. The area around the town is rich with megalithic tombs. The famous green/white "Connemara marble" (actually a type of verd antique) was a trade treasure used by the inhabitants of the prehistoric time. It continues to be of great value today. Even Celtic culture was able to thrive here for many years as no invaders were interested in the infertile soil, and Oliver Cromwell was the first to invade in the 17th century, although not for economic reasons. He forced his opponents into the western part of Connemara and onto

the nearby island of Inishbofin. As soon as you leave the coast, the landscape of Connemara is dominated by bogs, inhospitable mountains, and lakes. Strewn with granite boulders, the land yields not much more than peat and sheep's wool, but Connemara's landscape is a riot of hues: from the scarlet and brown heather at Killary Harbour to the deep green of lush ferns at Derryclare Lough, and the gray of the craggy cliffs near Maam Cross. Connemara's southern coast is extremely craggy and rugged, a damp stony desert interspersed with lakes that merge almost seamlessly with the sea, which is itself scattered with little islands. The author Padraig Pearse, one of the martyrs of the Republican Uprising in 1916, chose the tiny village of Rosmuck in this remote region for his summer residence. Dog's Bay and Gurteen Beach, two other western beaches near Roundstone, are known for their clear water and white sand. The three inhabited Aran Islands are easily reached from Connemara and have become the epitome of devotional, rustic life on the Irish Atlantic coast. The playwright John Millington Synge, a keen supporter of traditional Celtic culture, wrote about life on the islands in the 1890s and brought them to the attention of the world. Geologically, they are a continuation of the limestone plateau of the Burren, and seem to consist only of limestone and turf. Stone forts – prehistoric fortifications – are a common feature.

The Connemara National Park owes its geological history to sediments from an ancient warm sea which once covered the area. Although the sparsely populated valleys were soon covered in bogs and moors such as those surrounding the Owenmore River, the Twelve Bens and the Maumturk Mountains remained barren.

Ireland

THE BURREN

Location: West of Ireland (Clare)
Best time to travel: March–October
www.burrenbeo.com

An English officer who arrived with Cromwell's army in the *karst* landscape of County Clare cast a less than poetic eye over its unique beauty; he said there "was no water to drown a man, nor yet a tree from which to hang him, and no earth to bury him afterwards". The limestone plateau that occupies 250 sq km (96 sq mi) of the area is known as the Burren (from the Irish *boireann*, meaning "stony land"). At first glance it is indeed a bleak and desolate place, but in spring, an astonishing number of flowers including Alpine, Mediterranean and Arctic varieties sprout from the rock crevices.

Poulnabrone dolmen, a table-like stone tomb in which the skeletons of 33 people were discovered, is one of the most striking pieces of evidence remaining of early human settlement on the limestone plateau of the Burren.

CLIFFS OF MOHER

Location: West of Ireland (Clare)
Best time to travel: March–October
www.cliffsofmoher.ie
www.cliffs-moher.com

The stunning cliffs of Moher are Europe's highest coastal escarpment and extend for 8 km (5 mi) along a spectacular shoreline. Between Liscannor and Doolin the cliffs reach dizzying heights of more than 200 m (656 ft) and provide impressive panoramic views. Looking down from the vertiginous cliffs to the churning surf and rugged rock formations, you get a good idea of the immense forces at work in the Atlantic. Hikers will enjoy the beautiful footpath that follows the craggy coast for 35 km (22 mi) here. The southern end of Moher, near Hag's Head, is an ideal place to take in this extraordinary nature spectacle.

The Cliffs of Moher rank as one of the most popular tourist destinations in Ireland.

Ireland

CLONMACNOISE

Location: Central Ireland (Offaly)
Best time to travel: March–October
www.heritageireland.ie

The unique monastery settlement of Clonmacnoise is situated in a bend of the river Shannon, in County Offaly. Its isolated location long protected it from most attacks, but in 1552, pillaging English soldiers put an end to 1,000 years of thriving culture. In the Middle Ages, the monastery was renowned throughout Europe as a center for religion and scholarship. The complex includes two round towers as well as the ruins of the cathedral and eight smaller churches from various eras.

Another highlight is Ireland's most extensive collection of Celtic high crosses, the most precious of which date back to the first millennium AD.

ROCK OF CASHEL

Location: Southern Ireland (Tipperary)
Best time to travel: March–October
www.cashel.ie

An imposing limestone cliff topped with the ruins of a fortress complex towers over the broad lowlands of County Tipperary. Its strategic location has always meant the Rock of Cashel was of enormous importance. According to legend, the Rock of Cashel is said to have fallen from the devil's mouth when he flew over and saw Saint Patrick. The kings of Munster, whose rule extended across large parts of southern Ireland, used the fort (Irish: *caiseal*) as their residence from the 5th century onwards.

After being plundered in 1647 by troops commanded by Oliver Cromwell the complex lay abandoned for 100 years.

KING JOHN'S CASTLE

Location: South-west Ireland (Limerick)
Best time to travel: throughout the year
www.shannonheritage.com
www.limerick.ie

Limerick was originally a Viking settlement, and it was here that the mighty King John's Castle was constructed. King John himself travelled to the Shannon to attend to inauguration of the castle, which was considered impregnable. The Irish-speaking locals were obliged to live beyond its mighty walls in Irish Town, leading to a certain amount of friction between the two communities.

King John's Castle is a five-sided fortification with an imposing keep, three round towers, and a gatehouse with two turrets.

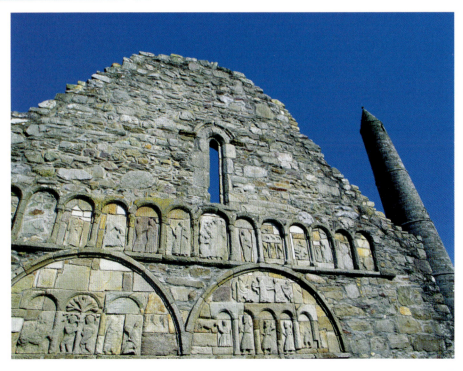

ARDMORE

Location: South-east Ireland (Waterford)
Best time to travel: March–October
www.waterfordtourist.com

Beside three old stone crosses on a hill on the outskirts of the village of Ardmore there is a well named after St Declan, and here pilgrims would refresh themselves. Modern-day pilgrims follow the 90-km (56-mi) St Declan's Way, which connects Ardmore with the Rock of Cashel shrine. Magnificent Romanesque carvings of scenes from the Old Testament on the west façade of Ardmore Cathedral have been preserved, although the church's roof is now missing.

The site of the saint's former monastery is now occupied by a 30-m (98-ft) high round tower and a 12th-century cathedral.

Ireland

DINGLE

Location: South-west Ireland (Kerry)
Best time to travel: March–October
www.dingle-peninsula.ie
www.dodingle.com

The approximately 50-km (31-mi) long Dingle Peninsula is the northernmost of five spits of land in County Kerry that point westward like fingers. With its gorgeous mountains, romantic rocky coast, and magnificent beaches it is one of Ireland's most beautiful and most popular regions. The mountains on either side of the Connor Pass, which at 456 m (1,496 ft) is the highest pass in Ireland, are a paradise for ramblers, while surfers will find excellent if chilly conditions on the 5-km (3-mi) beach near Inch on the peninsula's southern coast. The main town is Dingle to the south, a former fishing village which is now the haunt of divers.

BEARA

Location: South-west Ireland (Kerry)
Best time to travel: March–October
www.bearatourism.com
www.bearainfo.com

The Beara Peninsula is bounded by the Kenmare "river" (actually a bay) to the north side and Bantry Bay to the south. Beara was the ancestral home of the O'Sullivans, the lords of Dunboy Castle near Castletownbere. When English troops took the castle in 1601, 1,000 clan members began a march across Ireland to the county of Leitrim; only 35 of them made it. Subsequent waves of emigration further reduced the population and it continues to be a sparsely populated area.

The narrow road around the craggy Beara Peninsula (top right; below, a view of Ballydonegan Bay near Allihies) offers 140 km (87 mi) of fantastic views.

Ireland

Those who fancy remaining above the surface might like to visit Dingle's Oceanworld aquarium. Like everywhere in the west of Ireland, Dingle boasts relics of early Christendom. Especially impressive are the "beehive huts" lived in by early hermits. St Brandon, the patron saint of Kerry, is said to have prayed on Mount Brandon, which at 953 m (3,127 ft) is the second highest peak in Ireland after Carrauntoohill (1,041 m/3,415 ft), before setting off in a *curragh*, a traditional sailboat, with 14 other monks on his journey to America in the 6th century.

The coastal scenery of the Dingle Peninsula is as enchanting as it is romantic. Swathed in cloud, Mount Brandon fills the middle of the image, with the slopes of the "Three Sisters" visible along the steep coast beyond the mountain to the left.

IVERAGH

Location: South-west Ireland (Kerry)
Best time to travel: March–October
www.kerrytourist.com
www.discoverireland.ie

The drive around the Ring of Kerry takes you 170 km (106 mi) along the Iveragh Peninsula and is a highlight of any trip to Ireland. The ever-changing views of mountains and bays are simply breathtaking. A popular starting point for the tour of the Ring is Kenmare, a picturesque town of pastel-colored houses at the end of Kenmare Bay.

Puffin Island (above left), near the Bay of St Finan, is a popular nesting-place for puffins, gannets and boobies. Bottom: In a valley about 4 km (2.5 mi) from the south coast of Iveragh there is a 2,000-year-old ring fortification known as Staigue Fort.

Ireland

KILLARNEY

Location: South-west Ireland (Kerry)
Best time to travel: March–October
www.killarney.ie

Ice Age glaciers formed the Killarney Area, a mountainous lakeland area comprising more than 8,000 hectares (19,768 acres) near the town of the same name. Parts of the region have been made into a national park and the roads are closed to traffic. Any visit to the national park should include a trip by horse-drawn coach through the Gap of Dunloe, a mountain pass in the shadows of Purple Mountain, which owes its name to the heather that flowers here in late summer. The trip to the top of Carrauntoohil, Ireland's highest peak at 1,041 m (3,416 ft) is a little more demanding. The oak and yew trees that grow in the park are fairly rare in Ireland, since most of the forests were cut down centuries ago. The strawberry tree, a shrub with red, edible fruits that normally only grows in the Mediterranean, is just one of the unusual plants found in the region.

Built in the late 15th century, Ross Castle stands on a spit of land in Lough Leane. The three beautiful lakes of the Killarney Area (bottom) lie to the south-west of Killarney Town.

SKELLIG MICHAEL AND LITTLE SKELLIG

Location: South-west Ireland (Kerry)
Best time to travel: March–October
www.skelligexperience.com
www.skelligstrips.com

A rocky cliff rising from the Atlantic about 12 km (7 miles) from the Irish coast is the location of one of the most important archeological sites in the British Isles: the monastery complex dedicated to the Archangel Michael here was probably founded in the 7th century before being abandoned for unknown reasons in the 12th century. The walls of the prayer and accommodation cells are beehive-like structures built with no mortar, as was typical in early Irish architecture.

Besides the ruins of a 12th-century church there are also the remnants of a flight of 500 steps, which were intended to ease pilgrims' ascent to the highest point on the island. The nearby island of little Skellig is home to the world's largest gannet colony, with some 27,000 breeding pairs, and is also a nesting place for puffins. The surrounding waters teem with life also. Grey Seals are common, and Basking Sharks, Minke Whales, dolphins and Leatherback Turtles have also been recorded.

The highest point of Skellig Michael is 289 m (948 ft) above sea level.

Netherlands

AMSTERDAM

Location: Western Netherlands
Best time to travel:
throughout the year
www.iamsterdam.com
www.amsterdam.info

Amsterdam, the fourth-largest city in 17th-century Europe after Paris, London, and Naples, grew up around the delta at the mouth of the Amstel. The city owed its riches to the river, which facilitated importing and processing of commodities from the former colonies, and trading in spices and slaves. While controlling the seven seas beyond the city, Amsterdam's rich merchants concentrated on promoting the arts at home, building imposing townhouses which still dominate the skyline. Tree trunks were rammed as much as 30 m (98 ft) deep into the peaty ground to form the foundations of Amsterdam's Old Town, creating not only seventy islands on stilts, but also the romantic ambience of a town on the water – unsurprisingly Amsterdam was known as the "Venice of the North". There are 400 bridges in the city's historic center alone and the water level is kept constant with the help of a system of locks and pumps. Commercial cargo is still transported on the city's canals. Hundreds of houseboats lie at anchor on the quays of Amsterdam's 160 waterways as well. They have become an iconic element of city life, just like the bicycles and the flower stalls selling "tulips from Amsterdam". Although Amsterdam is the capital of the Netherlands and the most important center of education and culture, the government has its seat in The Hague to the south-west.

Construction of the crescent-shaped "Three Canal Belt" (right, the Keizersgracht canal) began at the height of the "Golden 17th Century".

Netherlands

THE HAGUE

Location: Western Netherlands
Best time to travel:
throughout the year
www.denhaag.nl

Holland's third-largest city is also the seat of both the Dutch parliament and the International Court of Justice, where UN war crimes trials are held. The Hague is the home of Queen Beatrix, and the States-General of the Netherlands. All foreign embassies and government ministries are located in the city, as well as the *Hoge Raad der Nederlanden* (Supreme Court), the *Raad van State* (Council of State) and many lobbying organisations. Its 750 years of history begin with just a few cottages built on the edge of the Count of Holland's hunting grounds. One of these 13th-century buildings, the Binnenhof, is now the political heart of the country. The classically styled Mauritshuis

GOUDA

Location: Western Netherlands
Best time to travel:
throughout the year
www.gouda.nl

It only takes a short stroll through this old town to show that it has much more to offer than the cheese market, which is held on the square between the town hall and the Renaissance Waag building every Thursday morning from mid-June to the end of August. There is the Gothic Stadhuis, built of gray blocks of stone on the market square, not to mention St Janskerk, built south of the market at the end of the 16th century, which at 123 m (404 ft) in length is the longest church in the Netherlands.

Gouda's Gothic-style town hall in the picturesque Old Town is really enchanting.

now houses an art gallery with works of incalculable value by Golden Age Dutch painters, and Flemish Old Masters. The house at 65 Zeestraat is the home of the Panorama Mesdag, a cylindrical painting 120 m (394 ft) long and 14 m (45 ft) high depicting the dunes at Scheveningen.

The nearby Museum Mesdag exhibits other works by the late 19th-century Hague School. The International Court of Justice (ICJ) has sat in the half neo-Gothic, half classical Peace Palace since 1945. The 15 judges of the International Court of Justice, which only hears pleas from states, not from private individuals, are elected by the Security Council and the General Assembly of the United Nations to a nine-year term of office.

The Hague's 13th-century Binnenhof is the seat of parliament and of a number of other government institutions.

UTRECHT

Location: Central Netherlands
Best time to travel: throughout the year
www.utrechtyourway.nl
www.utrecht.nl

The cathedral, which has been the icon of the city for 600 years, is built on the exact spot where a Roman military camp was once established. This camp was surrounded by a small civilian settlement from which modern-day Utrecht grew. Besides the cathedral, don't miss the pioneering Modernist house built by Gerrit Thomas Rietveld in 1924. Rietveld was a member of the *de Stijl* movement founded by the artists Piet Mondrian and Theo van Doesburg.

Dominating the skyline, the free-standing tower of the cathedral – the tallest church in Holland – is 112 m (367 ft) high.

Netherlands

DELFT

Location: South Netherlands
Best time to travel:
throughout the year
www.delft.nl
www.delfttoerisme.nl

Founded in the 11th century, Delft has a well-preserved historic Old Town, with canals and a number of late Gothic and Renaissance buildings. The Prinsenhof and the market square, lined with picturesque merchants' houses and featuring both the old town hall and the new church, are particularly worth a visit. No less than 46 members of the Dutch royal family lie buried in the church. Delft is also famed for the porcelain manufactured here in the 17th and 18th centuries (Delft faience).

Delft's historic market square still hosts markets and other events to this day.

KINDERDIJK

Location: South Netherlands
Best time to travel:
throughout the year
www.kinderdijk.nl
www.kinderdijk.com

The scenery of Kinderdijk-Elshout near Rotterdam is evidence of the Dutch mastery of drainage, being a typical mixture of reservoirs, dykes, pumping stations, monitoring buildings, and beautifully preserved wooden windmills. Simon Stevin, a Belgian, refined a technique for draining the *polders* in the early 17th century: erecting a neat row of windmills at Kinderdijk, he was able to create an ingenious system by which the water was "milled" away. This took place in two stages. First, water was transported from a lower canal to one that was higher up. It was then transferred to a system of locks that would remove it.

KEUKENHOF

Location: Western Netherlands
Best time to travel:
March–September
www.keukenhof.nl

Visitors to the Bollenstreek, or "bulb area" situated between Haarlem and Leiden can enjoy a drive through a veritable sea of flowers. The fields of around 8,000 nurseries specializing exclusively in the wholesale flower trade of are all on display here. The Tulip Route, as it is also known, will take you to the most important locations in the area. One such Mecca for flower-lovers is the Keukenhof, founded in 1949, where more than 700 varieties of tulip are exhibited at the world's largest flower show.

Keukenhof was once the kitchen quarters of a country house belonging to Countess Jacoba of Bavaria (1401–1436).

These windmills are still standing proudly today, ranged along the canals between Kinderdijk and Alblasserdam farther south. Such scenery, an essential part of Dutch culture, is also the largest and best-preserved collection of historic windmills in the country, and they are not there just for show – the majority of them have been in constant use since the 18th century. One of them has been transformed into a museum and is now open again to visitors. The windmills of Kinderdijk were placed on the list of UNESCO list of World Heritage Sites in 1997. √

The 19 windmills lining the canals between the towns of Kinderdijk and Ablasserdam to the south are like a string of pearls; the largest and best-preserved collection of historic mills in the country forms an essential part of traditional Dutch culture.

Belgium

BRUSSELS

Location: Central Belgium
Best time to travel:
throughout the year
www.bruxelles.irisnet.be
www.brussels.org

Brussels has grown from a 10th-century fortress town founded by a descendant of Charlemagne into a metropolis of more than one million inhabitants. Since the end of the Second World War, Brussels has been a main centre for international politics. Lying on the Senne River and linked to Antwerp by the Brussels Sea Canal, the Belgian capital and royal residence of Brussels is the seat of the European Parliament. Its hosting of principal EU institutions as well as the headquarters of the North Atlantic Treaty Organization has made the city a polyglot home of numerous international organisations, politicians, diplomats and civil servants. The Grand Place, a tantalizing mixture of public and private buildings, is one of the most beautiful squares on earth, with Victor Hugo calling it "a true miracle". The square is only 110 m (360 ft) long and 68 m (223 ft) wide, but the densely packed guild palaces squeezed into it make it one of the most outstanding architectural ensembles in Europe. When the rich guilds of Brussels took over control of the city from the aristocracy in the 15th century, they sought to build themselves a monument with this square and its precious guild palaces. The centerpiece of the square is the seven-storey Town Hall, the Maison des Ducs de Brabant, so-called after 19 ducal busts adorning the façade. The hall comprises six guild houses united by a single, monumental pilaster façade. The portals and façades of the other guild palaces to be admired on the square are also decorated with lively depictions of local scenes. Another of Brussels' claims to fame are Victor Horta's *art nouveau* buildings; the architect's town houses

and palaces have created a coherent stylistic atmosphere that is unique in Europe, and his old house and studio are now preserved as a museum. The Hôtels Tassel (1893–1895), Solvay (1894–1898), and van Eetvelde (1895–1897), as well as his house and studio (1898–1901), are early examples of Victor Horta's skill in expressing the basic principles of *art nouveau* in ever new variations. The buildings typically feature an open floor plan with the individual rooms arranged and decorated according to their particular function. The heart of the building is an open stairwell, lit from above, to enable quick and easy access to the various floors. The use of modern materials such as iron, steel, and glass for the interior and exterior was revolutionary for the time. Horta drew on every branch of the arts, from architecture and painting to sculpture and craft work, to decorate the interior, making his buildings a composite work of art.

The Palais Stoclet, a Viennese *art nouveau* gem built by Josef Hoffman for the Belgian art collector and banker of that name is also worth a visit. On 17 April 1958, the Belgian King Baudouin solemnly opened the first World's Fair since World War II and the icon of the exhibition was the 110-m (160-ft) high Atomium, a model of an iron crystal magnified 150 billion times; this symbol of the contemporary belief in unchecked technological and nuclear progress can still be seen today.

The Grand Place is lined with dozens of magnificent houses, such as the narrow, baroque guild houses with their sharply defined façades (top).
Behind the Italianate façade of the Maison des Ducs de Brabant (bottom), which was completed in 1698 and restored in the 19th century, there are six guild houses, each with their separate entrances.

Belgium

BRUGES

Location: North-west Belgium
Best time to travel:
throughout the year
www.brugge.be
www.flandern.com

The prosperous trade in textiles between medieval England and the European continent was mostly conducted in Bruges, where merchants from 17 countries owned factories. Bruges was transformed into a center of art and culture by Jan van Eyck and Hans Memling (and their generous patrons), reaching its zenith in the 15th century when the dukes of Burgundy, active supporters of late-Gothic court culture, took up residence within its walls. International trade, however, soon began to decline when the river Zweyn silted up, thus blocking access to the sea. The oval footprint of the town is punctuated by numerous canals and long streets with rows of gabled houses. These patrician mansions, the counting houses of the merchant princes, and the magnificent town hall, where the counts of Flanders were obliged to grant the rights to liberty demanded by the people, tell of the former prestige of the city. Bruges is also home to one of the most beautiful Flemish Beguinages, built here in 1245: these were semi-monastic institutions founded in many of the cities of north-eastern Europe at the end of the 12th and the early 13th centuries, and intended for single young women who wished to live a devout life without having to join one of the recognised – and oversubscribed – religious orders. Upon entering the beguinage, the women swore vows of chastity and obedience but were free to return to their secular lives at any time.

The belfry of the Lakenhalle (Drapers' Hall), an icon of the city's former glory and the Town Hall make up an interesting ensemble.

Belgium

GHENT

Location: Northern Belgium
Best time to travel:
throughout the year
www.visitgent.be
www.gent.be

A center of the textile industry since the Middle Ages, Ghent has managed to remain faithful to its traditions even in modern times. The second most important industry in the city is the cultivation of fruit, vegetables and flowers. The city's most famous sights nestle in the well-preserved historic heart of the city, between the Grafenburg and the 14th-century St

Bavo's Cathedral, which can be seen for miles around. Its greatest religious treasure is the famous "Ghent Altar" by the brothers Hubert and Jan van Eyck (15th century). The 95-m (312-ft) high bell tower opposite the church is a symbol of the rising power of the bourgeoisie in the 14th century. The

Drapers' Hall, the Great Meat House, the Grafenburg, and the Town Hall are also worth a visit.

The capital of the Belgian province of East Flanders lies at the confluence of the Scheldt and Leie rivers.

ANTWERP

Location: Northern Belgium
Best time to travel:
throughout the year
visit.antwerpen.be
www.antwerpen.be

The lifeblood of Antwerp, Belgium's second-largest city, is its bustling port. An array of car-making and chemical companies are based here, and as one of the busiest ports in the world it has cultivated an atmosphere of openness to the world for centuries – a fact that has contributed significantly to the rise of Antwerp as a world center for diamonds. Antwerp boasts a number of historic monuments and an exceptionally vibrant cultural life. Most of its sights are in the city center, which forms a semi-circle on the right bank of the Scheldt. The most remarkable sight in Antwerp is probably the Steen, an ancient fortress whose oldest sections date back to the 9th century. It now houses the National Maritime Museum, whose centerpiece is a fascinating 15th-century Flemish warship. The castle's viewing platform offers superb views across the Scheldt – which is more than 500 m (1,650 ft) wide at this point – to the bridges, old wharves, and, on the horizon, the countless freight cranes down at the port.

The north tower of the Cathedral of Our Lady is 123 m (404 ft) high; the church's interior is decorated with works by Peter Paul Rubens.

Luxembourg

LUXEMBOURG

Location: South Luxembourg
Best time to travel:
throughout the year
www.ont.lu
www.lcto.lu

Luxembourg is a landlocked country, bordered by Belgium, France, and Germany. It has a population of over half a million people in an area of approximately 2,586 sq km (999 sq mi). Luxembourg, the largest city and also the capital of the Grand Duchy, boasts a wealth of interesting architecture. Siegfried of Luxembourg founded the fortress of Lützelburg on a steep and strategically important mound called the Bock Fiels some time after 963, and the medieval city grew around its feet. The castle was continually extended until the 14th century, when Henry VII of Luxembourg took the Imperial and German crowns. The Spanish, who conquered Luxembourg in 1555, were the first to leave their mark on modern Luxembourg, building fortifications right across the city and mining tunnels which largely consisted of galleries and casemates blasted out of the rock. Other buildings of interest include the Grand Ducal Palace, the home of the family of the Grand Duke in the Old Town, St Michael's Church, the oldest surviving ecclesiastical building in Luxembourg, and the Cathedral of Our Lady, which is also known as Notre-Dame. This was designed as a church and Jesuit college by Jean de Blocq, a Jesuit priest, at the beginning of the 17th century. The church was completed and dedicated to the Immaculate Conception under Otto Herloy, another of the brotherhood, in 1621.

Grund, the lower town, extends along the banks of the Alzette. The area was once the preserve of handworkers, who needed the river water for their work.

PARIS

Location: Central France
Best time to travel:
throughout the year
www.parisinfo.com
www.paris.fr

No other city has been the subject of more songs, more films, more novels, or more plays – Paris, the city of light, and the city of love. The French capital casts a spell on its visitors, often in-spiring love at first sight, whether they are drinking *café crème* or *pastis* in the vibrant Latin Quarter, viewing the breathtaking panoramic view of the the cathedral square at Sacré-Coeur, taking a romantic river trip along the Seine, enjoying a relaxed stroll in the Jardin du Luxembourg, or even inspecting one of the major works of art in the museums – it's just a matter of preference. What is cer-tain is that it is almost impossible to resist the charms of this metropolis. A gigantic city has grown from the seed of a settlement on the Ile de la Cité, but its individual districts can still be explored on foot. Kings and presi-dents, artists and architects have all left their mark on the city over the centuries: the Roman baths in the Musée de Cluny, Notre-Dame cathe-dral, the Louvre, the Eiffel Tower, and the Grande Arche de La Défense all prove that Paris has always been a city with a plethora of traditions and yet also well ahead of its time, a place of monumental size and yet seduc-tive in its charm. Paris is a true world metropolis with a wealth of historic architectural gems and cultural high-lights. The area surrounding the Pont de Sully and the Pont d'Iéna is partic-ularly rich in history: it begins at the

Île Saint-Louis with its statue of St Geneviève, the patron saint of Paris, and continues to the west to the spiritual heart of the city, the cathedral of Notre-Dame and the Sainte Chapelle, a filigree masterwork of High Gothic style on the Île de la Cité. Next there is the Conciergerie, a former royal palace and prison, and part of the larger complex known as the Palais de Justice, which is still used for judicial purposes. The Louvre opposite houses one of Europe's most important art collections. From the 14th century until 1682, when Louis XIV moved his court to Versailles, the Louvre was actually the Paris residence of the kings of France. After that, the former town palace was transformed into one of the world's most important art museums. On the occasion of its 200th anniversary, the Louvre was remodeled as the "Grand Louvre", the largest museum in the world. Following the Seine downriver we find the Musée d'Orsay, the Grand and Petit Palais, and the National Assembly. Another fascinating destination is the world-famous Eiffel Tower, whose steel frame was revolutionary at the time of its construction and led the example.

The Alexandre III Bridge over the Seine was built for the World's Fair in 1900. Its steel frame crosses the river in a single span and guides traffic straight to Les Invalides, a complex of buildings containing museums and monuments, all relating to the military history of France, as well as the burial site for some of France's war heroes, notably Napoleon Bonaparte.

France

VERSAILLES

Location: Central France
Best time to travel:
throughout the year
www.chateauversailles.fr
www.mairie-versailles.fr

In 1661, King Louis XIV began the expansion of his father Louis XIII's hunting lodge, a site that was soon to serve him as the permanent seat of his government. The two leading architects, Louis Le Vau and later Jules Hardouin-Mansart, created a palace complex of roughly 700 rooms with vast manicured gardens – a work of art in themselves with plants, fountains and sculptures – as well as the auxiliary garden palaces of Petit and Grand Trianon. Versailles was the political heart of France for 100 years, with as many as 5,000 people living at court, including a considerable number of French aristocrats and up to 14,000 soldiers who were quartered in the outbuildings and in the actual town of Ver-

sailles. Of the many magnificent staterooms in the palace, the Hall of Mirrors has historically been seen as the most important. The room, which bewilders visitors with its sheer size – 73 m (240 ft) long and 11 m (33 ft) wide – is so named for the 17 giant mirrors reflecting the light from the windows opposite; it is here that the German emperor was crowned in 1871 and the Treaty of Versailles was signed in 1919 to put an end to the Second World War.

Versailles is the prototype of a residence designed for an absolute monarchy. Below: wrought-iron gates separate the Place d'Armes from the château itself. The Hall of Mirrors (bottom left), is part of a series of rooms created in 1678 which run the entire length of the garden façade. Bottom right: this portrait (now in the Louvre) by Hyacinthe Rigaud celebrates the majesty of the monarchy.

FONTAINEBLEAU

Location: Central France
Best time to travel: throughout the year
www.uk.fontainebleau-tourisme.com

In the 12th century, King Louis VII commissioned a small hunting lodge in the forest of Fontainebleau, about 60 km (37 mi) south of Paris. After it had lain abandoned for a while, Francis I had it rebuilt in 1528, and only a single tower from the original building was left standing. For the interior design work he hired Italian artists including Rosso Fiorentino and Francesco Primaticcio, both of whom were to become well known for their adaptations of the Mannerist style known as the "Fontainebleau School". The palace was subsequently remodeled on a number of occasions, in particular during the reigns of Henry IV and Napoleon. Today the palace houses some outstanding baroque, rococo and neoclassical works of art from Italy and France. The palace was eventually extended to contain five courtyards, all with differing designs. Among its most impressive rooms are the horseshoe-shaped main stair hall and the luxurious ballroom. The palace gardens are also well worth seeing.

The landscape architect André Le Nôtre – the creator of the park at Versailles – designed the Grand Parterre in the park at Fontainebleau in 1645. As a garden terrace with a few low plants, the area was intended for state occasions.

France

AMIENS

Location: Northern France
Best time to travel:
throughout the year
www.visit-amiens.com

Situated about 115 km (71 mi) north of Paris, Amiens is both a university town and a bishop's seat. The cathedral, Notre Dame d'Amiens, is one of the great French High Gothic churches, and its dimensions are awe-inspiring. Covering a total area of 7,700 sq m (82,852 sq ft), it is the largest church in France. Bishop Evrard de Fouilloy laid the foundation stone for the church in 1220 and Robert de Luzarches' plans had been nearly completed by the end of the 13th century.

Archbishops, cardinals, and other religious worthies all lie buried in the Cathedral of Notre-Dame at Amiens.

CHARTRES

Location: Central France
Best time to travel:
throughout the year
www.chartres-tourisme.com

Notre Dame de Chartres is the finest High Gothic cathedral bar none. This triple-aisled basilica with a transept and five-aisled choir is considered to be one of the first purely Gothic structures and was the model for the cathedrals in both Reims and Amiens. Construction began here in the early 12th century and the church was consecrated in 1260. The Crypt of St Fulbert, built in 1024, is the largest Romanesque crypt in France. New construction techniques were employed at Chartres, for example the use of flying buttresses to create such large window spaces.

Chartres boasts a wealth of fully preserved original features.

REIMS

Location: North-eastern France
Best time to travel:
throughout the year
www.reims-tourisme.com

Lying in the heart of the Champagne region, Reims can look back on a glorious history. Founded by the Gauls, it became a major city during the period of the Roman Empire. Clovis was anointed first king of the Franks here by St Remigius in around 500, and the archbishop's bones are interred in the 11th-century St Rémi Abbey Church, with its early-Gothic choir adjoining narrow nave and 12th-century windows. Construction of Notre Dame Cathedral, the coro-

nation church of the French kings, was begun 1211 on the site of an earlier church. The building is adorned with expressive stone sculptures and the lovingly restored stained-glass windows (including some by Chagall) are vibrant masterpieces of light and color. French kings traditionally spent the night

before their coronation in the archiepiscopal Palais du Tau, built around 1500.

Reims was the starting point for the Christianization of Gaul and for centuries a bastion of the Catholic Church, as exemplified by the Abbey Church of Saint-Rémi.

France

CHALKSTONE CLIFFS OF NORMANDY

Location: North-western France
Best time to travel: March–October
www.normandy-tourism.org

The countryside stretching along the English Channel coast of northwest France is not exactly delicate, but the wind-battered coast and verdant green hinterland have their own undeniable magic which is impossible to resist. The Atlantic surf, the rugged shoreline, the gleaming white chalkstone cliffs, and the long sandy beaches scattered across hundreds of bays along the spectacular Normandy coast represent a nature full of brute force and primordial beauty. Strewn throughout the area are sleepy fishing villages and lively port towns as well as elegant seaside spas and pleasant holiday resorts. The highlight of the Normandy chalkstone cliff landscape is to be found at Étretat. This tiny fishing village was "discovered" by artists in the 19th century, who thought it particularly picturesque. Situated in a quaint cove, it is romantically framed by alabaster-white cliffs with a series of bizarre rock formations extending along the steep coastline. They attract a lot of tourists every year.

The steep coastline between Le Havre and Le Tréport is known as the Côte d'Albâtre, the Alabaster Coast, because of its chalk cliffs, some of which are over 100 m (330 ft) high.
There is a famous eroded arch to the west of Étretat which with a little imagination resembles an elephant's trunk being dipped into the water.

MONT SAINT MICHEL

Location: North-western France
Best time to travel:
throughout the year
www.mont-saint-michel.net
www.ot-montsaintmichel.com

The miraculous history of Mont Saint Michel begins in the 8th century with the Vision of St Aubert: the Archangel Michael appeared to the bishop, and in thanks the bishop had a small prayer hall built for pilgrims. A new structure incorporating the original walls was built on top of the earlier church of Notre-Dame-sous-Terre in 1022, with the crypt and choir – possibly the first ambulatory without radial chapels – being built first. After its collapse, the church was rebuilt in a late-Gothic style. Work continued on the crossing piers and transept under Abbot Randulf of Beaumont in the 11th century and the nave was completed at the beginning of the 12th century under Abbot Roger I. The crossribbed vaults of the side aisles and central nave walls have been preserved only on the south side. The west front, with its twin towers, was completed in 1184, but burned down in 1776. People soon began to settle at the foot of the abbey and some houses from the 14th century are still standing today. Due to its shifting sands and strong currents, Mont Saint Michel was difficult to reach even at low tide – the island was besieged but never conquered.

The former Benedictine Abbey of Mont Saint Michel occupies an exclusive location on a craggy island about a kilometer (half a mile) off the Normandy coast and has become an icon of the region.

France

BRITTANY

Location: North-western France
Best time to travel:
June–September
www.bretagne.com

The civilization that grew up in Brittany before the Common Era still puzzles scientists to this day – who were the people of this megalithic culture? Did the menhirs, large stones erected between 5,000 and 2,000 BC, function as solar or lunar calendars? Or were they fertility symbols, religious sites or markers for processional routes? We can't even begin to answer these questions. The veil of mystery only begins to lift after 500 BC, when the Celts arrived and settled in Brittany, a region they fittingly called "Armor": land by the sea. Although they eventually converted to Christianity, many of their pre-Christian customs and legends have survived, as has the Breton language. Certain Celtic characteristics also live on: Bretons are quite imaginative people, and are said to be wilful and proud. Brittany, which covers roughly 27,200 sq km (10,499 sq mi) of north-western France, is dominated by fishing and agriculture – just about every sea bass or monkfish ("loup de mer") that lands on European plates comes from the Breton coast. Other local activities include the export of vegetables and the production of meat, milk and cidre. Its 1,200 km (746 mi) of coastline also ranks as one of the country's most popular tourist regions after the Côte d'Azur.

The Atlantic surf breaks constantly over the rocks: the ruins of the old Benedictine Abbey of Notre-Dame-des-Grâces and the village church of St Matthew both lie about 20 km (12 miles) west of Brest. Beside them there are a 36-m (120-ft) high lighthouse and a square signal tower on a 30-m (100-ft) high spit of land.

France

LOIRE VALLEY

Location: Central France
Best time to travel:
throughout the year
www.loiret.com

There is a unique concentration of historic monuments along the rough-ly 200-km (124-mi) stretch of the Loire Valley between Sully-sur-Loire to the east and Chalonnes to the west, a little way downstream from Angers. France's longest river meanders through sensational countryside to-ward the Atlantic, traversing the his-toric regions of Orléanais, Blésois, Touraine and Anjou. The growth of the towns along the Loire Valley be-gan between 371 and 397 when St Martin, Bishop of Tours and patron saint of the Franks died, and his tomb in Tours became an important pilgrim-age site. In 848, Charles the Bald was crowned in Orléans, and in the 10th and 11th centuries the river valley be-came the preferred place of residence for the ruling family of France. There are several important Romanesque landmarks on the Loire, among them the abbey churches of St Benoît-sur-Loire with its 11th-century narthex and crypt, Germigny-des-Prés (with a 12th-century mosaic), frescoes in Liget and Tavant, and Notre-Dame de Cunault. Fontevraud Abbey, one of Europe's largest monasteries, was to become the burial place of the Planta-genets. The coronation of Henry Plan-tagenet as King of England in 1154 created a massive empire whose cen-ters of power were at Angers and Chi-non. It was here, in 1429, during the Hundred Years' War, that Joan of Arc met the still uncrowned Charles VII and set off to liberate the town of Orléans, which was besieged by the English. Many beautiful châteaux were rebuilt or remodeled under Francis I.

**Chambord, the largest of the castles
on the Loire, which Francis I had
built as a hunting lodge in 1619.**

France

ORLÉANS

Location: Central France (Loiret)
Best time to travel:
throughout the year
www.orleans.fr
www.francethisway.com

The capital of the Centre region and the Loiret Département is situated on the middle course of the Loire. The Maison de Jeanne d'Arc, in which the city's liberator lived in 1429, was destroyed in World War II but has since been restored to its original appearance. The equestrian statue on the Place du Martroi is another memorial to Joan of Arc. The Hôtel Toutin was one of the few merchants' houses and aristocratic palaces to survive the devastating bombing of Orléans during the last war.

Sainte-Croix cathedral, whose origins are late Gothic, was built between the 13th and 19th centuries.

BLOIS

Location: Central France (Loir-et-Cher)
Best time to travel:
throughout the year
www.ville-blois.fr
www.chateaudeblois.fr

Beginning with Philip VI in 1328 and ending with Henry II in 1589, 13 members of the House of Valois became kings of France. Blois became the royal residence under Louis XII in 1498 and for a few years enjoyed the status of being the capital of France. Built in the middle of the town that it effectively controlled, the château of Blois comprises several buildings constructed from the 13th to the 17th century around the main courtyard. Its most famous piece of architecture is the magnificent spiral staircase in the Francis I wing.

A mighty bridge leads across the Loire into the old town of Blois.

AMBOISE

Location: Central France
(Indre-et-Loire)
Best time to travel:
throughout the year
www.ville-amboise.fr
www.chateau-amboise.com

Situated on top of a promontory over-looking the Loire, Château Amboise was commissioned by Charles VIII in 1490; the king hired Italian artists and landscape gardeners to build the magnificent palace on the founda-tions of an older castle, and Francis I later based his glamorous court here. An avid patron of the arts, the king invited Leonardo da Vinci to spend his last years in Clos Lucé, a mansion connected to the château via a tun-nel. He is said to be buried in the château chapel.

The castle at Amboise was built on a rocky plateau above the town.

SAUMUR

Location: Western France
(Maine-et-Loire)
Best time to travel:
throughout the year
www.ot-saumur.fr
www.ville-saumur.fr

Despite later enlargements, this de-fensive structure of four towers standing on a rocky promontory at the confluence of the Loire and the Thouet rivers has been more or less preserved in its original 14th-centu-ry state. Saumur palace now houses the Musée du Cheval, which docu-ments the history of equestrianism, as well as the Musée des Arts Déco-ratifs.

Château Saumur became world-famous as an illustration on a calendar page in the *Très Riches Heures*, the Duke de Berry's book of hours.

France

VILLANDRY

Location: Central France
(Indre-et-Loire)
Best time to travel:
throughout the year
www.chateauvillandry.com
www.chateaux-de-la-loire.fr

In contrast to many of the other castles on the Loire, the main attraction of Villandry, which lies about 15 km (9 mi) west of Tours and was completed in 1536, is not the building itself but the beautiful Renaissance grounds which surround it. Covering a total area of about 7 ha (17 acres), the garden is divided into sections for water, music, love, vegetables, and herbs. The gardens are laid out in formal patterns created with low box hedges.

The gardens at Villandry are watered via an underground irrigation system.

CHENONCEAU

Location: Central France
(Indre-et-Loire)
Best time to travel:
throughout the year
www.chenonceau.com
www.chateaux-de-la-loire.fr

The history of this romantic waterside castle, originally built as a fortified house with an adjacent windmill between 1513 and 1521, features a succession of strong women, and it is also known as the "Château des Dames". Its construction in the 16th century was overseen by Cathérine Briçonnet whilst her husband, Thomas Bohier, the king's financial secretary, was in Italy. After Bohier's death, the castle fell to the crown and Henry II gave it to his lover Diane de Poitiers, who extended the building with a bridge over the Cher. After Henry II's death, Catherine de Medici, his wife, re-

AZAY-LE-RIDEAU

Location: Central France
(Indre-et-Loire)
Best time to travel:
throughout the year
azay-le-rideau.monuments-
nationaux.fr
www.chateaux-de-la-loire.fr

This castle on the Indre has harmonious proportions and a romantic location right beside the waters of what used to be the moat. All this brought Gilles Berthelot, who built it, little luck. King Francis I, who did not like his subjects to flaunt their wealth, simply accused the him of treason and confiscated the castle. Over the centuries, it changed hands several times until the early twentieth century, when it was purchased by the French government and restored.

Azay-Le-Rideau was built between 1519 and 1524.

claimed the castle for herself, covering the bridge with a Florentine gallery. After her, the castle passed to Louise de Lorraine, the widow of the assassinated Henry III, who spent a lifetime of grief in what would otherwise be cheerful surroundings. The bourgeois Louise Dupin brought vibrant academic life to the castle in the 18th century and even saved it from the massive depredations of the Revolution which led to significant loss of heritage in other parts of France.

Château Chenonceaux is unique, thanks to its location and the extraordinary two-storey gallery straddling the river Cher. Built by Philibert Delorme, this major Renaissance structure was commissioned by Catherine de Medici. Its isolated *donjon* a classic keep which was a characteristic of French castles, is a relic from an earlier building.

France

FONTENAY

Location: Eastern France (Côte-d'Or)
Best time to travel:
throughout the year
www.abbayedefontenay.com

The Abbey of Fontenay, consecrated by Pope Eugene III in 1147 and located some 50 km (31 mi) north-west of Dijon, was partially rebuilt in the 18th century. However, the original model layout of a Cistercian monastery can still be clearly discerned: high walls surrounding a harmonious collection of buildings. The church and monastery combine to form an enclosed, almost featureless block, although various administrative buildings have grown up amongst the parks and trees surrounding the twin buildings.

The church at Fontenoy is run according to extremely strict Cistercian ideals.

SAINT-SAVIN-SUR-GARTEMPE

Location: Central France (Vienne)
Best time to travel:
throughout the year
www.abbaye-saint-savin.fr
www.art-roman.net

Lying some 35 km (22 mi) east of Poitiers, the Abbey Church of Saint Savin was miraculously spared the destruction and pillaging that other such buildings have suffered over the centuries, but fell into disrepair after the French Revolution. The writer Prosper Mérimée, who had become the official inspector of historic monuments in France in 1831, rediscovered the church in 1836 and placed it immediately under a protection order. The cycles of expressive murals created in the 11th and early 12th centuries were saved in the 1970s thanks to the modern techniques used during restoration

VÉZELAY

Location: Central France (Yonne)
Best time to travel:
throughout the year
www.vezelaytourisme.com

Built on a hill above the old town of Vézelay, about 100 km (62 mi) west of Dijon, the Basilica Sainte Madeleine, the largest monastery church in France, stands surrounded by mighty fortifications. It was built between the 11th and 13th centuries on the foundations of a 9th-century church in which the relics of St Mary Magdalene are said to have been kept. Vézelay became a major religious center during the Crusades, but when the supposedly genuine relics of the penitent saint were discovered in Provence, it spelled the end of the abbey's heyday.

The *tympanon* of the narthex is particularly skilfully carved.

work. The barrel vaulted nave is supported on magnificently-scaled column with foliate capitals. The paintings adorn the vaults of the central nave, covering an area of more than 400 sq m (4,304 sq ft) and representing a coherent account of the Old Testament from Genesis to Exodus. The murals in the gallery and narthex depict the life of Christ and the Apocalypse of St John. Below the church is the Crypt of St Savin and St Cyprian, also frescoed with the lives of these two saints. Aside from these inestimably precious murals, the abbey church also houses valuable Romanesque altarpieces.

Saint-Savin-sur-Gartempe, often described as the "Romanesque Sistine Chapel", boasts beautiful 11th- and 12th-century frescos forming the largest Romanesque cycle in France; shown here is the depiction of Noah's Ark.

France

NANCY

Location: Eastern France
(Meurthe-et-Moselle)
Best time to travel:
throughout the year
www.ot-nancy.fr

Stanislas Lesczinski, the deposed King of Poland, became the nominal ruler of Lorraine in 1737. The generously proportioned Place Stanislas in Nancy was named after this "king without a kingdom". Originally laid out and built between 1752 and 1755 by the Nancy-born architect Emmanuel Héré de Corny (1705–1763), the square was intended as an architectural link between the Old Town and the New Town to the south, forming a new city center for Nancy as the Place Royale. The most noticeable building here is the Hôtel de Ville on the southern side of the square; its lavishly appointed interior features a charming staircase which is made to look larger by the *trompe-l'oeil* paintings on its sides. The square is adorned with a triumphal arch leading to the elongated Place de la Carrière, also laid out in the 16th century, and also the work of Emmanuel Héré de Corny. Construction of the Place d'Alliance, with its impressively regular house façades, began in 1753, and this style of housing continues into the surrounding streets. The "École de Nancy", a group of artists and architects founded by the glassmaster and furniture maker Émile Gallé, worked in the Art Nouveau style at the end of the 19th century and the early 20th century. It was principally their work which made Nancy a centre of art and architecture that rivaled Paris and helped give the city the nickname "Capitale de l'Est".

Thanks to its magnificent buildings, Nancy, Lorraine's ancient capital, has managed to maintain the appearance of a royal city to this day. The image shows the Arc de Triomphe on the Place Stanislas.

France

STRASBOURG

Location: Eastern France (Bas-Rhin)
Best time to travel:
throughout the year
www.strasbourg.eu

Situated on the Grande Île, an island in the River Ill, the medieval city of Strasbourg is a mixture of historic buildings and districts drawing on both French and German influences. Strasbourg's icon is its cathedral, one of the most important sacred buildings of the European Middle Ages. Begun in about 1015, it was originally Romanesque in style, but as it took several centuries to complete, the cathedral also features Gothic elements. The west front, praised for its proportions and ornate portal sculptures, is an especially important element of the structure; it became a way for the citizenry, who took over the financing of the edifice in 1286, to create a monument to this achievement. Further highlights include the magnificent stained-glass windows and its astronomical clock. The cathedral square is lined with half-timbered houses, some of which are up to five stories high, including House Kammerzell and Palais Rohan, built around 1740 in a Louis XV style. The historic cityscape also includes La Petite France, the 16th- and 17th-century tanners' district, the Ponts Couverts (bridges which were once roofed over), and the Vauban Weir.

La Petite France, the old tanners' quarter in the Old Town, begins at the Ponts Couverts (top), The mechanism of the astronomical clock (above left) with its apostle figures in Strasbourg's Minster is a miracle of precision engineering. Middle, the west façade; right, one of the stained-glass windows.

COLMAR

Location: Eastern France (Haut-Rhin)
Best time to travel:
throughout the year
(September/October: grape harvest)
www.ot-colmar.fr
www.colmar.fr

Colmar's location at the junction of two important valleys in the Vosges, the Vallée de Munster and the Valée de la Fecht, on the Rhine's flood plain allowed it to become the third-largest city in Alsace after Strasbourg and Mulhouse. It is an ideal base from which to explore the Vosges or head south along the Route du Vin. The capital of the Haut-Rhin Département, which grew up from a small royal court and, is first documented as *Columbarium* ("dovecote") in 823, combines all of the delights of the region, which is as well-known for its beautiful half-timbered houses as it is for its wine industry. The river Lauch flows through the Old Town, which boasts some very picturesque and romantic sights such as the St Martin Collegiate Church, the tanners' district, and "Little Venice". Art lovers typically head straight for the renowned Unterlinden Museum to see Matthias Grünewald's famed altar piece of the Passion of Christ which was probably finished between 1512 and 1516. The highlight of the nearby Dominican Church is Martin Schongauer's grand *Madonna of the Rosebush* (1473).

At the heart of the museum's collection of medieval art is the altarpiece created by Matthias Grünewald for the monastery of Isenheim near Guebwiller between 1512 and 1516. This powerful masterpiece was intended to end the "fevers of hell", an epidemic sickness.

France

BEAUNE

Location: Eastern France (Côte-d'Or)
Best time to travel: throughout the year (September/October: grape harvest)
www.ot-beaune.fr

First-time visitors to the ancient wine town of Beaune invariably head for the Hôtel-Dieu: its well-proportioned columns, shaded arcades around a courtyard, ornamental gable roofs, and the lavish decoration of its wards and kitchens have gained it the reputation of being the most beautiful Renaissance hospital in Europe. It was without doubt a selfless act on the part of Nicolas Rolin, the chancellor of Burgundy, and his wife Guigone to found the institution; their intentions have survived and the initials N and G feature heavily throughout the house's decoration. There is much more in Beaune than can be seen in two days: monasteries and churches, wine cellars and restaurants, and the famed Musée du Vin de Bourgogne. There is also the Musée Marey, commemorating the invention of chronophotography, a technique which enabled Étienne-Jules Marey, a doctor, to record 12 frames a second onto a glass plate – in 1882.

The inner courtyard of the Hôtel-Dieu in Beaune is filled with life again for a brief period when the Festival International d'Opéra Baroque de Beaune performs here for several weeks in June.

MASSIF CENTRAL

Location: South-eastern France (Côte-d'Or)

Best time to travel: throughout the year (November–April: Ski season)

www.parcs-massif-central.com

The romantic Massif Central is a largely barren chain of mountains in the south of the heartland of France. You are unlikely to run into anyone in its deep, steep valleys, although you will see otters and crystal-clear streams. Bordered to the west by the Limousin, to the east by the Rhône-Alpes, and to the south by the Causses, Aubrac and the Cévennen, the watercourses in the largest and oldest volcanic area in Europe still seem to be unpolluted.

The region's geological location means that the typical local flora and fauna are still in much the same form as would be recognised by the Avernes, the Celtic tribes who came to this magical area in the 6th century BC. The highest peak in the Monts Dôme volcanic chain, Puy de Dôme, has been regarded as sacred since the earliest times.

The Puy de Dôme (1,464 m/ 4,803 ft) is now an iconic symbol of the Auvergne. Water and fire in the form of rivers and volcanoes have conspired to form smooth humps of lava, now covered with green velvet, granite formations folded up into jagged teeth, and volcanic cones whose craters form gentle depressions.

France

LYON

Location: Eastern France (Rhône)
Best time to travel:
throughout the year
www.lyon.fr
www.lyon-france.com

Lyon, one of the largest cities in France, grew up as a result of the silk-weaving trade – now commemorated in the museum – and book-printing in the 16th century, and it became one of the most important trade fair venues in Europe. France's first stock exchange was founded here in 1506 and Lyon is still a major banking center. Fourvière, Lyon's oldest district, the Roman *forum vetus*, is a maze of lanes and medieval buildings. The cathedral of St-Jean, whose construction lasted from the 12th to the 15th century, features remarkably early Gothic stained glass and a 14th-century astronomical clock. There are also a number of impressive Renaissance house façades nearby. The hill overlooking the Saône chosen as a strategic location by the Romans for their city is now dominated by the pilgrimage church of Notre-Dame-de-Fourvière, built in the 19th century. The town hall, the 17th-century Palais des Arts – a former Benedictine monastery – the stock exchange, and several late medieval churches are all located on a 5-km (3-mi) long peninsula between the two rivers; this is the heart of Lyon and at its center there lies the Place Bellecour. The 12th-century Saint-Martin-d'Ainay, Lyon's oldest church, which dates back to a 6th-century basilica, is to be found just to the south of the square. Lyon is a major centre of business with a reputation as the French capital of gastronomy and having a significant role in the history of cinema due to Auguste and Louis Lumière.

Lyon's town hall stands on the Place des Terreaux with its 69 fountains. The Batholdi Fountain is one of the highlights of this square.

MONTBLANC

Location: French Alps, eastern France
Best time to travel: throughout the year (October–May: Ski season)
www.chamonix.com

The "White Mountain" (4,807 m/ 15,771 ft) is the highest peak in the Alps, and the area is popular for mountaineering, hiking, skiing and snowboarding. Most climbers make the ascent from the west, following the usual route from the Nid d'Aigle. The first recorded ascent of Mont Blanc was on 8 August 1786 by Jacques Balmat and the doctor Michel Paccard. This climb, initiated by Horace-Bénédict de Saussure, who gave a reward for the successful ascent, traditionally marks the birth of modern mountaineering. The first woman to reach the summit was Marie Paradis in 1808. From the summit of Mont Blanc on a clear day, the Jura, the Vosges, the Black Forest and the Massif Central mountain ranges can be seen, as well as the principal summits of the Alps.

The cable-car to the Aiguille du Midi crosses a sharp crest of snow at the Cosmiques hut before beginning the ascent to the summit.

France

PARC NATIONAL DES ÉCRINS

Location: Alpes-Provence, South-east France
Best time to travel: throughout the year
www.ecrins-parcnational.fr

The Parc National des Écrins is not only the largest, it is also the highest national park in France, and the *massif* of the same name has the highest peak south of Mont Blanc, the 4,102-m (13,458-ft) high Barre des Écrins. The park's area of 918 sq km (354 sq mi) is almost doubled by the territory lying at its borders. At its very center there lies the tiny mountaineering village of La Bérarde, an ideal base from which to hike and climb in the area.

The Barre des Écrins is the southernmost and westernmost peak over 4,000 m (13,100 ft) in France.

HAUTES ALPES, ALPES MARITIMES

Location: South-eastern France
Best time to travel: throughout the year (October–April: Ski season)
www.hautes-alpes.net
www.leshautesalpes.com

The southern Alps begin at Briançon (1,321 m/4,334 ft), which sells itself as the "highest town in Europe". With 300 days of sun a year, the area is wild, diverse, almost exotic, with a mixture of colorful rocks sparkling from jagged cliffs, and mighty gorges such as those at Cians or Daluis. Alpes-Maritimes includes the famous French Riviera coastline on the Mediterranean Sea with the important towns and cities of Cannes, Nice, Saint-Jean-Cap-Ferrat, and Antibes.

Many shades of green: the Parc National du Mercantour.

MASSIF DE LA VANOISE

Location: Graian Alps, South-east France
Best time to travel: throughout the year (October–April: Ski season)
www.parcnational-vanoise.fr

The Massif de la Vanoise is an Alpine region of great contrasts; its northern slopes have been opened up for skiing, whilst to the south it is strictly protected as the Parc National de la Vanoise. The area is the largest nature reserve in western Europe, home to a growing population of ibex. The *Tour de la Vanoise*, a five-day hike from hut to hut, crosses beautiful unspoilt mountain pastures which in late June and July are carpeted with a spectacular display of mountain flowers.

The peaks of the Massif de la Vanoise can reach heights of up to 3,855 m (12,648 ft).

GRAND CANYON DU VERDON

Location: South-eastern France (Alpes-de-Haute-Provence)
Best time to travel: March–October
www.verdon.de

The largest gorge in the Alps lies in the Provençal foothills at the extreme south-west of the chain, where there is a feeling of being closer to the sea than to the mountains. The Grand Canyon du Verdon is around 25 km (16 mi) long and in places up to 900 m (2,953 ft) deep. Its walls are completely vertical at some points and are a famed mountaineering challenge. The Route Panoramique affords beautiful views for motorists driving around the spectacular canyon.

The little Verdon river flows between vertiginous cliffs to the west of Castellane.

LUBÉRON

Location: South of France
Best time to travel:
March–November
www.parcduluberon.fr

The expansive limestone plateau of the Lubéron, a rocky landscape of lonely oak groves, tiny mountain villages, and stone huts that has lost none of its impressive natural beauty lies to the east of Avignon, halfway between the Alps and the Mediterranean. The mountains reach 1,125 m (3,691 ft) and contain some largely uninhabited stretches of land with more than 1,000 different species of plants. The "Parc Naturel Régional du Lubéron" was founded in 1977 to protect this unique environment. Despite the remoteness of many parts of the Lubéron, people have always lived on the limestone ridge, which was formed in the Tertiary period. The villages huddled in the hollows and valleys here date back to the Middle Ages. The houses have thick walls and churches served as both places of worship and refuge. The inhabitants of the Lubéron generally scraped a living as farmers – when the harvests began to fail, the villages on the north side were abandoned.

Blooming fields of lavender are iconic images of Provence. The peak period is from mid June to mid July.

AIX-EN-PROVENCE

Location: South of France
(Bouches-du-Rhône)
Best time to travel:
throughout the year
www.aixenprovencetourism.com
www.aix-en-provence.com

The spa and university town of Aix-en-Provence has been the capital of Provence for centuries: the Romans founded the spa colony of Aquae Sextiae Saluviorum on the ruins of the Celto-Liguric settlement of Entremont in 122 BC. Aix first became an important center for the arts and learning at the turn of the 13th century. The Old Town extends from the Cours Mirabeau, an avenue of plane trees and beautiful 18th-century city mansions to the Cathedral of St Sauveur, whose baptistery dates back to the Merovingians. Other sights worth seeing include the 17th-century town hall, the Musée des Tapisseries and Paul Cézanne's studio; the subject that the city's most famous son returned to was Mont St Victoire to the east of Aix-en-Provence, and it is certainly worth a detour to discover the landscapes which inspired the painter.

The Cours Mirabeau was laid out on the southern edge of the Old Town in 1651. Enjoy the bustle of the weekly market.

France

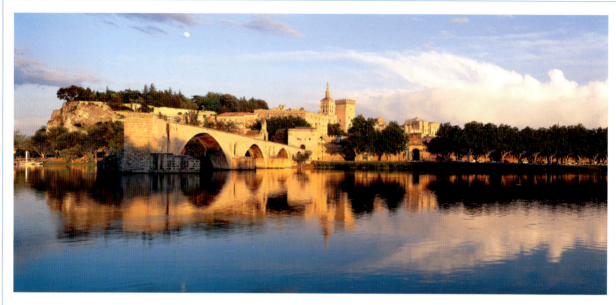

AVIGNON

Location: South of France (Vaucluse)
Best time to travel: throughout the year
www.ot-avignon.fr

Catholic history was made in the 14th century in this southern French town on the Rhône when the Roman curia sought refuge here from the political turmoil in Rome, going into "Babylonian exile" between 1309 and 1376. The papal residence consists of an Old and a New Palace, with the 12th-century Roman cathedral of Notre Dame-des-Doms adjoining them to the north. The Petit Palais, built in 1317 and intended to compensate the archbishop for the demolition of his original palace, is also part of the episcopal seat. Avignon was surrounded by an imposing town wall at the beginning of the 14th century and this was reinforced with fortified towers such as the Tour des Chiens and the Tour du Châtelet. The latter controlled access to the world-famous Saint-Bénézet bridge, the "Pont d'Avignon", of which now only a section remains.

The view of Avignon from the other side of the Rhône with its famous "Pont d'Avignon".

ARLES

Location: South of France (Bouches-du-Rhône)
Best time to travel: throughout the year
www.arlestourisme.com

The "Gateway to the Camargue" has been settled by Celts, Greeks, and Romans during its long history; the emperor Constantine even had a villa here, where he convened a council in 314. The most impressive buildings in Arles are Roman. Some 136 m (446 ft) long and 107 m (351 ft) wide, the oval amphitheater could seat 20,000 spectators, and even the semi-circular theater could seat 12,000. The portal of the Romanesque church of St Trophime dates back to the 11th century and is a masterpiece of Provencale masonic skill; the Romano-Gothic nave is considered the most beautiful in Provence.

The Roman Consul Marius had a canal built in 104 BC to link Arles and Fos, thus creating a direct connection to the Mediterranean. Arles has gone down in art history as one of the places painted by Vincent van Gogh who was taken by the strong sunlight there.

France

ORANGE

Location: South of France (Vaucluse)
Best time to travel:
throughout the year
www.ville-orange.fr

Orange enjoys a history of more than 2,000 years going back to the Romans, who originally founded the town of Arausio on the site of a conquered Celtic settlement in the Rhône Valley. Completed in about AD 25, the triumphal arch here is the most completely preserved Roman archway in Gaul. The Théâtre Romain was one of the largest in Roman antiquity, with a façade measuring 103 m (330 ft) by 37 m (150 ft) which impressed even King Louis XIV.

The Théâtre Romain (left, a statue of the Emperor Augustus; right, the Arc de Triomphe) in Orange is one of the most important Roman ruins in Europe.

LES BAUX DE PROVENCE

Location: South of France (Bouches-du-Rhône)
Best time to travel:
throughout the year
www.lesbauxdeprovence.com

Although now only a ruined castle, medieval Les Baux was the seat of mighty feudal lords who claimed descent from the Three Kings of the East. The Bible story is commemorated in the Feast of the Shepherds, in which local herdsmen congregate in the church every Christmas Eve to bring the new-born Savior a lamb. It has a spectacular position in the Alpilles mountains, set atop a rocky outcrop crowned with a ruined castle overlooking the plains to the south.

The surviving buildings mostly date back to between the 14th and 17th centuries.

PONT DU GARD

Location: near Remoulins,
South of France (Gard)
Best time to travel:
throughout the year
www.pontdugard.fr

This famous three-tier aqueduct was
built between AD 40 and 60 to supply
water to the fast-growing ancient
town of Nemausus, present-day
Nîmes. The bridge, was considered a
daring feat of engineering at the time
and is still a very impressive sight. The
bottom level has six arches, which
vary in width from 15 to 24 m (49 to
79 ft). The middle level has a total of
11 arches. The 35 arches on the top
level, which is 275 m (900 ft) long, are
about 5 m (16 ft) wide and support
the actual water duct.

**The Pont du Gard was built during
the reigns of the emperors
Claudius and Nero.**

NÎMES

Location: South of France (Gard)
Best time to travel:
throughout the year
www.ot-nimes.fr
www.nimes.fr

Nîmes, a town of temples, hot springs,
and theaters, was founded by the emperor Augustus as Colonia Augusta
Nemausus in the year AD 16. The most
impressive Roman structure here is
the amphitheater with its oval arena
and rising rows of stone seats which
can accommodate up to 25,000 spectators. The many bathhouses, temples,
and the theater are grouped around
the Jardin de la Fontaine.

**The Maison Carrée, or "square
house", features Corinthian
columns and an impressive decora-
tive frieze. It is one of the best-
preserved Roman temples in Europe
and an icon of Nîmes.**

France

SAINT-TROPEZ

Location: South of France (Var)
Best time to travel:
throughout the year
www.ot-saint-tropez.com
www.beyond.fr

Dense forests of pine, oak and chestnut push their way down to the coastline between Fréjus and Hyères and the hills drop off steeply toward the sea, leaving no room for construction or development along the Corniche des Maures. The coast road is all the more attractive because of it, winding along the wooded hills often half way up the incline and frequently offering superb views across the sea. Tiny old fishing villages huddle together in the numerous coves and bays having lost little of their original charm. One of these, on the southernmost shores of the Gulf of St Tropez at the eastern foot of the Massif des Maures was known to the Greeks as Athenopolis.

NICE

Location: South of France
(Alpes-Maritimes)
Best time to travel:
throughout the year
www.nicetourisme.com
www.nice.fr

This, the secret capital of the Côte d'Azur – and actual capital of the Département Alpes-Maritimes – enjoys a fantastic location on the Baie des Anges, surrounded by the foothills of the Alpes Maritimes. Nice is a town of contrasts: while the grand boulevards cling to memories of the Belle Époque, life in parts of Nice's Old Town resembles scenes in a village in Italy. The Greeks founded what they referred to as Nikaia, the "victorious town", in the 5th century BC, while the Romans preferred a location higher up in the hills for their settlement, Cemenelum, present-day Cimiez.

France

The Romans called it Heraclea Carcabaris and the present name is said to derive from a Roman legionary who died a Christian martyr's death under Nero. During World War II, on 15 August, 1944, it was the site of a military landing called Operation Dragoon, the Allied invasion of southern France. The motto in Saint-Tropez is "see and be seen", the exclusive village first became famous through the film *And God Created Woman*, which was shot here in 1956 by the director Roger Vadim and featured Brigitte Bardot, his wife of the time. In latter years, it has been a resort for the European and American jet set and the inevitable hordes of tourists in search of a little Provençal authenticity and an occasional celebrity sighting.

The jet set discovered the once sleepy fishing village of St Tropez in the 1950s.

The iconic image of Nice is the Promenade des Anglais, built in the 1830s along the waterfront by wealthy English folk who by the mid-19th century had already recognized the attractions of Nice as a desirable place to retire. The most impressive edifices from that period are the famous Hotel Négresco and the Palais Masséna. The Old Town features narrow, winding alleyways and houses with a distinctly Italian feel and the main square, Cours Saleya, has an attractive farmers' market. From the castle on the hill there are amazingly beautiful views of the Old Town and the Mediterranean.

The Cours Saleya (opposite) is one of the most attractive and atmospheric squares in town. Left, the marina, which was built in 1750 under the name Port Lympia.

France

CAMARGUE

Location: South of France
Best time to travel:
March–November
www.camargue.fr

The delta between the two main arms of the Rhône comprises 140,000 hectares (346,000 acres) of swamps, meadows, and grazing land, as well as dunes and salt marshes – it is one of Europe's largest wetlands. Agricultural use, mostly the cultivation of rice, is concentrated in the northern part of the Camargue; salt is harvested in shallow lagoons in the south-eastern portion. The Camargue is home to more than 400 species of birds; its brine ponds provide one of the few European habitats for the greater flamingo. The marshes are also a prime habitat for many species of insects. The distinctive features of the black Camargue bulls are their lyre-shaped horns. Their companions, the half-wild white horses of the Camargue, were depicted in the ancient cave paintings of Solutré. The fully-grown horses typically have a squat body, a square head, and a thick mane, acquiring their white coloration only as five-year-olds.

If Camargue horses can be broken in for saddle and tack at an early age, they make tireless mounts and serve the local cowherds well.

CANNES

Location: South of France
(Alpes-Maritimes)
Best time to travel:
throughout the year
www.cannesinfo.com
www.cannes.fr

The Celts and Romans established settlements around the Golfe de la Napoule during their stays, but the bay did not become a popular destination until the arrival of the British in the 19th century. They built beautiful villas for themselves, followed these with up-market hotels, and The Boulevard La Croisette was constructed along the entire bay. Le Suquet, the Old Town, stands on Mont Chevalier (67 m/220 ft), a tiny hill that rises above the old port and whose summit is crowned by a watchtower dating back to the 11th century. Next to it, the Musée de la Castre displays relics from antiquity.

The Gothic Notre Dame de l'Espérance dates back to 1648. Magnificent views of the entire bay of Cannes unfold from the viewing platform behind the church, and there is a giant hall on the edge of the Old Town that houses the Forville Market. Cannes is of course also a town of festivals; the month of May is firmly set aside for the Film Festival, when the Palme d'Or is awarded for the best film, and the international advertising industry meets in Cannes in June to select the best cinema and TV advertising spots. TV bosses from around the world gather here in the fall to buy and sell their programs. The venue for all these activities is the Palais du Festival at the western end of the Croisette.

Not a bad address: the luxury Carlton Hotel on the Croisette in Cannes.

MARSEILLE

Location: South of France (Bouches-du-Rhône)
Best time to travel: throughout the year
www.marseille-tourisme.com

Marseille, France's third-largest city and most important port, boasts more than 2,500 years of history. Its importance as a major gateway for military campaigns in North Africa is also mirrored in the composition of its population. The town of Massalia was originally founded by Greeks from Asia Minor on the hill where Notre Dame de la Garde now stands. After an initial Graeco-Roman alliance, Caesar finally conquered the Greek republic in 49 BC. The port town experienced its first major period of prosperity in the 12th century, when armies of Crusaders brought lucrative business to the city as they prepared for their journey to Jerusalem, and it was to become the most important port in the Mediterranean in the centuries that followed. Two large forts flank the entrance to the Old Port - Fort Saint-Nicolas on the south side and Fort Saint-Jean on the north. Further out in the Bay of Marseille is the Frioul archipelago which comprises four islands, one of which, If, is the location of Château d'If, made famous by the Dumas novel The *Count of Monte Cristo*.

La Canebière, the city's main boulevard, begins its winding journey in the old port.

CARCASSONNE

Location: South of France (Aude)
Best time to travel:
throughout the year
www.carcassonne.org

Even before the Romans, the Iberians had settled on the hill above the river Aude along the old trading route linking the Mediterranean and the Atlantic. The Gallo-Roman town of Car-

casso fell to the Visigoths in 418, who built the inner town fortifications in 485. The Moors conquered the town in 725, followed by the Franks in 759. Carcassonne fell to the French crown in 1229. The impressive Romanesque basilica of St Nazaire was built between 1096 and 1150 during the course of the town's expansion in the Middle Ages. It was remodeled in the

Gothic style in the 13th century, and the magnificent stained glass windows date from the 14th to the 16th century. Château Comtal was integrated into the inner town wall complex around 1125. Construction of the outer wall and its fortified towers began at the end of the 13th century. An imposing gate known as the Porte Narbonnaise was added later, and the

Pont d'Avignon is from the 12th century. The outdated fortifications fell into a state of disrepair after about 1660 but reconstruction was begun in 1844; the restoration project was not to be completed until 1960.

Two crenelated curtain walls and a ring of towers surround the fortress town.

France

CASTELNAU-BRETENOUX

Location: South of France (Lot)
Best time to travel:
throughout the year
http:/castelnau-bretenoux.
monuments-nationaux.fr

The Dordogne Valley forms a deep cleft between the Limousin and Quercy regions. The area around the gentle Dordogne River was once settled by the Petrocorians, a Gallic tribe, and for this reason the region is still known as the "Périgord" today. The Château de Castelnau-Bretenoux is just one of the highlights of this magnificent landscape. The castle, dating back to the 13th century, was extended to its present size during the Hundred Years' War.

Visible from afar: the three round towers and triple curtain wall of Château de Castelnau-Bretenoux.

SAINT-CIRQ-LAPOPIE

Location: South of France (Lot)
Best time to travel:
March–November
www.saint-cirqlapopie.com

This village owes its double name to Saint Cyrus, the village's patron saint, and to the aristocratic La Popie family, who ruled both castle and village in the Middle Ages. The once powerful fortress was demolished by Henry of Navarre in 1580. Magnificent views unfold from the ruins at the highest point on the rock. The sturdy village church was built as a fortified structure in the 16th century, and the narrow alleyways of the small town are lined with Gothic half-timbered houses that are sagging with age.

Saint-Cirq-Lapopie is overlooked by a castle, a fortified church and an 80-m (260-ft) cliff.

France

LASCAUX

Location: Western France (Dordogne)
Best time to travel: March–November
www.lascaux.culture.fr

Four children playing on a hill above the village of Montignac in the Vézère valley on 12 September 1940 happened to stumble upon an archeological sensation: proof that the hunter-gatherers who settled in southern France during the Ice Age 30,000 years ago had produced the earliest art recorded in Europe. The caves have been closed since 1963 to preserve the paintings, but reproductions can be viewed in the adjacent Lascaux II cave.

The "Great Hall of Bulls" in the Lascaux caves depicts a partially drawn bull amongst a herd of horses.

ROCAMADOUR

Location: South-western France (Lot)
Best time to travel: March–November
www.rocamadour.com

Until the Reformation, the pilgrimage to celebrate Saint Amadour – an obscure saint whose existence is not even certain – was among the most famous in Christendom. The miraculous "Black Madonna" has been here since the 13th century as well, and is now venerated in the Chapelle Notre Dame. There are a wealth of frescoes to admire at the Chapelle Saint Michel. To get an idea of the full size of the entire complex, visitors should climb the 233 steps of the Via Sancta, visiting the Francis Poulenc Museum of Sacred Art on route.

Rocamadour clings to the walls of a cliff 150 m (494 ft) above the Alzou.

LOURDES

Location: South-western France (Hautes-Pyrénées)
Best time to travel: throughout the year
www.lourdes-france.com

Lourdes, a small town of only 15,000 inhabitants at the foot of the Pyrenees, owes its fame to a local girl: Maria Bernarda Soubirous, later to be canonized as St Bernardette, to whom the Virgin Mary is first said to have appeared in the Massabielle grotto in 1858. Lourdes soon became a popular pilgrimage for those seeking healing and five million people now visit the town every year, of which some two million are pilgrims.

The girl who was to become St Bernardette is said to have had visions of the Mother of God in the grotto at Massabielle.

CIRQUE DE GAVARNIE

Location: South-western France
Best time to travel: April–October
www.gavarnie.com

The Cirque de Gavarni, an imposing enclosed valley at an elevation of 800 m (2,600 ft) above sea level, has a diameter of a little more than 4 km (2.4 mi). Originally formed by a glacier, it is now one of the most popular tourist destinations in the Pyrenees. The valley is enclosed by the peaks of Grand Astazou (3,071 m/10,075 ft), Marboré (3,248 m/10,656 ft), Pic de la Cascade (3,073 m/10,082 ft), and Taillon (3,114/10,217 ft). The romantic picture is completed by waterfalls such as the Grande Cascade, one of the highest in Europe with a drop of 422 m (1,385 ft).

The Grande Cascade is one of the highest waterfalls in Europe.

BORDEAUX

Location: South-western France (Gironde)
Best time to travel: throughout the year
www.bordeaux-tourisme.com
www.bordeaux-city.com

Although it is about 50 km (31 miles) from the Atlantic coast, Bordeaux's position on the river Garonne has made it an important port since Roman times. One of its most important exports is the wine for which the town and the surrounding region are famous. Bordeaux preserved its medieval character until the early 18th century when the prevailing intellectual climate of the Enlightenment prompted the redesign of the town as a coherent neo-Classical cityscape. As a first step, Jacques Gabriel designed the Place de la Bourse in 1730. The Marquis of Tourny, Louis-Urbain Aubert who ran the municipality between between 1743 and 1757, replaced the medieval city gates and added a number of buildings, including the Place Gambetta, the Place d'Aquitaine, the Place de Bourgogne and the Place Tourny. He also laid out new streets as well as gardens and parks. The façades along the quays of the Garonne were also built during this period, and many new public buildings were erected. The first stone bridge across the Garonne was built between 1810 and 1822. The old port on the left bank has been preserved in its original form.

The historic Old Town follows the crescent-shaped left bank of the Garonne.

SAINT-ÉMILION

Location: South-western France
Best time to travel:
throughout the year
(September/October: grape harvest)
www.saint-emilion.org

This small town in the Gironde region of Aquitaine originally grew up around a grotto where the Breton monk Émilion lived as a hermit in the 8th century. He was soon joined by several other Benedictine monks, and an underground church, the Église Monolithe, was hewn out of the rock near the hermitage; a direct path links the church to the catacombs where St Émilion is said to be buried. Other historic buildings worth seeing include the Cloître de la Collégiale with its magnificent cloisters and the Chapelle de la Trinité, which was built in honor of St Émilion, the patron saint of vintners. Saint-Émilion is one of the principal red wine areas of Bordeaux along with the Médoc, Graves and Pomerol. The primary grape varieties used are the Merlot and Cabernet Franc.

The bell-tower of the church overlooks Saint-Émilion, the leading wine village in the Bordelais.

CÔTE D'ARGENT, ARCACHON

Location: South-western France (Gironde)
Best time to travel:
April–September
www.arcachon.com

The section of coast between the Arcachon Basin, a vast bay of about 200 sq km (77 sq mi) and the elegant seaside resort of Biarritz, where the coastline merges into the Spanish-French Côte Basque, is known as the Côte d'Argent. It has a mild climate said to be favourable for invalids suffering from pulmonary complaints. Aside from swimming and water sports, the main attraction here is the fascinating landscape, in particular the Dune de Pilat, Europe's largest and highest sand formation. The dune measures some 2.7 km (2 mi) in length, is 500 m (1,640 ft) wide, and varies in height between 105 and 120 m (345 and 393 ft).

The almost triangular Arcachon basin, which is protected from stiff Atlantic breezes by the spit of land at Cap Ferret, features wide mudflats laced with creeks and the highest sand dune in Europe. The Atlantic surf attracts aventurous water freaks as well.

BIARRITZ

Location: South-western France
(Pyrénées-Atlantiques)
Best time to travel: April–October
www.biarritz.fr

Biarritz is a luxurious seaside town and is popular with tourists and surfers. It was here that France's wealthiest class gathered during the Belle Époque. The Empress Eugénie chose the town as her favorite spa in the 1850s and the rest of high society followed suit. Many of the hotels, such as the Hôtel du Palais, still exude an aura of that period. Two popular destinations for strolls along the es- planade include the 44-m (144-ft) lighthouse built north of the town in 1834, and, further south and accessi- ble via a jetty, the Rocher de la Vierge, a rock crowned with a statue of the Madonna. The *art deco* Musée de la Mer, which has excellent views, is al- so on the seafront.

The former fishing village of Biarritz is now one of the most exclusive and best-known seaside resorts on the Atlantic. The Casino Bellevue on the Grande Plage, which extends as far as the white lighthouse at Pointe St-Martin, is especially famous.

CORSICA

Location: North of Sardinia
Best time to travel:
March–November
www.corsica.net

With the white limestone near Bonifacio, the red granite rock of the calanche, and the green wilderness of the Castagniccia, it is no surprise that the Greeks once called Corsica "Kalliste", meaning "the beautiful". The island is not just a collection of wide beaches and tiny swimming coves in a beautiful setting, there are 50 peaks higher than 2,000 m (6,600 ft) here, and green forests, preserving a landscape that has remained unspoilt despite the all-pervading influences of civilization. No other Mediterranean island is as green as Corsica, and the heady aromas of ilex, eucalyptus, black pines, and lavender waft through the air. The most beautiful part of the island is the coast, 1,000 km (620 mi) long, with its beaches of pure white sand and blue fjords between steep cliffs and rocks. Tourism is particularly concentrated in

the area around Porto Vecchio and Bonifacio in the south of the island and Calvi in the northwest. Napoleon, Corsica's most famous native son, was born in Ajaccio in 1769, but he left his island home only ten years later, in 1779. After various military vic-
tories he assumed power in France and had himself crowned Emperor in 1804, with a view to conquering Europe. After the "great Corsican" was defeated in his Russian campaign of 1812 and the Battle of the Nations at Leipzig in 1813, he was exiled to Elba.
He escaped and returned to power a year later, but was defeated again at Waterloo in 1815. He died in exile on the island of St Helena six years later, on 5 May 1821. The mountainous Mediterranean island is a true gem and attracts a lot of tourists.
Bonifacio, the southernmost town on the island of Corsica, was built on a narrow cliff surrounded by water on three sides. The rock has been hollowed out at its base by the action of wind and water over centuries.

Spain

MADRID

Location: Central Spain
Best time to travel:
throughout the year
www.turismomadrid.es
www.feelmadrid.com

Madrid has been occupied since pre-historic times, in the Roman era this territory belonged to the diocese of Complutum (present-day Alcalá de Henares). There are archeological remains of a small village during the visigoth epoch. This metropolis, declared the capital of Spain in 1561 by Philip II, was the political creation of a king who wished to rule "from the geographical center". Thus the court was moved from Toledo to the southern foothills of the Sierra de Guadarrama Castilian highlands in the middle of the country, which are known for their hot summers and cold winters. Although the town, which had grown up around a Moorish fortress on the Río Manzanares, lacked all the necessary prerequisites for natural development as a city, the royal will was unshakable, and throughout the 19th and 20th centuries the town grew in leaps and bounds, aided by the railways and a modern road network, to become the intellectual and cultural center of the country. Modern Madrid is vibrant city, receiving visitors warmly and Madrileños could not imagine living anywhere else. With its famous universities, renowned museums, stylish bars, and cool cafés, this city of more than three million has a charm that has made it one of the greatest cities in Europe. The Gran Via ("Great Road"), one of Madrid's main arteries, was opened in 1910. The most interesting architecture here is to be found between the traffic of the Red de San Luis interchange and the Calle de Alcalá and includes urban icons such as the Capitol Movie Theater, jutting out like a ship's prow on the Plaza de Callao, the Telefónica building on the Red de San Luis, and the

Metropolis House on the Calle de Alcalá. Here, the Gran Via feeds into the Plaza de la Cibeles, the junction of the north-south and east-west axes of Madrid. The spot is marked by the Cibeles Fountain with its statue of Greek fertility goddess Kybele driving a chariot drawn by lions. The Plaza Mayor, laid out in the 17th century, is the impressive heart of the city. Intended as a show ground for important events, the square was once used for bullfights, executions, and processions. The Palacio Real, Madrid's royal palace, was built high above the Río Manzanares, having been commissioned by Philip V after an earlier building had been consumed by fire. Joseph Bonaparte, the eldest brother of of Napoleon I, wanted a clear view from the palace and had all the houses to the east demolished to make way for the square. An equestrian statue of Philip IV adorns the middle of the Plaza de Oriente to the east of the Teatro Real. Madrid's most impressive ecclesiastical building is also one of the few to survive from the 16th century: the Monasterio de las DesCalzas Reales ("Royal Monastery of the Discalced Order") was founded by Joan of Austria, the daughter of Charles V. The popular recreation sites of the Parque del Retiro and the Palacio de Velázquez, built behind the Museo del Prado for an exhibition in 1887, were originally a royal park used for chivalric tournaments and reconstructions of sea battles. The cultural highlight of any visit is of course the world-famous Museo del Prado itself, one of the greatest galleries in the world, featuring works by Goya and many others. The best known work on display at the museum is Las Meninas by Velázquez.

Spain's capital (left, the Gran Via with the Metropolis House and the Plaza de la Cibeles) is not only the geographic heart of the Iberian peninsula, but at one point was also the center of an empire on which "the sun never set".

Spain

CABO DE FINISTERRE

Location: North-western Spain (Galicia)
Best time to travel: April–October
www.galiciaguide.com

Cape Finisterre – Cabo de Finisterre in Spanish, Cabo Fisterra in Galician – is sometimes said to be the westernmost point of the Iberian Peninsula. However, this is not correct, since other locations are farther west. Verdant Galicia is a landscape of rugged coasts interrupted by long fjords reaching far inland, and the people here live largely from the bounty of the sea. Traditional agriculture is still practised on the tiny farms with their modest fields and dry stone walls.

If you are lucky, the fogs will lift to reveal the beaches and steep cliffs in all their glory.

A CORUÑA

Location: North-western Spain (Galicia)
Best time to travel: throughout the year
www.galinor.es
www.coruna.es

The four provinces of northern Spain are Galicia, Asturias, Cantabria and the Basque Country, and it was here, in small duchies in these remote hinterlands, that Christians were able to hold out against the onslaughts of the Moors of North Africa in the early Middle Ages. A Coruña, Galicia's vibrant capital, is situated on a spit of land in a bay formed by the El Ferrol, Ares, Betanzos, and A Coruña rivers. The Old Town is surrounded by medieval walls.

The façades and balconies of the houses overlooking the marina can breathe in the smell of the sea.

Spain

VIGO

Location: North-western Spain (Galicia)
Best time to travel: throughout the year
www.vigo.com

Vigo was an important harbor for the Romans as they traveled between the Mediterranean and Britannia. It is now a major shipping hub for international commerce and a fishing port for tuna and sardines. In recent years it has also become a popular leisure marina. Vigo boasts a natural harbor basin and a lively Old Town of charming narrow alleyways, small bars, and picturesque little plazas. The superb beaches and the Parque Nacional de las Islas Atlántica on the small islands off the coast are equally attractive.

Oyster farmers have set up their platforms in the bay off Vigo.

PONTEVEDRA

Location: North-western Spain (Galicia)
Best time to travel: throughout the year
www.pontevedra-virtual.com
www.concellopontevedra.es

The town of Pontevedra lies only a short distance from Vigo, at the end of a fjord-like inlet extending deep into the green, hilly landscape. The many churches, city palaces, and aristocratic palaces in the romantic Old Town were built in a mixture of Gothic, Renaissance, and baroque styles. The Museo Provincial (Praza da Leña), which is housed in two 18th-century townhouses, is certainly worth a visit.

The Plaza de la Herrería, with its 16th-century fountain of the same name, lies at the historic heart of Pontevedra.

Spain

ALTAMIRA

Location: Northern Spain (Cantabria)
Best time to travel: throughout the year
http://museodealtamira.mcu.es
www.spain.info

The Cave of Altamira located in the hills above Santillana del Mar was rediscovered in 1879. At first, the paintings found here were believed to be fakes – it was hard to believe that Stone Age man would have possessed such advanced artistic skills. Only further research and the discovery of additional caves whose paintings were easier to date finally proved beyond doubt that they were genuine. The ceiling painting in one of the auxiliary caves is especially famous: a herd of bison is depicted on a surface area of 18 m (60 ft) by 9 m (30 ft), picked out in brown, yellowish and red ochre paints, with shades of black manganese oxide and charcoal. The shape of the natural rock has even been incorporated into the images, giving the animals an almost three-dimensional effect. The entire work has acquired the nickname of the "Sistine Chapel of the Stone Age". The most recent investigations have shown that the drawings date from the Paleolithic period, around 16,000 years ago. They are now considered to be the most important relics of prehistoric art in the world. The original cave is more or less closed to the general public to protect the works – very few visitors are allowed in and there is a waiting list – but a faithful replica has been reconstructed in a museum. The cave with its paintings has been declared a World Heritage Site by UNESCO.

The paintings in the Cave of Altamira are evidence of the acute observation and artistic excellence of the early settlers.

Spain

BILBAO

Location: Northern Spain **Best time to travel:** throughout the year www.leon.es www.idealspain.com

A unique program of urban renewal in which famous architects were asked to develop a new look for the city has transformed Bilbao into one of the world's greatest cities of art and architecture. The most beautiful old buildings are in the Old Town's Siete Calles with its streets of 19th-century neoclassical buildings, bay windows, and wrought-iron balconies. The most important new contributions include the Puente del Campo Volantin pedestrian bridge and the futuristic airport, both designed by Santiago Calatrava, and Sir Norman Fos-

ter's metro stations. Bilbao's main attraction is however the Guggenheim Museum by the architect Frank O. Gehry. Towering over the banks of the river Nervion, the metal roof of this structure, which is made of limestone, titanium and glass, and cost over 100 million US dollars, is known by locals as the "metallic flower. It is set between two levels: the river level and the city level. The plot is crossed by the Puente de la Salve bridge, embraced by a sculptural tower that makes it part of the compound. It has wide stairs that connect the different levels. **Dxhibitions of artists such as Roy Lichtenstein, Robert Rauschenberg, Jeff Koons, Jackson Pollock, and Andy Warhol have made the Guggenheim Museum world-famous.**

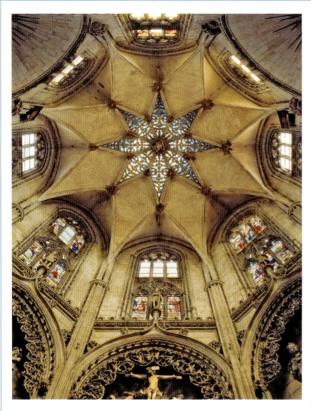

CAMINO DE SANTIAGO DE COMPOSTELA

Location: Northern Spain
(Castile and León)
Best time to travel:
throughout the year
www.leon.es
www.turismoburgos.org
www.idealspain.com

Over the centuries, countless pilgrims have trudged along the Way
of St James from the foothills of the
Pyrenees to the tomb of their
beloved saint in Santiago de Compostela. The important role played
by this path in encouraging cultural
exchange can be seen from the outstanding buildings that have been
erected along its route. The Way itself consists of a network of several
paths spread along the entire northern coast of Spain. Historically, royal protection and support from
wealthy monasteries ensured safe
passage through the Basque country, Cantabria and Asturias and on
to Santiago. The two main routes of
the Way also served as a cultural
link between the somewhat isolated reaches of the Iberian Peninsula
and the rest of Europe.

León und Burgos are major stations
on the Way of St James. The Old
Town of León is dominated by the
Santa Maria de Regla (right), built
at its center in the 13th and 14th
centuries. Burgos Cathedral was
built between 1221 and 1539. A
cupola in the form of an eight-
pointed star has been erected over
the tomb of the royal general Pedro
Hernández de Velasco (top).

Spain

SANTIAGO DE COMPOSTELA

Location: North-western Spain (Galicia)
Best time to travel: throughout the year
www.galiciaguide.com
gospain.about.com

Legend has it that pious 8th-century Christians rescued the bones of the apostle St James the Greater from the Saracens in St Catherine's Monastery on Mount Sinai and brought them to Galicia, where the relics were buried in a purpose-built church. The town of Santiago (derived from Sanctus Jacobus) de Compostela grew up around the church. James became the patron saint of the Spanish Christians in their adamant struggle against the Moorish invaders, and victory in the Battle of Clavijo in 844 was credited to his divine intervention. The news spread quickly throughout Europe and Santiago soon became the most important pilgrimage destination after Rome and Jerusalem. Thousands of modern pilgrims come here to venerate their saint on the Feast of St James in July. The cathedral above the Apostle's grave dates back to the 11th and 12th centuries and is Romanesque in style, but was enlarged and altered several times before the 18th century. It is the largest Romanesque church in Spain and even one of the largest in Europe. Tucked away behind the portal of the façade you will find the Pórtico de la Gloria, a narthex by Master Mateo housing a Romanesque sculpture group, that was completed in 1188.

The cathedral was consecrated in 1211 and later extended to include further chapels, a dome, and a transept. The building's highlight is the baroque façade at its end. The Pórtico de la Gloria narthex dates back to the Romanesque period.

Spain

PAMPLONA

Location: Northern Spain (Navarre)
Best time to travel: throughout the year (July: Running of the Bulls)
www.pamplona.es

Pamplona, also known as Iruña ("the great city"), is situated on a plateau near the River Arga. It is the capital city of Navarre, Spain and of the former kingdom of Navarre. The extensive ruins of its old city wall, demol-

ished at the time of Charlemagne in the 8th century, are extremely impressive, and don't miss the nearby Museo Arqueológico de Navarra. The fortified church of San Nicolás and the Cámara de Comptos Reales counting house are just two of the public buildings surviving from the town's thousand years of history. A stroll through the labyrinth of tiny lanes lined with aristocratic palaces

in the Old Town is a very special experience. The baroque Palacio de Navarra with its imposing throne room and original canvases by Goya lies behind the Jewish Quarter on the other side of the Plaza del Castillo. Leave the Old Town of Pamplona to the north-east and you will soon find the Parque de la Taconera, where the historical backdrop merges seamlessly into charming scenery.

The city is famous worldwide for the San Fermín festival, from July 7 to 14, in which the running of the bulls through the Old Town to the arena, or *encierro* is one of the main attractions. This fiesta, known as Sanfermines to the local population, was first brought to widespread attention by Ernest Hemingway in his first novel, *The Sun Also Rises*.

HUESCA

Location: North-eastern Spain (Aragon)
Best time to travel:
throughout the year
www.huescaturismo.com

The city of Huesca (population approximately 50,000) lies at the edge of the Ebro Basin. The capital of the province of the same name was founded as "Osca" in the first century BC and grew to be one of the principal cities in Roman Hispania. It was chosen as the capital of the independent state founded by the rebel Sertorius and even had a Senate and the first school for young Iberians. The cathedral in the upper part of the Old Town conceals a wealth of art treasures.

The 11th-century Castillo de Loarre is considered the most important Romanesque structure in Spain.

LA RIOJA

Location: Northern Spain
Best time to travel: March–October
www.lariojaturismo.com
www.spanish-living.com

Spain's most famous wines and the province where they are made both owe their name to the River (Río) Oja, a tributary of the Ebro, which flows across the region. The harvesting of wine in La Rioja has an ancient lineage with origins dating back to the Phoenicians and the Celtiberians. The climate of moderate rainfall, mild conditions, and stable temperatures is ideal for viticulture. The soil is also important: there is a good supply of chalk and clay in just the right proprtions.

La Rioja (left, vineyards at Haro) has a thousand years of wine-making history. Its traditional grape variety is the *tempranillo*.

Spain

NATIONAL PARKS IN THE PYRENEES

Location: Northern Spain, South of France
Best time to travel: throughout the year (October–April: Ski season)
www.parc-pyrenees.com
www.spain.info

Much like the Alps, the Pyrenees were created some 50 to 100 million years ago as so-called fold mountains. The chain extends for about 435 km (270 mi) from the Bay of Biscay in the Atlantic Ocean to the Golfe du Lion on the Mediterranean. Peaks in the range reach heights of more than 3,000 m (9,843 ft). Two large expanses on the Spanish side have been declared national parks to protect the landscape, animals and plant life: the Parque Nacional de Ordesa y Monte Perdido, and the countless lakes and rich flora and fauna of the Parque Nacional d'Aigües Tortes at the foot of rugged mountains further to the west. The name of the latter means "contorted waters" and refers to the streams that wind their way through the deep gorges and valleys. The heart of the Parque Nacional de Ordesa y Monte Perdido in the upper valley of the river Arazas is a gorge whose walls are roughly 1,000 m (3,281 ft) high. In the spring, snow melt rushes down the mountains from peaks whose summits are covered by eternal snow. The footpaths of the Circo de Soaso are best explored between May and September.

The Pyrenees form a natural border between Spain and France, with only the little principality of Andorra to the east interposed between them. The 2,380-m (7,808-ft) summit of Estany d'Amitges towers over the Parque Nacional d'Aigües Tortes (right).

COSTA BRAVA

Location: North-eastern Spain (Catalunya)
Best time to travel: April–October
www.tossademar.com
www.girona.cat

For most visitors, a visit to the Costa Brava means relaxing on golden beaches with clear waters, picturesque fishing villages, small towns, and excursions into the mountainous hinterland. With its mild climate and low rainfall, this coast was an early discovery for tourists, and here they found the little village of Cadaqués, tucked into a charming bay. Artists such as René Magritte, Pablo Picasso and Henri Matisse all made short stays here, and Salvador Dalí bought a house. Girona, the largest town on the Costa Brava, lies further inland on both banks of the River Onyar; its twelve bridges make river crossings easy. One of the most attractive villages is Tossa de Mar, where Marc Chagall lived for a while; some of his paintings are exhibited in the Museu Municipal in the old town. The name of the little town is derived from the Roman settlement of Turissa, the ruins of which can be inspected at an archeological site. Tossa has retained much of its charm over a thousand years of history and is considered the flagship of the Costa Brava, which extends away to the north from here. The town is reached along a winding coast road, and stops at the many viewing points are recommended.

Surrounded by the round towers of the well preserved city walls, the Old Town of Vila Vella (left) overlooks the bay of Tossa de Mar.
The Dalí Museum in Figueres (top) is the most popular museum in the country after the Prado in Madrid.
The surrealist painter lived in Cadaqués for some time, attracting a number of like-minded artists to the pretty fishing village (above).

Spain

BARCELONA

Location: North-eastern Spain (Catalunya)
Best time to travel: throughout the year
www.barcelonaturisme.com
www.bcn.es

The city has a lively history: said to have originally been founded by Hannibal's father, it eventually became an important Roman stronghold. During the Middle Ages, it was in the hands of the caliph of Córdoba before becoming the residence of the kings of Aragón. Modern Barcelona is a city of culture, industry and trade. Artists such as Joan Miró, Salvador Dalí, Antoni Gaudí, and Pablo Picasso have lived here and left their mark. The 1992 Olympic Games bequeathed the town Port Olimpico, and the Olympic Quarter, whose restaurants enjoy an unrivalled view of the marina at Barcelona. Port, Vell, the Old Port, lies at the bottom of the Ramblas beside the Custom House (1902) at the Portal del Pau, Barcelona's old port entrance. The five distinct sections of the magnificent Ramblas connecting Plaça de Catalunya with the port are always pulsing with life in the evenings and at weekends. The Barri Gòtic, the Gothic Old Town, is the heart of the city; it extends from the port to the old cathedral and marks the spot where the Romans first established their settlement under Augustus. Construction of the cathedral in the Barri Gòtic began in 1298 but was not completed until the end of the 19th century. The magnificent La Boqueria market is one of the most beautiful in Europe. The medieval Plaça del Rei is the site of the palace of Catalan and Castilian kings. The Palau de la Música Catalana (Palace of Catalan Music) is the most important concert hall in Barcelona. Designed by Domènech i Montaner in 1908 for the "Orfeo Catalá" chorus, the steel frame of this *art nouveau* building is clad in shiny, colorful materials, including ceramics and stained

glass. Some famous artists of the Catalan *art nouveau* style joined in the design of the interior as well, making the harmonious combination of light and space a particularly impressive element. Also noticeable are the lavish flowers and climbers ornamenting the ceiling. Architect Antoni Gaudí i Cornet is considered an outstanding representative of Modernism, or Catalan *Art Nouveau*. He created some of his most magnificent buildings in Barcelona, such as the Sagrada Familia, a church originally designed in the neo-Catalan style in 1882 which has still not been completed. Gaudí designed an idiosyncratic city mansion, the Palau Güell, for Eusebi Güell, and this was completed in 1889. Typically for the artist, ornamentation and organic forms dominate here. The Parc Güell was conceived as a small garden city. Although the park was created according to detailed plans from 1900 to 1914, it seems to have grown naturally. The Casa Milà, built between 1905 and 1911, is a multi-story apartment block whose bizarre design makes it hard to distinguish between architecture and sculpture. The Casa Batlló is a magnificent city mansion with a roof adorned with mosaic chimneys, designed by Gaudí to represent a large dragon. For the interior design of the Casa Vicens, Gaudí adapted some ideas from Mudéjar architecture. He was only able to complete the crypt of the Colonia Güell Church, but an existing drawing by the master gives an idea of how the structure was supposed to have looked in its final form.

Scenes from Barcelona. Opposite: bottom, Plaça del Rei, one of the most amazing places in the Gothic quarter; top, the proscenium arch of the Palau de la Musica Catalana features Catalan *art nouveau* mosaics. Page right: Gaudí's buildings in Barcelona (top, the Sagrada Familia; bottom, the Casa Milà) are stunning examples of the age of Moderism.

MONTSERRAT

Location: North-eastern Spain (Catalunya)
Best time to travel:
throughout the year
www.abadiamontserrat.net
www.barcelona-tourist-guide.com

About halfway to the 1,236-m (4,055-ft) summit of the "serrated mountain", the literal translation of the peak's name, you will find the lofty buildings housing the most famous shrine in Catalunya: the legendary monastery of Montserrat (Monestir de Montserrat). The basilica, the museum, and the Plaza de Santa María with its Gothic cloisters are certainly worth seeing, but the main attraction is La Moreneta ("the little dark one"), a remarkable 12th-century wooden figure of the Madonna which has been attributed to St Luke, although this is unlikely as the statue is not old enough. Restoration

POBLET

Location: North-eastern Spain (Catalunya)
Best time to travel:
throughout the year
www.poblet.cat

The abbey at Poblet was founded by the Duke of Barcelona and much like the nearby monastery of Santa Creus served the rulers of Aragón as a retreat for centuries. The name "Poblet" is probably derived from *populetum*, the Latin for poplar, of which there are considerable forests nearby. This monastery was the first of three sister monasteries, known as the Cistercian triangle, that helped consolidate power in Catalonia in the 12th century. The abbey itself is enclosed by three curtain walls and access from the first ring to the second is via the 15th-century Puerta Daurada, the "golden gate". The monastery area itself is reached through the Puerta Real, an

work has shown that the "Black Madonna" is not made of dark wood at all, but has been blackened by centuries-old soot. The monastery has been run by Benedictine monks since 1409, and several of the buildings are more than 1,000 years old. The Basilica houses a museum with works of art by many prominent painters and sculptors including very precious works by El Greco, Dalí, Picasso and more. Montserrat's highest point, Sant Jeroni, can be reached by an easy footpath from the topstation of the funicular Sant Jeroni.

The imposing massif of Montserrat about 50 km (31 mi) north-west of Barcelona conceals a monastery (opposite) on a rocky outcrop at an elevation of 725 m (2,379 ft). The16th-century basilica, which was restored in the 19th and 20th centuries, guards the famous statue of the Madonna (left).

important example of 14th-century military architecture. The adjacent church of St Catherine was built at the same time during the 12th century as the monastery buildings with their Romanesque-early Gothic cloisters, but its originally Romanesque buildings were altered and extended in the 13th and 14th centuries, eventually receiving a baroque façade in 1670. The two large, richly decorated 14th-century stone sarcophagi dominating the church's interior contain the remains of the rulers of Aragón and were finally restored in the 19th century.

Work began on the abbey of Santa María de Poblet, the most important royal monastery, after Catalunya and Aragón were united by a political marriage in 1137. The highlight of the monastery, which was inhabited by Cistercian monks into the 19th century, are the beautiful cloisters.

Spain

TARRAGONA

Location: North-eastern Spain
(Catalunya)
Best time to travel:
throughout the year
www.tarragonaturisme.cat
www.tarragonaguide.com

The ruins of the old Roman provincial town of Tárraco in modern Tarragona give a picture of a lively administrative and trading center which was the base for the Romanization of the Iberian Peninsula. The ruins of the fortifications, once 4 km (2.4 miles) long, also date back to the time of the town's foundation. An archeological information trail known as the Passeig Arqueològic runs along the 1,000 m (3,300 ft) of wall that remain.

As the capital of the Roman province of Hispania Citerior, ancient Tárraco was equipped with sturdy fortifications.

LLEIDA

Location: North-eastern Spain
(Catalunya)
Best time to travel:
throughout the year
www.paeria.es
www.lleidatur.com

The Iberian settlement of Lleida was Romanized in the second century BC. A Roman bridge across the River Segre will lead you through a gate and along the Carrer Major, the main road into town. The Cavallers road to the left will take you up to the Zuda, the ruins of the Moorish castle, and to La Seu Vella, the 13th-century cathedral, which was used as a barracks between 1707 and 1949. The building still retains a cloister which is laid out like the courtyard in front of a mosque.

The armies of Caesar and Pompey once faced each other at Lleida.

ZARAGOZA

Location: North-eastern Spain (Aragon)
Best time to travel:
throughout the year
www.zaragoza.es
www.spain.info

Lying on both banks of the Ebro, the two halves of the royal residence of Zaragoza (Saragossa) in Aragon are connected by many bridges (including the Puente de la Almozara and the Puente de Santiago). The town has always been an important staging post for traffic between the Pyrenees and Castile. The riverside Basílica del Nestra Señora de Pilar with its 11 tiled domes, and a 15th-century statue of the Madonna are both worth a visit.

Zaragoza's baroque pilgrimage church has become an icon of the city.

TERUEL

Location: North-eastern Spain (Aragon)
Best time to travel:
throughout the year
www.teruel.com
www.teruel.org

Situated on a plateau surrounded by gullies beside the Río Turia, Teruel grew out of the Iberian settlement of Turba, which was sacked by the Romans in 215 BC. Even after Spain was reconquered from the Moors, Arabs continued to live here, enjoying special rights and living without restrictions. They left their mark with the so-called Mudéjar style, which typically features glazed tiles and *azulejos*.

The Cathedral of St Martin, with its Christian-Islamic interior, is typical of the Mudéjar buildings in Teruel.

Spain

SEGOVIA

Location: Central Spain
(Castile and León)
Best time to travel:
throughout the year
www.turismodesegovia.com
www.segoviaturismo.es

Straddling a mountain ridge almost 100 m (330 ft) above the Eresma and Clamores rivers, the medieval Old Town of Segovia boasts a rich architectural heritage that includes more than twenty Romanesque churches. The Old Town is a distillation of everything that is plesant about a trip to Castile – picturesque houses and lanes, beautiful churches, and an impressive castle. In order to channel fresh water from the Río Frío to Segovia over a distance of 18 km (11 mi), the Romans built an impressive aqueduct with a total length of 730 m (2,395 ft). The bridge, erected in the 2nd century AD, rests on 118 arches

SALAMANCA

Location: Eastern Spain
(Castile and León)
Best time to travel:
throughout the year
www.salamanca.es
www.aboutsalamanca.com

Salamanca was conquered by the Romans in the 3rd century BC and named "Salamantica" before being sacked on several later occasions by the Moors. It achieved great importance after 1085, when it was reconquered by King Alfonso VI of Spain. The university, founded in 1218 by Alfonso IX, was regarded as one of the four most important universities in the West along with Oxford, Paris and Bologna. Its façade is a masterpiece of the Plateresque Renaissance style. Situated on the right bank of the Río Tormes, Salamanca is also rich in Romanesque and Gothic buildings. The 12th-century Old Cathedral is one of

and was built from specially designed granite blocks without the use of mortar. After rule by the Visigoths and the Arabs, the Counts of Castile established a new settlement here and Segovia was the residence of choice for Castilian monarchs for many years. The city's many Romanesque churches are remarkable for their characteristic ambulatories, which served as meeting places for guilds and fraternities. Work on Segovia's late-Gothic cathedral was begun in 1525 on the site of an earlier structure that had been destroyed by fire. After the death of Henry IV in 1474, the coronation of Isabella of Castile took place in the Alcázar fort, which stands high above the town on a rock.

Silhouetted against the Sierra de Guadarrama, two striking buildings overlook Segovia's Old Town: the Gothic cathedral and the Alcázar.

few surviving churches to show Romanesque- Byzantine influences. The church was eventually incorporated into the complex of the New Cathedral, which was begun in 1513 and features late-Gothic, Plateresque and baroque elements. Thanks to its Renaissance sandstone buildings, Salamanca received the nickname La Ciudad Dorada ("The golden city"). Its golden glow is unique in Spain.

Laid out between 1729 and 1755, the Plaza Mayor in the middle of Salamanca was built to designs by Alberto Churriguera to form a courtyard enclosed by four arcades. The buildings are several storeys in height and topped with a balustrade. The bell tower of the Town Hall (in the middle of the image) is a later addition. Bullfights were held here in the "municipal arena" until well into the 19th century.

EL ESCORIAL

Location: Central Spain (Madrid)
Best time to travel:
throughout the year
www.elescorial.es
www.turismomadrid.es

Eager to express his hunger for power and bolstered by his successes in the war against France in 1561, Philip II commissioned the construction of a vast palace in Escorial, only some 60 km (37 mi) north-west of Madrid. After the death of Juan Bautista de Toledo, the original architect, the project was taken over by Juan de Herrera in 1567, who supervised construction until near completion in 1584. The rectangular complex covers a vast area of more than 30,000 sq m (7 acres) and provides space for sixteen courtyards. It also contained nine towers, 400 rooms, 15 cloisters, and a basilica built in 1576. The composition of the buildings was inspired by the Temple of Jerusalem, and thanks to its perfect symmetry it remained for a long time the leading prototype for many other extravagant palaces across Europe. The magnificently furnished royal mausoleum has housed the mortal remains of all Spanish monarchs since Philip II.

Besides the countless private and state rooms of the royal family, the comprehensive library contains many priceless volumes.

ÁVILA

Location: Central Spain
(Castile and León)
Best time to travel:
throughout the year
www.avilaturismo.com
www.avila.com

Ávila is perhaps the most attractive example of a medieval town in all of Spain. It is built on the flat summit of a rocky hill, which rises abruptly in the midst of a veritable wilderness: a brown, arid, treeless table-land, strewn with immense grey boulders, and shut in by lofty mountains. Ávila's Gothic cathedral rises like a bastion above the battlements of the perfectly preserved town fortifications. Construction of the town walls was started as early as about 1090, but it was not until the 12th century that they received their present appearance, which is based on a rather simple rectangular plan. The *ciborro*, the mightiest of its towers, also serves as the church's apse. The church, which is incorporated into the fortifications like a bulwark, is one of the oldest cathedrals in Spain. There are also some remarkable medieval churches outside the town walls, the most interesting of which is probably the 12th-century San Vicente with its historically significant collection of Romanesque sculptures.

The mighty cathedral of Ávila has been incorporated into the eastern fortifications of the city.

Spain

TOLEDO

Location: Central Spain
(Castile-La Mancha)
Best time to travel: all the year
www.toledo-turismo.com

The Middle Ages still seem to live on wherever you go in this city above the Tagus. The panoramic view from the opposite bank of the river gives you some insight into Toledo's architectural gems: the cathedral, the Alcázar (from the Arabic for fort), and a number of medieval structures combine to form a wonderful ensemble, and narrow alleyways typify the Old Town, which is surrounded by a wall with towers. Toledo is a treasure chest of Spanish architectural jewels. The town's icon is the Cathedral, built from the 13th to the 15th centuries on the site of a former Visigoth church and an old Moorish mosque. While its exterior displays the typical features of pure French Early Gothic, the building's interior, which is a stately 110 m (350 ft) in length, is a fine example of Spanish Late Gothic. The three portals on the main façade are richly adorned with reliefs and sculptures. The Capilla Mayor shows a multitude of biblical scenes in which the life-size figures are carved from larch pine and then painted or gilded. At the highest point in the town is the Alcázar. The façade of this almost square building dates mostly from the 16th century. The way up to the fortress starts from the Plaza de Zocodover, the true heart of the city. Other attractions in Toledo include the Franciscan San Juan de los Reyes Monastery (15th-17th centuries) and the Casa El Greco; the painter, who was born in Crete, lived in Toledo for nearly forty years.

Toledo's Old Town stands on a gentle cliff surrounded on three sides by Tagus river, which runs far below in a deep gorge.

Spain

ARANJUEZ

Location: Central Spain (Madrid)
Best time to travel:
throughout the year
www.arannet.com

The town, which was laid out according to a strictly geometric plan, is famous for its gardens, as well as for Rodriguez' *Concierto de Aranjuez*. The largest park is the Jardín del Príncipe in the north-east, which was created from plans by French landscape gardeners in 1763. The Casa del Labrador, a small palace in the garden, is definitely worth visiting. Another building nearby, the Casa de Marinos, has six royal boats on display.

The royal palace was rebuilt after two fires in the 17th century. Its main façade combines elements from the Renaissance and the baroque.

CUENCA

Location: Central Spain
(Castile-La Mancha)
Best time to travel:
throughout the year
www.turismocuenca.com
www.vercuenca.com

The Old Town of Cuenca was laid out beside a steep cliff which falls away on both sides to the valleys of the Río Júcar and the Río Huécar. The town is most famous for its *casas colgadas*, the "hanging houses", and the Museo de Arte Abstracto Español has been established in one of these to accommodate one of the largest collections of modern Spanish abstract art. The highest point on the plateau is occupied by the Torre de Mangana, once the castle watchtower.

Flanked by two rivers, the Old Town lies on the edge of a sheer cliff.

CONSUEGRA

Location: Central Spain
(Castile-La Mancha)
Best time to travel: April–October
**www.turismocastilla
lamancha. com**

Most Spanish windmills, can be found in the province of Castilla-La Mancha in central Spain. "In a certain village of La Mancha, which I shall not name ..." Thus begins the first chapter of a novel which reports the "happy victory" of the "doughty Don Quixote in his terrible and miraculous battle with the windmills ..." Quite where the story took place will forever remain a mystery, but even imagining it was here in Consuegra is enough for some.

There are still 11 windmills and a restored 12th century castle on the hill in Consuegra.

VALÉNCIA

Location: Western Spain (Extremadura)
Best time to travel: throughout the year
**turismo.caceres.es
www.visitextremadura.co.uk**

Only portions of the city wall of the Roman settlement of Colonia Norbensis Caesarina have survived. The Almohad dynasty who ruled here in the 12th and 13th centuries built the fortifications we can still see today, reinforcing them with numerous towers, of which the largest is 30 m (100 ft) tall. Little of the Moorish rulers remains to be seen in the city itself, but an Arabic influence is discernible in the layout of the streets and inner courtyards.

The wealth of the town is apparent in the silk exchange (La Lonja de la Seda).

Spain

MÉRIDA

Location: Western Spain (Extremadura)
Best time to travel: throughout the year
www.visitextremadura.co.uk

Mérida's name was made by the Romans, and not far from the town you will find the best preserved ruins from the Roman period and the early Middle Ages. Augusta Emerita was founded in AD 25 as a colony for veterans of the Vth and Xth legions to live out their days. It soon flourished, becoming the capital of Lutania and a cultural and political center with a population of about 50,000; before long it was the greatest Roman city in Iberia and one of the largest in the entire empire. The emperor Agrippa contributed the semi-circular Roman theater, which seated 6,000 spectators, and the nearby amphitheater

GUADALUPE

Location: Western Spain (Extremadura)
Best time to travel: throughout the year
www.visitextremadura.co.uk
www.pueblos-espana.org

Legend has it that a 13th-century shepherd found an icon of the Virgin Mary, supposedly fashioned by St Luke himself, buried in the ground. A hermitage was built on the spot where it was discovered, and here Alphonse XI commissioned a larger monastery in thanks for his victory at the Battle of Salado in 1340. The fame of Our Lady of Guadalupe soon spread throughout the Hispanic world.

The Black Madonna of Gudalupe is displayed under a canopy on the high altar of the monastery church. Carved out of oak, the figure is cloaked in a plush brocade gown.

which was completed in 8 BC seated no less than 14,000. The Circus Maximus was probably built at the turn of the 1st century. With more than 400 m (1,300 ft) by 100 m (330 ft), it could accommodate a crowd of 30,000. Taverns and several guest-houses for visitors to the Roman attractions can still be seen today. One citizen's house with its floor mosaics and frescos has survived in good condition, giving an excellent insight into life as a retired Roman legionary.

The Roman bridge over the Río Guadiana was built during the reign of the emperor Augstus. It is 792 m (2,598 ft) long and is supported by 60 granite arches. Mérida preserves more important ancient Roman monuments than any other city in Spain (including a triumphal arch of the age of Trajan).

CÁCERES

Location: Western Spain (Extremadura)
Best time to travel: throughout the year
turismo.caceres.es
www.visitextremadura.co.uk

Only portions of the city wall of the Roman settlement of Colonia Norbensis Caesarina have survived. The Almohad dynasty who ruled here in the 12th and 13th centuries built the fortifications we can still see to-day, reinforcing them with numerous towers, of which the largest is 30 m (100 ft) tall. An Arabic influence is discernible in the layout of the streets and inner courtyards. It was the first city in Spain to become a listed UNESCO World Heritage site.

Little of the Moorish rulers remains to be seen in Cáceres itself.

SEVILLA

Location: Southern Spain (Andalusia)
Best time to travel: throughout the year (Easter Week: Semana Santa)
www.sevillaonline.es

Seville is one of the most beautiful cities in Spain, a great Andalusian beauty with an Arabic past. Moorish invaders from North Africa built the Great Mosque after their initial conquest of Seville in 712, but it was ultimately destroyed during the Reconquest in the year 1248. The chapels of the cathedral house important paintings by Murillo, Velazquez and Zurbarán. The mighty Alcázar (from the Arabic for fortress) is clear survivor from Moorish times and features detailed ornamentation in its beautiful courtyards. Goods from the Spanish colonies overseas changed hands here, bringing great wealth to the city.

Large image: the Casa Lonja (1583 to 1598) was once the main market and exchange for goods imported from the colonies; it was converted into the Archivo General de las Indias in 1785 to house documents connected with the exploration of the Americas.
This page, from top: Santa María de la Saede, Seville's five-naved cathedral, is 117 m (384 ft) long, 74 m (243 ft) wide, and 40 m (130 ft) high, making it the third-largest church in Christendom. The sarcophagus of Christopher Columbus has been here since 1900; as the seafarer wished never to lie in Spanish soil, his stone coffin is held aloft on the shoulders of four heralds representing the kingdoms of León, Castile, Navarre, and Aragón. The Reales Alcázares de Sevilla, Seville's royal palace, is a gem of Mudéjar architecture; the walls are decorated with Arabic patterns and calligraphy, but you will also find Christian symbols such as St James' mussel shell in the magnificent rooms.

Spain

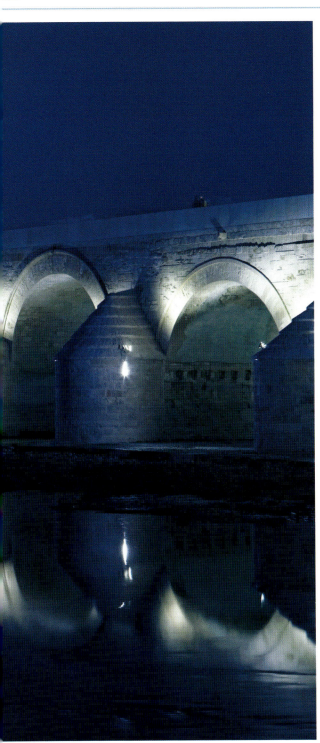

CÓRDOBA

Location: Southern Spain (Andalusia)
Best time to travel: throughout the year (Easter Week: Semana Santa)
www.turiscordoba.es
www.turismodecordoba.org

Córdoba was an important center of politics and culture even in Roman times, as is evidenced by the Puente Romana bridge across the river Guadalquivir. With its 16 arches, it was once part of the Via Augusta, a road stretching from Cádiz to the Pyrenees. One of Córdoba's most important sons was the Roman philosopher Seneca. In the year 929, the Caliphate of Córdoba rose as the shining star of Al-Andalus and thus competed for fame with Baghdad, also a major world city. As in many cities at the time, Jewish, Arabic and Christian cultures lived peacefully together here while science and philosophy flourished. In the Old Town, around the Mezquita, some of this spirit can still be experienced today. At its height, Córdoba was a powerful city of one million inhabitants with great influence within the Caliphate. It is now a provincial capital with a population of only about 300,000, but Córdoba is still a magical city.

In particular, the Old Town with its narrow alleyways, whitewashed houses, and flowery courtyards is truly idyllic. In the center stands the Mezquita, the mighty fortress that was once a mosque and is now a cathedral. The vast former prayer hall of the Great Mosque has 856 ornate columns and a wonderful ambience. The Alcázar de los Reyes Cristianos, a royal residence built as a fortress in the14th century, is set in spectacular grounds, and the bullfighting museum and the old synagogue are certainly worth a visit.

**The 16 arches of the Puente Romana bridge were once part of the Via Augusta (opposite).
Below: 19 naves and 36 transepts, splendid Moorish ornamentation and the mysterious light between the columns make any visit to the Mezquita an unforgettable one.**

Spain

UBEDA AND BAEZA

Location: Southern Spain (Andalusia)
Best time to travel:
throughout the year
http://ubedaturismoy
patrimo nio.es
www.baezamonumental.com

These ancient towns were originally 9th-century Moorish settlements with a fortress (*alcázar*), and few alterations were made to the basically Arabic architectural forms after the *Reconquista* in the first half of the 13th century. Things were to change only as the Renaissance began: the 15th century brought a certain prosperity – if only to a small minority of aristocrats and the Church – and ushered in a period of frenetic building. The walls separating the *alcázar* from the rest of the town were torn down and new buildings in the style of the Italian Renaissance were erected on the land exposed. Both towns are now considered shining examples of Spanish Renaissance architecture; Ubéda is laid out on a square plan and surrounded by a wall, and the Plaza de Vázquez Molina is particularly worth seeing. Built in the 13th century, the church of Santa María de los Reales Alcázares on the Plaza Vázquez de Molina in Ubéda conceals a number of lavishly decorated Gothic chapels and a Renaissance choir screen created by Maestro Bartolomé of Jaén. Baeza is also surrounded by a wall, but has an oval town plan with the cathedral, built in 1570, at its center. The ancient Córdoba and Úbeda gates, and the remarkable arch of Baeza, are among the remains of its Moorish fortifications.

The sister towns of Ubéda and Baeza lie no more than 10 km (6 mi) apart, The central point of Baeza is the little Plaza del Pópulo (right).

Spain

GRANADA

Location: Southern Spain (Andalusia)
Best time to travel:
throughout the year
www.turgranada.es
www.andalucia.com

The south of Spain remained under Moorish rule even after the so-called Caliphate of Córdoba had ended in 1031. In 1238, for example, Granada became an independent Islamic kingdom, and its rulers built the magnificent complex of the Alhambra. In 1492, the town was the last Moorish possession to be "reconquered" by Christian Spanish rulers. Probably the most famous part of the Alhambra is the Patio de los Leónes, the Court of the Lions. In the middle of the patio, surrounded by richly decorated arcades, is a fountain supported by 12 lion sculptures the likes of which are extremely rare in Islamic art outside of the Iberian Peninsula. They endow the ensemble with a very special character. After the 16th century, the fortress palace of Alhambra grew more and more dilapidated until a large part was lavishly restored in the 19th century. The cathedral, which was built after the end of Moorish rule, contains the graves of the Spanish kings. In the Alhambra district stands the uncompleted palace of Charles V, which was begun in 1526, with total disregard for the existing Moorish structure. The most beautiful declaration of love for Granada was probably that made by the writer Federico Garcia Lorca, who not only said that the city was made for "dreams and dreaming", but that it was the place where a lover "could better write the name of his love in the sand than anywhere else on earth".

Overlooked by the snow-capped peaks of the Sierra Nevada, Granada (left) is bounded to the west by a plateau and to the south by the banks of the Rio Genil. The most famous part of the Alhambra is the Court of the Lions (bottom). In the middle of the patio, surrounded by richly decorated arcades (below), is a fountain with 12 lion sculptures.

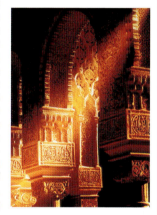

Spain

RONDA

Location: Southern Spain (Andalusia)
Best time to travel: throughout the year (April–June: bullfighting)
www.turismoderonda.es

Once described by the poet Rainer Maria Rilke as an "ideal city", Ronda is divided into three districts. La Ciudad, the oldest of these, is situated in the middle of a chalk plateau and separated from the others by a Moorish wall and steep cliffs. The streets of San Francisco, the district lying at the foot of the cliffs, are lined with farmhouses, and the modern suburb of El Mercadillo, where most of the population of 35,000 actually live, is on the other side of the Tagus valley. The Casa del Rey Moro in the Old Town is one of the city's major attractions, and there is a staircase of 365 steps carved out of the rock which leads from this Moorish palace to the valley floor below.

CÁDIZ

Location: Southern Spain (Andalusia)
Best time to travel: throughout the year
www.gotarifa.com
cadiz.costasur.com

Cádiz, founded by the Phoenicians as an important trading port west of the Strait of Gibraltar, is one of Europe's oldest towns. The golden dome of the New Cathedral towers above the Old Town. While the Old City's street plan consists largely of narrow winding alleys connecting large plazas, newer areas of Cádiz typically have wide avenues and more modern buildings. In addition, the city is dotted by numerous parks where giant trees supposedly brought to Spain by Columbus, flourish.

Cádiz is located at the the end of a spit of land extending for about 9 km (6 mi) into the Atlantic.

The Arabic ornamentation in the cathedral, the Palacio de Mondragón, and the Casa del Gigante are also worth seeing. Built in 1785, the bullfighting arena is one of the oldest in Spain. The partially intact Baños árabes ("Arab baths") are found below the city and date back to the 13th and 14th centuries.

Ronda is a good base from which to explore the famed *pueblos blancos* ("white villages") in the surrounding area, including Zahara, Prado del Rey with its grid of streets, Ubrique, the capital of the Sierra de Cádiz, Setenil, whose hanging houses cling to the vertical cliffs like great eagles' eyries, and Olvera, with its 12th-century castle.

Ronda lies at the edge of a highland plateau which has been split into two by a 200-m (660-ft) deep valley. The Puente Nuovo linking the two two parts of the town is 98 m (322 ft) high.

GIBRALTAR

Location: South of the Iberian Peninsula (British sovereign territory)
Best time to travel: throughout the year
Beste Reisezeit: ganzjährig
www.gibraltar.gi
www.gibraltar.gov.gi

This British enclave, covering only about 6 sq km (2 sq mi), is inhabited by some 30,000 people. Its name derives from "Djebel al-Tarik", the "Mountain of Tarik", named after the Moorish conqueror who arrived in 711. The Straits of Gibraltar have been called the "Key to the Mediterranean" as they represent a strategically important link between the Atlantic and the Mediterranean Sea.

The rocky cliffs of Gibraltar rise up out of the sea at the southern tip of the Iberian Peninsula.

Spain

THE BALEARICS

Location: Eastern Spain
Best time to travel: April–October
www.mallorca.com
www.visitbalears.com
www.illesbalears.es

"If you like Paradise," wrote Gertrude Stein, "Majorca is paradise". Every year, this Mediterranean island is visited by millions of tourists, and yet it still has some quiet bays and breathtaking landscapes. Majorca is an island like an entire continent, with wilderness and surprisingly high mountains in the north, vast almond plantations and cornfields in the interior, and miles and miles of beaches and coves in the south. A holiday paradise with an area of 3,640 sq km (1,405 sq mi), surrounded by turquoise seas, its capital Palma with the La Seu Cathedral towering high above the port is the most prosperous town in Spain by gross national product. Those who wish to escape the bustle of the coastal resorts between Andratx and Arenal, and discover the beauty of nature and meet the people in the small villages, only have to go a short way inland. The mountain village Valldemossa, for example, boasts a charterhouse whose monks' cells were converted into small apartments in the 19th century. In 1838/39, Frédéric Chopin and George Sand lived there, a fact that has attracted music lovers from around the world ever since. Near the Port de Valldemossa is the majestic Son Marroig, former summer residence of the Austrian Archduke Ludwig Salvator. Covering an area of 716 sq km (276 sq mi), Menorca is only about one fifth the size of Majorca.

Cap de Formentor (opposite), Majorca's northernmost point; right, from top to bottom: Cala Macarelleta, a bay in Menorca; Formentera, Ibiza; La Seu Cathedral in Palma de Majorca.

Spain

CANARY ISLANDS

Location: Eastern Central Atlantic
Best time to travel: April–October
www.turismodecanarias.com
www.visitenerife.com
www.grancanaria.com
www.turismolanzarote.com
www.gomera-island.com
www.lapalmaturismo.com
ww.fuerteventura.com
www.elhierro.es

Gran Canaria is an island of contrasts. The Tamadaba Nature Park on the west coast of the island is a superb adventure. The subtropical north with its lush vegetation is contrasted by the desert landscape of Maspalomas in the south. The landscapes of Tenerife are as varied as its climate zones, and range from verdant green in the north to rugged mountains and desert-like expanses in the south. Life in the coastal towns is modern European. San Cristóbal de La Laguna is a lively university town and the cultural capital of the island. In the more isolated mountain villages, people still lead more traditional lives. Thanks to its species-rich vegetation, many visitors regard Tenerife as the most beautiful of the Canary Islands. The Teide National Park, for example, is not only home to Spain's highest mountain, Pico del Teide at 3,718 m (12,199 ft), but also to a fascinating volcanic landscape with a vast variety of flora and fauna.

Large picture: Columnar cacti at the rocky coast of Los Gigantes on Tenerife, in the background the summit of Mount Teide.
This page: More than a fifth of Lanzarote's surface area is covered with a layer of lava and ash (top). The slopes of the Alta de Garajonay on Gomera are covered with dense ancient forest. (middle). This finger of rock (bottom), which has been defying the elements for thousands of year, is known as the Dedo de Dias, the "finger of God".

Portugal

LISBON

Location: West Portugal
Best time to travel: throughout the year
www.visitlisboa.com
www.lisboa-cidade.com

A sea of houses climbs from the wide estuary of the river Tagus up the steep hills of the "white city". Lisbon, the capital of Portugal, has a superb location that attracts visitors from around the world. Particularly worth seeing is the Alfama, Lisbon's oldest and most picturesque neighborhood, a labyrinthine Old Town on Castle Hill, which is crowned by the ruins of the Castelo de São Jorge. Between the castle ruins and the medieval Sé Cathedral are two of many miradouros, attractive viewing platforms that Lisbon is famous for and from which you can enjoy spectacular views across the city. Author Fernando Pessoa, a native of Lisbon, said of his city there exists "no flowers that can match the endlessly varied colors of Lisbon in the sunlight". Lisbon is divided into an upper town (the bairro alto) – the entertainment quarter with its lively pubs, traditional restaurants and fado bars – and a lower town (the baixa), which was rebuilt after the devastating earthquake of 1755 according to the city's original plans and is today the banking and shopping district. The best view of the baixa can be enjoyed from the Elevador de Santa Justa.

Built in 1901, the Elevador de Santa Justa (left), a wrought-iron elevator between the upper and lower towns, has the best views of the Baixa. Opposite: a good way to explore the "white city" on the banks of the Tagus is to take a trip on one of the old Eléctricos, the old trams which make their bumpy, creaking way through the narrow lanes of Lisbon.

Portugal

HIERONYMITES MONASTERY, BELEM TOWER

Location: West Portugal
Best time to travel:
throughout the year
www.mosteirojeronimos.pt

The richly adorned tower of Belém was built in 1521, on the orders of Manuel I, as a watchtower to protect the Tagus estuary – the location where Portuguese sailors once embarked on their journeys of exploration. With its many balconies and battlements, Belém is an impressive example of Manueline architecture and also one of Lisbon's most famous landmarks. Over the centuries, the Tagus silted up so much that the tower today no longer stands at the estuary but on the riverbank. There are superb views from the highest platform at 35 m (115 ft). Emanuel I the Fortunate, king of Portugal from 1495 to 1521,

was an avid supporter of the country's maritime explorations, in particular those of Vasco da Gama and Pedro Cabral, credited with the discovery of the sea route to India and Brazil, respectively. Indeed, during his reign, the arts and sciences flourished. To honor Vasco da Gama, in 1502, he commissioned the enormous Hieronymites Monastery. This massive building, which later also served as a feared state prison, clearly shows Moorish, Gothic, and Moroccan influences.

The fortified Tower of Belem, today the city's icon, was originally built as a a ceremonial gateway to Lisbon. The charming interior of the monastery church is a mixture of late Gothic vaulting, magnificent stained glass, and richly decorated columns.

TOMAR

Location: Central Portugal
Best time to travel:
throughout the year
www.cm-tomar.pt

The Convento de Cristo, Portugal's largest monastery complex in Tomar, was used by the Knights Templar as a fortress, during the 12th century. The modern monastery complex is based on a castle donated to the Templar Order by King Alphonse in 1159. The minster of Santa María do Olival is said to have been modeled on the Church of the Holy Sepulcher in Jerusalem. No other monastery in Europe has 7 cloisters like Tomar.

The fortress-like 16-sided rotunda, the oldest part of this monastery in the little town of Tomar on the banks of the Rio Nabão, is decorated with magnificent frescos.

ALCOBAÇA

Location: West Portugal
Best time to travel:
throughout the year
www.cm-alcobaca.pt

The Santa María Monastery was founded in Alcobaça, located in the Alcoa and Baça river valleys about 100 km (62 miles) from Lisbon, as a reward for the victory over the Moors in Santarém. Its origins date back to 1153, the year of the death of Bernard of Clairvaux, the Order's founder, but the buildings have since been much enlarged and altered.

The minster (17th/18th century), Portugal's largest religious building, houses the ornate sarcophagus of King Pedro I and his lover, Ines de Castro, who was executed for treason by Pedro's father, Alphonse IV.

SINTRA

Location: West Portugal
Best time to travel:
throughout the year
www.cm-sintra.pt

Lying at the foot of a densely forested cliff, this old Moorish town and former summer residence of the Portuguese monarchy is a mixture of charming *quintas*, picturesque nooks and corners, and a maze of winding lanes, with the royal palace towering over the Old Town. The lavishly decorated rooms of this imposing complex of buildings date back in part to the 14th century but have been significantly extended since. The Palácio Nacional da Pena castle, a 19th-century faux-medieval mixture of Gothic portals, Manueline windows, Byzantine ceilings, minaret-like turrets, Moorish *azuelos*, and other Romanesque and Renaissance elements, looks down on Sintra from the highest point of the town and can be seen for miles around. The castles and palaces in the Serra de Sintra are surrounded by extensive and exotic grounds; one of the most impressive of these is the garden surrounding the Moorish-looking folly at Monserrate with its sub-tropical vegetation. The town is a UNESCO World Heritage Site on account of its 19th century Romantic architecture.

The high, strangely shaped kitchen chimneys of the the royal palace at Sintra display distinctly Islamic influences. It is the best preserved medieval Royal Palace in Portugal. It is an important tourist attraction.

COIMBRA

Location: West Portugal
Best time to travel:
throughout the year
www.turismodecoimbra.pt
www.turismo-centro.pt

The city on the steep banks of the Rio Mondego is one of the oldest university cities in Europe (13th century) and was actually the only one in Portugal until 1910. The city center is home to the fortress-like Old Cathedral (Sé Velha), Portugal's largest Romanesque structure dating back to the 12th century. On the hill behind the church is the Old University, which is also the former royal palace. The showpiece here is the world-famous Joanina Library (1716–1728), Portugal's most beautiful baroque building, which is color-coded for each area of specialization. Not far from the library is the Museu Machado de Castro, located in the former bishop's palace. Towering opposite the museum is the Sé Nova (New Cathedral), a former Jesuit church built around 1600. A short walk through the city's winding alleyways will take visitors to the Mosteiro de Santa Cruz, a former Augustinian monastery where the Parque de Santa Cruz offers a lovely place to relax. It is also home to the Quinta de Lagrimas, where the love story between Spanish crown prince Pedro and his lover, Ines, came to its tragic end.

Founded in 1290 on a hill at Alcácova, the University of Coimbra is the oldest in Portugal and one of the oldest in the world. I was founded by King Dinis and confirmed by Papal Bull.

Portugal

PORTO, ALTO DOURO

Location: North-western Portugal
Best time to travel:
throughout the year
www.portoturismo.pt
www.cm-porto.pt
www.visitportugal.com

This port city on the Rio Douro estuary on the Atlantic has much to offer its visitors. Five bridges link Porto with Vila Nova de Gaia, its sister city on the opposite banks and home to most of the port wine cellars. The Ponte de Dom Luís I railway bridge was designed in the offices of Gustave Eiffel. The streets and houses of Porto's Old Town cling tightly to the steep granite rocks beneath it. In the heart of the town, at the bottom end of the Avenida dos Aliados, is the Praça Liberdade with the Torre dos Clerigos, the highest church steeple in Portugal at 75 m (246 ft). At the top of the hill is the town hall with its 70-m (230-ft) bell tower. At the São Bento station, the giant azulejo murals are especially worth seeing. The name of these brightly hand-painted and glazed floor and wall tiles, which decorate all types of buildings in Porto including the Capela das Almas, is probably derived from the Arabic word "al-zu-layi", meaning small polished stone, or possibly from the word "azul", meaning blue. On the way to the Ponte de Dom Luis I you come to the cathedral with its superb silver altarpiece. From there you can descend into the Bairro da Sé quarter, Porto's oldest district. The Praça da Ribeiro and the Praça Infante Dom Henriques are the center of the Ribeira district, here rich and poor clash harshly — the stock exchange sits among narrow dingy alleyways.

The Ponte de Dom Luis I (top) was designed by Gustav Eiffel's architecture practice. Bottom, *azulejos* **on the Capela das Almas.**

Portugal

ÉVORA

Location: Central Portugal
Best time to travel:
throughout the year
www2.cm-evora.pt
www.rt-planiciedourada.pt

The Corinthian columns of a temple dedicated to Diana still stand at the heart of the Roman settlement of Évora. In addition to that, the preserved remains of an aqueduct and a castellum also remind us of the town's former significance in Roman commerce on the Iberian Peninsula. The town also has some Moorish influence from hundreds of years of rule that ended in 1165. The Jesuit university houses a seminary and a collection of valuable manuscripts.

Construction of the triple-naved cathedral (right, a view of the 70-m/230-ft long interior) was begun in 1186.

GUIMARÃES

Location: Northern Portugal
Best time to travel:
throughout the year
www.cm-guimaraes.pt

Guimarães is considered the cradle of the nation and in the 12th century was the first capital of the newly founded kingdom; Alphonse I was born in Guimarães. The special building techniques and styles developed here in the Middle Ages were to influence architecture throughout Portugal's colonies, and there are a number of well preserved examples from the period in the picturesque historic city center. The *castelo* on the hill is also one of the best-preserved Romanesque fortifications in the country.

The Largo da Oliveira lies at the heart of the well-preserved center of Guimarães.

BATALHA

Location: West Portugal
Best time to travel:
throughout the year
www.golisbon.com

After defeating the armies of Castile, King John fulfilled a vow by founding the monastery of Santa María da Vitória. The building was more or less completed in 1402 to a design by Alfonso Domingues and handed over to the Dominican order. The workers who built the monastery also made up the town's first inhabitants. Batalha, Tomar, and Alcobaça are the three greatest royal monasteries on the northern edge of Estremadura.

Breathtaking from within and without: Batalha monastery with its "Royal Cloisters" and carved stone figures on the north portal of the monastery church.

Portugal

ALGARVE

Location: Southern Portugal
Best time to travel:
throughout the year
www.visitalgarve.pt

The south of Portugal is a popular destination for many holidaymakers with its superb white sand beaches, crystal clear water, and charming little coves. The fascinating sandstone formations at the Praia de Dona Ana beach and the rocky cliffs on the Ponta da Piedade about 2 km (1.3 mi) south of there are typical of the Algarve. The town of Lagos was once a major staging point for Portuguese explorers setting sail for the New World, and since the days of Henry the Navigator (1394–1460) it has been a center of shipbuilding. The darker side in its history involved the transshipment of captured African slaves. The first recorded auctions took place here on the Praça da República in 1443. Sagres was once the location of Henry the Navigator's legendary nautical school, commemorated by a giant stone compass with a diameter of 43 m (141 ft), on the rocky Ponta de Sagres, not far from the Fortaleza de Sagres. Cabo de São Vicente is almost visible from Sagres jutting out to sea with its 24-m (79-ft) high lighthouse. It is Europe's south-westernmost point. The cliffs, which are up to 60 m (197 ft) high, were still thought of as the "end of the world" in the days of Christopher Columbus.

The magnificent beaches, picturesque rock formations, and turquoise waters of the Algarve are especially attractive in spring, drawing Europeans who are sick of winter to the coast. With some 3,000 hours of sunshine a year, it is no surprise that the Algarve has become one of the most popular tourist destinations in Europe both for sunseekers and golfers.

Portugal

MADEIRA

Location: island off North-west Africa
Best time to travel: April–October
www.madeira-web.com
www.madeiraislands.travel

Green banana plantations, bright flowers in the gardens, lovely parks, giant exotic trees, and dense laurel woods – Madeira simply radiates fertility. Funchal, the capital of Madeira boasts grand avenues ranked on both sides by fragrant jacaranda trees. The heart of Funchal is the Sé Cathedral, the interior of which was dedicated in 1514, and features an astonishing, finely carved wooden ceiling with ivory marquetry. In stark contrast to the cathedral stands the Zona Velha, the former fishing district, where low houses fringe the narrow alleyways, and elegant restaurants welcome visitors in the former harbor dives. From the Zona Velha, a cable car takes you up the Monte to the Nossa Senhora pilgrimage church, a popular annual pilgrimage site. In the old and slightly run-down fishing village of Câmara de Lobos, people are proud of their wharf, where ships are still built according to traditional models. The Nossa Senhora da Conceição Chapel is said to have been donated by the Portuguese explorer of the Madeiras,

João Gonçalves Zarco in 1419. West of Câmara, the steep cliffs of Cabo Girão rise 580 m (1,903 ft) almost vertically from the sea, offering magnificent views. A strong wind usually blows around the lighthouse at the Ponta do Pargo, but the view of the cliffs on the west coast is breathtaking. When it gets too chilly, an original English teahouse invites visitors to warm up with pastries and small snacks. Originally, Madeira was covered by dense forest, but logging has decimated much of it. Luckily, however, the Laurisilva laurel tree still survives in some large tracts of primary forest. Found at altitudes 600 to 1,300 m (1,969 to 4,265 ft), these forests – like those in the Garajonay National Park on the Canary Island of La Gomera – are remnants of the once vast laurel woods found in the Mediterranean region. These woods are central to the island's water supply: the leaves on the trees collect moisture from the clouds which is then held in the foliage, eventually finding its way into the local rocks.

Right: Funchal marina.
Below: Exotic giant trees, dense laurel forests, and bubbling waterfalls – the unique beauty of the island of Madeira, a pearl in the Atlantic

Portugal

AZORES

Location: Island chain in the
Atlantic
Best time to travel:
May–September
www.destinazores.com
www.visit-azores.com

Created many years ago by powerful
forces in the earth's interior, the island chain of the Azores is located in
the middle of the Atlantic Ocean,
1,500 km (930 mi) west of Lisbon,
the capital of Portugal, and 3,600 km
(2,200 mi) east of North America.
There are nine populated islands and
a few uninhabited islets with a
total surface area of more than
2,300 sq km (888 sq mi). These are
arranged in three groups running
from the north-west to the east: Flo-
res and Corvo to the north-west, Ter-
ceira, Pico, Faial, São Jorge, and Gra-
ciosa in the middle, and São Miguel
and Santa Maria to the east. Much
like Madeira, the Azores became an
autonomous region as a result of the
"Carnation Revolution". Ponta Del-
gada is the port capital of São
Miguel, the largest and most densely populated island in the archipelago, and Pico, the second-largest island, lies 250 km (155 mi) to the
west. The island is often referred to as
the *Ilha Montanha*, the "isle of mountains", as it is overshadowed by the
mighty volcanic peak of Pico, Portugal's highest summit (2,351 m/7,713
ft), whose volcanic genesis took place
more than 250,000 years ago. Wine
has been grown on the slopes of Pico since people first arrived here in
the 15th century, and dry stone walls
have been built to protect the vines
and the grapes from strong winds.

**The entire archipelago of the
Azores is of volcanic origin, as
can be seen from a number of
geographical features such as the
Lagoa do Fogo on São Miguel.
They are also visited for whale-
watching.**

Germany

BERLIN

Location: Eastern Germany
Best time to travel:
throughout the year
www.berlin.de
www.visitberlin.de

"Great Berlin, the open city – it should not be just a German city," wrote Mexican author Carlos Fuentes, before adding, "It is our city, a city of the whole world". History has been made in this city on the river Spree and is still being made today, combining the past with the present to construct the immediate future. This old and new capital has changed radically since the fall of the Wall. The Bundestag and Senate now sit here, making it the center of political power in Germany, and its museums, theaters, and architectural highlights bring it to the cultural avant-garde of the German republic. The city is recognized for its festivals, diverse architecture, nightlife, contemporary arts, public transportation networks and a high quality of living. Berlin has evolved into a global focal point for young individuals and artists attracted by a liberal lifestyle and modern *zeitgeist*.

Tradition and modernism in peaceful harmony: the Band des Bundes ("Federal Strip") on both banks of the Spree (top right) is an attempt by the architects Axel Schultes and Charlotte Frank to unite east and west. A strip 100 m (330 ft) wide and a kilometer (half a mile) wide on both sides of the river is dedicated to governmental and parliamentary buildings. The history of the Brandenburg Gate (right) is a reflection of German history; badly damaged during World War II – the Quadriga was almost completely destroyed – it was isolated behind the wall after 13 August 1961. The gate has since been restored to its former glory.

Germany

HELIGOLAND, AMRUM, SYLT

Location: German Bight, North Friesian Islands (Schleswig-Holstein)
Best time to travel: May–September
www.helgoland.de, www.amrum.de, www.sylt.de

You have to catch a boat if you want to visit Heligoland, with its famous red sandstone formations and breed-ing grounds for guillemots and kitti-wakes. Germany's only solid rock, high-seas island was actually in British hands for many years before becoming German in 1890, when it was swapped for the island of Zanzibar. South-west of Föhr lies the quiet island of Amrum, about 20 sq km (8 sq mi) in size and featuring dunes up to 30 m (98 ft) high. Amrum also has a sandy beach that is up to 2 m (1.3 mi) wide and 15 km (9 mi) long – the famous Kniepsand beach. The small island has a population of roughly 2,200 people living in five villages, of which the Friesian village of Nebel is the best known and most popular. Sylt is the northernmost point in Germany and little village of List the northernmost community. The island was separated from the mainland by a flood about 8,000 years ago but was reconnected by the Hindenburg causeway in 1927.

Top to bottom: Heligoland's famous sandstone rocks, dunes on Armun, and the lighthouse on the Ellenbogen peninsula, on the island of Sylt.

SCHLESWIG-HOLSTEIN – WADDEN SEA

Location: North-west coast of Germany
Best time to travel: May–September
www.wattenmeer-nationalpark.de
www.nordwest.net

The Wadden Sea is an annual stopover for more than two million migratory birds as well as a summer retreat for about 100,000 breeding shelducks, eider ducks, seagulls and swallows. In addition, the tidal area is a breeding ground for herring, sole and plaice as well as a habitat for gray seals, harbor seals and harbor porpoises. In an area covering more than 4,000 sq km (1,544 sq mi), from the Danish border to the estuary of the river Elbe, Wadden Sea National Park provides more than 3,000 different animal and plant species with an ideal environment. Schleswig-Holstein was the first German state to place the northern stretches of the Wadden Sea under protection, declaring it a national park in 1985, and then a biosphere reserve in 1990. The Wadden Sea is a perfect ecosystem that is rich in nutrients, and many animal and plant species have even found a habitat on the salt flats.

Schleswig-Holstein (seen here, the Westerhever lighthouse) was the first province to place the northern reaches of the Wadden Sea under protection.

Germany

HAMBURG

Location: North Germany
Best time to travel:
throughout the year
www.hamburg.de
www.hamburg-tourism.de

Think of Hamburg and you will think of the port, the Elbe, and the Alster. Michel, the famous fish market, might get a look-in, or perhaps HSV and FC St Pauli, Hamburg's soccer teams, or the magnificent Elbe boulevards and the legendary Reeperbahn. But the city is much more than all this: it is a throbbing commercial metropolis, a center of international trade, and a diverse city of media and culture. The "Gateway to the World" has not been spared from hard knocks in its more than 1,000 years of history, yet despite its eternal flux it has remained true to its Hanseatic traditions. The view from the Lombard Bridge across the Inner Alster to the Jungferstieg with its warehouses, townhouses, and the Alster Pavilion is one of the most beautiful panoramas on earth. The people of Hamburg have the emperor Frederick Barbarossa to thank for their port – on 7 May 1189 they received a royal warrant granting them immunity from taxation on the lower course of the Elbe. Despite the fact that this warrant has since turned out to be a 14th-century forgery, the people of Hamburg nonetheless celebrate the anniversary of their port's foundation.

Enterprising 19th-century Hamburg merchants built the *Speicherstadt*, an imposing warehouse complex on the banks of the Elbe, to store fresh fruit, coffee, tobacco, tea, valuable carpets, and rum. The old customs zone is now office space and sacks of coffee have been exchanged for cappuccino machines. Coffee tastings are very popular there.

BREMEN

Location: North Germany
Best time to travel:
throughout the year
www.bremen.de
www.bremen-tourismus.de

Bremen is the capital of a province of the same name (which also includes Bremerhaven) and is not only the largest car exporter and fishing port in Europe, but also the home of the Alfred Wegener Institute for Polar and Oceanic Exploration. Many of the sights in Bremen are found in the Altstadt (Old Town), an oval area surrounded by the Weser River, to the southwest, and the Wallgraben, the former moats of the medieval city walls, to the northeast. The oldest buildings and most famous statues in the city are all to be found on the market square. Here Gerhard Marck's Bremen "town musicians" are silhouetted against the 17th-century façade of the 15th-century Town Hall, and nearby there is the "Roland", created in 1404 as a symbol of the city's independence and jurisdiction. St Peter's Cathedral dates back to the 11th century. The gabled houses on the Böttcherstrasse and the *Schoorviertel*, the oldest residential area with its artists' colony, are both worth a look.

Two of Bremen's sights face one another across the market square: the Gothic brick building of the Town Hall and the 10-m (33-ft) high *Roland* as an emblem of former city liberties.

EAST FRIESIA

Location: North-western Germany
Best time to travel:
May–September
www.ostfriesland.de
www.ostfriesen-info.de

The sea and the tides have been the limiting factor for life on the broad coastal plains between the Weser and the Ems rivers. The region has produced many seafarers and whalers, from which towns like Emden grew rich, but further inland there are wide plains with extensive moors and meadows. East Friesia is a Mecca for fans of historic windmills, and these can be seen for miles around on the local flat terrain. Wind power was harnessed relatively early for drainage purposes, to grind corn, and to press oils, and large wind farms now produce energy for East Friesia. The local canals are extremely charming and have also made the bogs arable. Greetsiel is a local model community, and even its name is very traditional; a *siel* was an opening in a sea dyke used to drain the land in the interior.

There is a chain of islands off the coast, called the East Frisian Islands. These islands are (from west to east) Borkum, Juist, Norderney, Baltrum, Langeoog, Spiekeroog and Wangerooge. Most of the East Friesian islands have a single settlement; the rest are just islets covered in reed-covered dunes, such as Juist (above).

HARZ

Location: North Germany
Best time to travel: May–September
www.harzinfo.de
www.quedlinburg.de
www.wernigerode.de
www.goslar.de

Immortalized in print by Heinrich Heine, the Harz mountains are the northernmost chain of mountains in Germany. The Upper Harz mountains in Lower Saxony were an important commercial area in the Middle Ages, and their wooded slopes and steep valleys have made them equally popular with modern-day hikers and winter sports enthusiasts. The highest peak is the Wurmberg (971 m/3,186 ft). There has been logging and mining in the Upper Harz mountains for a thousand years, and there are plenty of old mining museums, the old silver town of Goslar, and the Mining College at Clausthal-Zellerfeld as evidence of this tradition. The agricultural land at the foot of the Harz is less well known, and Salzgitter and Wolfsburg are the two largest commercial towns. The scenery between Göttingen and Hannover is typified by the low peaks of the Hils, Ith, and Elm hills.

Castle Herzberg (opposite), a beautiful half-timbered structure, was first documented in 1154. This page: Werigerode Town Hall (top), with its two prominent oriel windows, narrow slate spires, and imposing façade, is another stunning example of half-timbering. The Upper Harz (middle) is known for its bizarre rock formations. A stroll through the medieval streets of Goslar will attest to its lasting prosperity (bottom). Sights include the town hall (16th century) and the ancient mines of the Rammelsberg, which houses now a mining museum.

Germany

LÜBECK

Location: North Germany
(Schleswig-Holstein)
Best time to travel:
throughout the year
www.luebeck.de
www.luebeck-tourismus.de

This famous trading town was founded in 1143 by Count Adolf II von Holstein. Lübeck's most famous icon is the Holstentor gatehouse, built in 1478 and one of only two remaining city gates (the other one is the Burgtor). Visitors to Lübeck's Old Town will enjoy a journey back in time to the Middle Ages through a maze of alleyways from Holstentor to Burgtor and the cathedral district.

The brick buildings of Lübeck's Old Town are surrounded by water (seen here with the towers of the Church of St Mary in the background).

SCHWERIN

Location: North-east Germany
(Mecklenburg-Vorpommern)
Best time to travel:
throughout the year
www.schwerin.de
www.schwerin.com

After the fall of the Berlin Wall, the state of Mecklenburg-West Pomerania needed to designate a new capital for itself. As a result, the small town of Schwerin was chosen despite Rostock's greater size. Schwerin was and still is a ducal residence and with a picturesque location amid charming lakes, a largely restored Old Town, and a fairy-tale palace on the Schlossinsel island. The provincial theater, art gallery of the provincial museum, and the castle festival in the summer have made it a cultural hotspot.

The castle became the seat of the provincial parliament in 1990.

ROSTOCK

Location: North-east Germany
(Mecklenburg-Vorpommern)
Best time to travel:
throughout the year
www.rostock.de

Rostock has an obsession with the number seven. The "Rostocker Kennewohrn", or the seven symbols of Rostock, is a poem from 1596 that extolls the seven icons that define the cityscape, each of those in turn having seven tell-tale features. After Danish King Valdemar destroyed it in 1161, this former village was given its town charters in 1218. Soon after, in 1229, it became the main principality in the Mecklenburg Duchy of Rostock and by the 14th century had become the most powerful member of the Hanse.

Seen from the Warnow, Rostock's silhouette is a mixture of imposing warehouses and high towers.

WISMAR

Location: North-east Germany
(Mecklenburg-Vorpommern)
Best time to travel:
throughout the year
www.wismar.de

Wismar is a town that resembles an open-air museum of the Hanseatic League. Many of its churches, burghers' mansions and the market square date back to this period, as do the harbor basin and the "Grube," an artificial waterway to Schwerin lake. After the Hanseatic League came the Swedes who ruled Wismar for 250 years. The high spires of the town churches of St Mary and St Nicholas are evidence of the town's close connections with sea, and were used as navigation features by sailors.

The well in the Old Town was replaced with the "Wasserkunst", an ornamental fountain, in 1602.

Germany

VORPOMMERN LAGOON AREA NATIONAL PARK

Location: North-east Germany (Mecklenburg-Vorpommern)
Best time to travel:
May–September
www.nationalpark-vorpommer
sche-boddenlandschaft.de

The area between Darsswald and the Bug peninsula, part of Rügen, was protected as a nature reserve shortly after Germany's re-unification. Much of the area is covered in water, although this is only knee-deep. The Low German word *Bodden* refers to such shallow coastal waters, and these provide a unique habitat for many animal species. Storks in particular need areas of shallow water and often rest here during the migration to their summer and winter homes – they are safe from foxes and other predators and there is plenty of food. Their renowned mating dances can be observed early in the morning and their trumpeting voices carry across the marshes. The stork has become an iconic symbol of the region and is even used to promote sustainable tourism.

The stork has always been seen as a messenger of heaven, and its arrival in Mecklenburg-Vorpommern heralds an early spring. More than 60,000 of the creatures stop to rest in the national park every year. The season has been extended to include the stork's return journey to Southern Europe in November.

HIDDENSEE

Location: Island off coast of north-east Germany (Mecklenburg-Vorpommern)
Best time to travel: May–September
www.hiddensee.de

Dat söte Länneken, is how this small island is lovingly described in Low German, and a "sweet little land" it is indeed. Hiddensee and its four villages, Grieben, Kloster, Neuendorf and Vitte, is a miniature world of its own without cars, spa resorts or even a pier. Just under 1,100 people live here in what some would consider self-imposed isolation. Many outsiders like it here as well, howev-er, and visit the island to find peace and tranquility. In 1930, Gerhard Hauptmann purchased "House See-dorn" in Kloster and came every summer until 1943. A memorial re-members the Nobel Prize winner. Lo-cated to the west of Rügen it is a flat island in the Vorpommern Lagoon Area National Park, that has virtually no forest, but features salt marshes, reed belts and heathland. The sea buckthorn also grows here, which is used to make Hiddensee specialties such as jam, juice and liqueur.

Island life on Hiddensee: the very picturesque historic "Thornbush" lighthouse (1888).

Germany

RÜGEN

Location: Island off coast of northeast Germany
(Mecklenburg-Vorpommern)
Best time to travel:
May–September
www.ruegen.de
www.m-vp.de

Rügen, Germany's largest island, has an area of 976 sq km (377 sq mi), and actually comprises five islands that have grown together over the course of centuries. Jasmund, isolated between sea and shallower coastal waters is only reachable via two spits of land and was the first of the five. The forested northern half of Rügen is home to the Jasmund National Park established in 1990. At only 30 sq km (12 sq mi) it is Germany's smallest. The chalk cliffs are a real highlight. Cape Arkona juts far into the Baltic Sea and is one of the sunniest places in Germany. Its exposed location on Rügen's northernmost tip make it important for shipping. When visibility is low or navigation errors occur, ships are in danger of running aground there. No wonder then, that Cape Arkona is home to the oldest lighthouse on the Baltic Sea. Built by Schinkel in 1826, the 21-m (69-ft) tower was operated until 1905. Beside the neoclassical old tower is its successor, which is still in use. More than 100 years old, it isn't exactly a new feature here either.

The Selliner Pier (right) was destroyed in 1941 by drift ice and only rebuilt in 1998. Opposite: the romantic chalk cliffs of Rügen (top) were painted by Caspar David Friedrich. The 21-m (69-ft) high Schinkelturm lighthouse (middle) was in use until 1905. Besides its bustling tourist towns, Rügen also has plenty of quiet places for romantics to seek out, such as the marina at Gager on the Thiessow Peninsula in the south-east of the island (bottom).

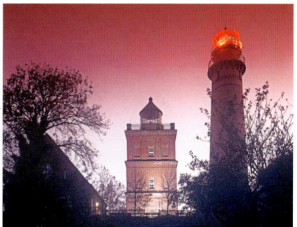

Germany

SANSSOUCI

Location: Potsdam, East Germany (Brandenburg)
Best time to travel:
throughout the year
www.spsg.de
www.potsdam.de

"Sanssouci" ("without worries") – that is how Frederick the Great wished to live in his summer palace in Potsdam. With that goal in mind, he had Georg Wenzeslaus von Knobelsdorff build him a graceful retreat among the vineyard terraces in 1747, partly according to his own designs. A single-storey structure, it is considered a masterpiece of German rococo and the most important sight in Potsdam. Adorned with ornate sculptures and rich furnishings, the palace also bears witness to its occupant's lively interest in the arts: in his music room the king liked to play his flute; in his magnificent library he would hold debates with Voltaire, the French philosopher of the Enlightenment. Maxims such as the following bear witness to his literary interests: "Thus do I say sedulously / Enjoy every moment / Today the heavens may smile upon us / We do not know if they will grumble tomorrow". More buildings were added later such as the New Chambers and the New Palace. Frederick's successors were active as well, adding the Orangery and the Charlottenhof Palace. In 1816, landscape architect Peter Joseph Lenné began the elaborate transformation of the spacious park, which extends all the way up to the Pfaueninsel (Peacock Island) and the parks of Glienicke and Babelsberg.

The annual Potsdam Castle Festival requires the participation of hundreds; actors, such as those shown here, musicians, dancers, and writers in historic costumes entertain the audience against a romantic backdrop.

Germany

HALLE, NAUMBURG, AND THE SAALE VALLEY

Location: East Germany
(Saxony-Anhalt)
Best time to travel:
April–September
www.halle.de
www.naumburg-tourismus.de

The catchment area of the Saale and Unstrut rivers is an attractive leisure area of vineyards and impressive cas-

tles, with museums full of treasures, and a range of facilities for sports enthusiasts. The largest town in the area is Halle, A Hanseatic town with more than a thousand years of history, which flourished many years ago as a salt-producing center and later became an industrial hub under the East German regime. Many of the medieval and earlier buildings have been

remarkably well preserved. This municipality on the Leipzig Plain on the edge of the Harz Mountains, was brought much renown as a town of music by George Frederick Handel, its most famous son. Surrounded by vineyards, Naumburg is located south of the confluence of the Unstrut and the Saale and has become famous for the 12 carved figures of patrons of

the church in the west choir of the Cathedral of St Peter and St Paul.

George Frederick Handel greets visitors to Halle market square from his pedestal (left). Naumburg's main attraction is the early Gothic cathedral with the world-famous statues of its patrons (right).

WITTENBERG

Location: East Germany
(Saxony-Anhalt)
Best time to travel:
April–September
www.wittenberg.de

Located on the northern banks of the
Elbe beside the southern foothills of
the Fläming hills, the town is inextricably linked with the life and work of

the great reformer Martin Luther
(1483–1546). Luther came to Wittenberg in 1508 as an Augustinian
monk, and from 1512 he taught theology and philosophy at the university, which had been founded by
Prince Elector Frederick the Wise ten
years previously. The publication of
his 95 Theses condemning clerical
behaviour in October 1517 heralded

the Reformation, and he was excommunicated and outlawed in 1521.
His patron, Prince Elector Frederick
the Wise, offered him refuge at the
Wartburg, and in the same year
Luther translated the New Testament
into German here, becoming one of
the most influential German writers
of all time in the process. Wittenberg
has commemorated its most famous

son with a monument on the market
place beside the remarkable façade
of the Town Hall and the Church of
St Mary.

**The Luther House in Wittenberg,
Collegienstrasse, was the main
place where Martin Luther lived
and worked for almost 35 years
between 1508 and 1546.**

LEIPZIG

Location: East Germany (Saxony)
Best time to travel: throughout the year
www.leipzig.de

Another chapter was written in the thousand years of history of this city, when the "Monday demonstrations" held here in the years 1989 and 1990 signalled the end of the East German regime. The city has always had many strings to its bow. Publishers such as Baedeker, Brockhaus, and Reclam trace their roots here, the "Exchange of German Book Dealers", the forerunner of the current book fair in Frankfurt am Main, was also established here in 1825, and the city is the cradle of German printing. It is also a city of music – Johann Sebastian Bach, Felix Mendelssohn-Bartholdy, and Robert Schumann all composed in the city, and the St Thomas' Choir and the Gewandhaus Orchestra are based here. Ferdinand Lasalle founded the German General Workers' Association in the city in 1863, creating the first worker's union in Germany. Founded in 1409, the university is the second-oldest in Germany after Hei-delberg (1386) and there is plenty of industrial activity in the area. The city has been best-known since the Middle Ages as a location for trade fairs.

The glass and steel of the New Trade Fair Hall is a symbol of Leipzig's unbroken tradition as a venue for trade shows. The famous trade fair city has been refurbished.

DRESDEN

Location: East Germany (Saxony)
Best time to travel:
throughout the year
www.dresden.de

"The Venice of the East", "Saxon Serenissima", "Florence on the Elbe", "Pearl of the Baroque" – the epithets that have been used to describe the capital of the Free State of Saxony over the centuries are as numerous as they are effusive. And with good reason, for the former seat of the Great Elector is without doubt one of the great European centers of culture. Seat of the Albertiner government from 1485, it developed into one of the most magnificent baroque centers of power in the German states under Elector Augustus the Strong. In the late 18th and early 19th centuries, intellectuals made Dresden a center of German Romanticism. However, the devastating bombing raids of World War II brought the glorious city to her knees and the Old Town was destroyed. Thankfully, many buildings have been lavishly rebuilt including the city's most famous icon, the Frauenkirche (Church of Our Lady), the Zwinger, the Semper Opera House, the Residenz (Dresden Palace), the Hofkirche (St Trinitatis Cathedral), and the Brühlsche Terrasse.

The view of the city from the Elbe (top and middle). The grounds of the Zwinger are surrounded in turn by galleries and pavilions housing museums (bottom).

Germany

UPPER ELBE VALLEY

Location: East Germany (Saxony)
Best time to travel:
April–September
www.sachsen-tourismus.de

Broad river islands, vineyards, parks and gardens, picturesque towns such as Pirna or Radebeul, and mighty cas- tles such as those at Moritzburg, Seußlitz, Pillnitz, and Albrechtsberg are just some of the highlights which make the area around the Elbe in Saxony a place of culture of the first order. Meissen is another gem: the "cradle of Saxony", where the Kais- ers established the first German settlement on Slavic soil, was the res- idence of the Wettin dynasty during the 12th century and managed to re- tain its medieval feel throughout World War II. The historic Old Town with its half-timbered houses is dom- inated by two symbols of worldly and spiritual power – the Gothic cathe- dral of St John and St Donatus, and Albrechtsburg castle, where porce- lain was manufactured.

Pillnitz: a flight of steps leads from the banks of the Elbe to the old summer palace of the former Saxon royal court.

SAXON SWITZERLAND

Location: East Germany (Saxony)
Best time to travel:
April–September
www.saechsische-schweiz.de

Some 360 sq km (140 sq mi) of the sandstone mountains around the Elbe which continue on into Czech territory have been preserved as a nature park, and the lush greenery here has become a habitat for a range of flora and fauna. To get the best view of the bizarrely shaped rocks lining the twisting river valley to the south-east of Dresden, you will need to take a boat trip, but there are good views to be had of the region's jagged plateaus from the road as well. Saxons consider the local scenery (the Lichtenhain Falls, typical rock formations, and a lynx) to be "as beautiful as Switzerland, just smaller") and at least two Swiss have been inclined to agree – the painters Adrian Zingg und Anton Graff took their sketchbooks to every corner of this fairytale landscape in the 18th century and are said to have coined the name "Saxon Switzerland".

Picturesque sceneries for painters of nature and wild animals

Germany

ERFURT

Location: East Germany (Thuringia)
Best time to travel: throughout the year
www.erfurt.de

Erfurt has preserved an intact medieval city centre. The city is known for its two churches, Erfurt Cathedral (*Mariendom*) and *Severikirche*, which stand side by side and together form the emblem of the city. Both churches tower above the townscape and are accessible via huge open stairs called *Domstufen*. Pass by the half-timbered houses of the Marktstrasse and you will reach the fish market beside the imposing neo-Gothic Town Hall and the statue of Roland (1581). The Krämer Bridge has spanned the Gera since 1472.

The Cathedral of St Mary and the Church of St Severus.

WEIMAR

Location: East Germany (Thuringia)
Best time to travel: throughout the year
www.weimar.de

Stroll through the trim streets of the little town of Weimar in Thuringia and it is difficult not to feel the weight of the town's history and spiritual legacy. A good part of this fame is due to Goethe and Schiller, the godfathers of German Classicism, but there was no shortage of genius in the centuries before and after them. Other inhabitants of note include Luther, Cranach, Bach, Liszt, Böcklin, Liebermann, and the founder of the Bauhaus movement, Walter Gropius, with an exhibition of more than 300 objects.

The Juno Room in the Goethe House with a flair of Classicism

WARTBURG

Location: Eisenach, East Germany (Thuringia)
Best time to travel: throughout the year
www.wartburg-eisenach.de
www.eisenach.de

"Just you wait, mountain – I shall make a castle of you". The Thuringian, Count Ludwig, is supposed to have said this in 1067 when he first saw the Wartberg mountain, punning on the German words *Burg* and *Berg*. The Wartburg was first documented in 1080 and

the town of Eisenach grew up in its shadow, soon becoming the center of the Dukedom of Thuringia. Count Hermann I (d. 1217) extended the fortress into a magnificent rural seat. Martin Luther lived in the castle between 1521 and 1522, adopting the name of Squire Jörg under the protection of Prince Elector Frederick the Wise, and it was here he began his famed translation of the Greek New Testament. His room has not changed at all, although the ink stain which is said to have come about when he threw his inkwell at

the Devil is no longer to be seen. By the time the German student associations gathered here for the Wartburg Festival in 1817, the castle was largely dilapidated and its extensive grounds and many buildings were not destined to be restored until the second half of the 19th century. Its two courtyards feature beautiful 15th- and 16th-century half-timbered houses and imposing neo-Romanesque and neo-Gothic structures; the oldest part of the castle is a late-Romanesque palace. The minstrels' gallery, knights' hall, fire-

places, and the chapel dedicated to St Elizabeth (canonized 1235) will transport visitors back into the High Middle Ages.

Towering over Eisenach in Thuringia, the Wartburg is not only a classic castle in its location and architecture, it has become an iconic image of German history, and was designated a national monument in 1817 when the German student fraternities made the first declaration of German unity there.

Germany

COLOGNE

Location: West Germany
(North Rhine-Westphalia)
Best time to travel:
throughout the year
www.koeln.de

Three words sum up Germany's westernmost metropolis: churches, art and kölsch (the local beer). A Roman settlement was the original nucleus of this cosmopolitan city on the Rhine. During the reign of Charlemagne, Cologne became an archbishopric, and by the early Middle Ages it had become one of Germany's leading cities. Romanesque and Gothic churches still bear witness to the former spiritual and intellectual importance of Cologne, most important of all, of course, the famous Kölner Dom (Cologne Cathedral). Art also seems more present here than anywhere else in Germany. Its important galleries and museums are numerous and include the Museum Ludwig and the Wallraf Richartz Museum. The local *joie de vivre* is legendary all year round, not just during the Rose Monday (Carnival) celebrations. People from Cologne often sum up their philosophy of life with two sentences: "Et kütt, wie et kütt." and "Et hätt noch immer jot jejange" ("Things happen the way they do" and "In the end things have always turned out all right"). People take things the way they come in Cologne because they are convinced that in the end all will turn out just fine. If you reflect on 2,000 years of history, you can understand such equanimity. After all, the locals have outlasted the ancient Romans as well as the occupation by the French in the 19th century.

Cologne's main artery is the Rhine with the cathedral. This panorama has a special charm at night, shown here the view from the Deutz Bridge past Great St Martin's to the cathedral. The cathedral contains masterpieces of great value.

BRÜHL

Location: West Germany
(North Rhine-Westphalia)
Best time to travel:
throughout the year
www.bruehl.de
www.schlossbruehl.de

The main sights in the town of Brühl, situated around 15 km (9 mi) south of Cologne, are the palaces of Augustusburg and Falkenlust. Construction on Augustusburg was begun in 1725, as a residence for Clemens August von Wittelsbach, Elector and Archbishop of Cologne. A unified work of art created by Johann Conrad Schlaun, François de Cuvilliés and Dominique Girard, the palace documents in detail the transition in style from baroque to roco-co. The furnishings in the magnificent staterooms are of the most remarkable quality, and the imposing staircase was the work of Balthasar Neumann. All of the rooms in the palace face toward the gardens, which gives it the feel of a summer residence. Falkenlust was begun in 1729 according to plans by Cuvilliés and Leveilly, and was used for falconry, one of the elector's hobbies. The rooms are fairly private in character, but are nevertheless magnificently appointed.

The harmonious juxtaposition of the baroque sunken garden and the Augustusburg palace brings out the grace and beauty of both.

AACHEN

Location: West Germany
(North Rhine-Westphalia)
Best time to travel:
throughout the year
www.aachen.de
www.aachendom.de

Aachen, the former residence of
Charlemagne, was one of the most
important cities in Europe during the
Middle Ages. The Romans had already settled here for the prized local
hot springs, and those healing waters are probably the reason why,
over 1,200 years ago, in the winter
of 794, Charlemagne decided to ex-
pand the existing royal mansion in
Aachen. After his return from Rome
in 800, Charlemagne was crowned
emperor here before dying in 814.
Otto I was crowned king here in 936
and from then on Aachen was to remain the coronation site of German
kings for more than 600 years until
the coronation of Charles V in 1531.
Numerous historical buildings still
bear witness to the great days of emperors and kings, for example the
town hall and the octagonal Palatine
Chapel, the core of Aachen Cathedral.

**The greatest architectural feat in
Aachen is the imperial cathedral,
whose inception is closely linked
with Charlemagne. The image
shows the imperial throne.**

Germany

MOSELLE VALLEY, TRIER

Location: West Germany
Best time to travel: April–October
(September/October: grape harvest)
www.mosel.com
www.trier.de

The Mosel is one of Germany's most capricious rivers, despite the fact that it rises in France, where it is called the Moselle. With its source in the heart of the Vosges Mountains, the Mosel snakes past Metz before reaching Luxembourg and finally enters German territory for the last 243 km (151 mi) of its 544-km (338-mi) total length. More than 2,000 years ago, the river was part of the Roman realm and called the Mosella. Indeed, the Mosel probably has a longer history than any other "German" river. After all, Germany's oldest town, Trier, was founded on its banks. The Mosel is a meandering river that flows past famously steep vineyards and numerous castles such as Cochem, originally built in 1100, destroyed by French soldiers in 1688, and rebuilt in its present neo-Gothic style in the 19th century. It sits perched above the town of the same name. Records document that Trier was founded in the year 16 BC by the Romans during the reign of Emperor Augustus, and subsequently named "Augusta Treverorum", the town of the Treveri. Trier was initially the capital of the Roman province of Belgica before becoming the capital of the divided Western Roman Empire.

The almost fairytale mountain medieval castle Burg Eltz (opposite) in one of the valleys adjoining the Moselle. This page: Cochem Castle overlooks the town of the same name on the Moselle (top). A bend in the Moselle at Bremm (middle). The Porta Nigra in Trier, the best-preserved Roman city gate north of the Alps (bottom).

Germany

FRANKFURT

Location: Western Germany (Hessen)
Best time to travel:
throughout the year
www.frankfurt.de
www.frankfurt-tourismus.de

Known as "Mainhattan" for its sky-line, Frankfurt am Main looks more the part of a stylish international metropolis than any other city in Germany. One skyscraper after an-other heaves into view as you ap-proach, and the building boom of the last 20 years has completely al-tered the appearance of a city with a thousand years of history. The skyline is dominated by the Main tower, the Messe tower, and DZ Bank's Kronenhochhaus, not to mention the offices of the Deutsche, Dresdener, and Commerz banks. Historic Frankfurt (Charlemagne first mentions Franconofurd in 794) has held its own in the shadow of the skyscrapers, however, and at the heart of old city is the 13th cen-tury cathedral, where German kings and emperors were elected and crowned, and the Römer, a row of townhouses which includes the Old Town Hall. The first German national assembly met in nearby St Paul's Church in 1848–9. St Leonhard's church and the Alte Nicolaikirche (Old Church of St Nicholas) are ex-cellent examples of ecclesiastical architecture, as is the Lieb-frauenkirche (Church of Our Lady) with its adjoining Capuchin monastery. Goethe's painstakingly reconstructed birth house is a must for fans of the famous writer. The archeological garden between the cathedral, the Schirn exhibition hall, and the Town Planning Office is a display of the ruins of a Roman mil-itary camp with its hot spas, and the Carolingian imperial palace.

The cathedral of St Bartholomew stands out proudly against the modern Frankfurt skyline.

Germany

LIMBURG

Location: Western Germany (Hessen)
Best time to travel:
throughout the year
www.limburg.de

Lying close to the border with the Rhineland-Palatinate, the ancient bishop's seat of Limburg is one of the finest cultural gems in the Lahn valley. Consecrated in 1235, the cathedral is a harmonious mixture of the late Roman and early Gothic with a lavishly decorated interior. The castle built by the Isenburger dynasty on the same limestone cliffs above the Lahn now shares several buildings with the cathedral. There is a feast of half-timbered houses in the Old Town at the foot of the hill, especially in the Corn Market.

The towers of the Cathedral of St George have towered over Limburg since the early 13th century.

SPEYER

Location: Western Germany (Rhineland-Palatinate)
Best time to travel:
throughout the year
www.speyer.de

This ancient imperial and episcopal seat on the Rhine is a masterpiece of Romanesque architecture. Built between 1030 and 1061, St Mary's cathedral was the personal chapel and burial place of the Salic dynasty of emperors, and at the time, the largest church in Christendom. Located at the confluence of the Speyerbach river and the Rhine, the town's highlights include an 11th-century Jewish *mikveh*, the late baroque Church of the Holy Trinity, and the 55-m (180-ft) high Altpörtel town gate.

Four emperors lie buried in the imperial vault in the crypt of Speyer's cathedral.

WORMS

Location: Western Germany (Rhineland-Palatinate)
Best time to travel: throughout the year
www.worms.de

Worms, an imperial bishop's seat on the Rhine, is inextricably linked to the tale of the Nibelungs, a creation of German High medieval culture. The Nibelung Museum contains a wealth of information separating the myths from the historical truth. The site of the old imperial palace is now occupied by the 19th-century Heylshof with its excellent art galleries. The old Jewish Quarter lay to the north of the Old Town and here you will find the synagogue, reconstructed after its demolition in 1938, and the Jewish Museum.

Worms Cathedral was built in the 11th and 12 centuries.

MAINZ

Location: Western Germany (Rhineland-Palatinate)
Best time to travel: throughout the year
www.mainz.de

The capital of the federal state of Rhineland-Palatinate owes its origins to the Roman fort of Moguntiacum which was built opposite the confluence of the Main and the Rhine at about the time of the birth of Christ. St Boniface made the town his see in 742 and the first university in Mainz was founded in 1477. The city's most famous son is Johannes Gutenberg, who invented printing here in 1450.

The Cathedral of St Martin and St Stephen, located in Mainz city center is one of the greatest achievements of Romanesque architecture.

Germany

BLACK FOREST

Location: South-western Germany
(Baden-Württemberg)
Best time to travel:
April–September
www.schwarzwald.de

The locals call their homeland "God's chemist" but you could just as easily call the northern and central Black Forest an enchanted wood from a fairy-tale, or the land of milk and honey – all these names would fit: the mountain air and the many thermal springs are good for your health, the charming valleys and villages seem to be full of characters out of Hans Christian Andersen, and the food? You won't eat better food anywhere else in Germany. Wood-carving is a traditional cottage industry in the region and carved ornaments now are produced in substantial numbers as souvenirs for tourists. The southern Black Forest, the High Black Forest, begins where the forest is especially black and some of the peaks rise to more than 1,000 m (3,300 ft). Here you will find aromatic pine forests, highland valleys, remote lakes, wild streams, farmhouses – and Black Forest gateau. The region is rich in natural spectacles of one size or another, such as the Wutach Gorge, the "Grand Canyon of the Black Forest", or the peaceful summits of the Hoher Belchen (1,414 m/4,639 ft) or the Feldberg (1,493 m/4,898 ft), where mountain goats still graze. Further south, at the lower edge of the Hotzenwald, the Rhine forms the border with Switzerland.

With its romantic waterfalls, the valley of the Lotenbachklamm (opposite) in the Wutach Gorge is heaven for hikers. This page from top: the view south from the Hoher Belchen, with the Western Alps on the horizon, a Black Forest chalet in the Gutach valley, and the Hexenlochmühle ("Witches' Mill") at St Märgen.

Germany

HEIDELBERG

Location: South-western Germany (Baden-Württemberg)
Best time to travel: throughout the year
www.heidelberg.de

Although Heidelberg is now part of Baden-Württemberg, the city is actually the historic capital of the Rhineland-Palatinate, and this misappropriation still causes many a Rhinelander to shed a tear. The Old Town, the castle, and the Neckar combine to make the city Germany's capital of Romanticism, and the counts palatine chose this picturesque location for their family seat. Ruprecht I founded the university in 1386 and enlarged the castle, and this was later to become the seat of the prince electors of the Palatine.

A famous ruin: the city's iconic Heidelberg Castle.

MAULBRONN

Location: South-western Germany (Baden-Württemberg)
Best time to travel: April–September
www.maulbronn.de
www.kloster-maulbronn.de

Anyone can enter "Paradise" in Maulbronn, as this is the name given to the 800-year-old early Gothic narthex of the monastery church. Once run by the Cistercians, the church itself is even older; construction of the abbey, which is thought to be the best-preserved monastery complex north of the Alps, began in 1147. The cunning irrigation system thought up by the monks of Maulbronn is still a feature of the region to this day.

Even 450 years after the end of monastic occupation here it is easy to imagine Cistercian life.

FREIBURG

Location: South-western Germany
(Baden-Württemberg)
Best time to travel:
throughout the year
www.freiburg.de

Freiburg Minster, can be seen from as
far away as the Vosges Hills, and its
defined, elegant, but witty architectural style seems to have had an effect on the outlook of the citizens:
people enjoy life here, especially art
and wine. The city was founded by the
Zähring dukes in 1120 but has spent
most of its history (1368–1806) in the
possession of the Austrian house of
Hapsburg; its motto has always been
"take it easy". Freiburg's climate lend
the town a Mediterranean charm.

**The 116-m (381-ft) Gothic spire of
Freiburg Minster stands out from
this university town like an exclama-
tion mark.**

BADEN-BADEN

Location: South-western Germany
(Baden-Württemberg)
Best time to travel:
throughout the year
www.baden-baden.de

With its clattering roulette tables, liv-
eried pages opening the doors of lim-
ousines, and the soft burbling of water in marble fountains, Baden-Baden
is like a German Monte Carlo. The
town had gained renown even in Roman times, and the ruins of the ancient bath houses can still be seen today. The first casino opened here in
1810 and nearby Iffezheim has been
parting racing enthusiasts from their
money since 1858. The Festival Theater in Baden-Baden is one of Europe's most prestigious venues.

**A statue of Bacchus in a verdant
and blooming rotunda in the
spa park.**

Germany

LAKE CONSTANCE

Location: South-western Germany (Baden-Württemberg)
Best time to travel: throughout the year
www.bodensee.eu
www.meersburg.de
www.konstanz.de
www.reichenau.de
www.birnau.de

Lake Constance consists of three bodies of water: the *Obersee* ("upper lake"), the *Untersee* ("lower lake"), and a connecting stretch of the Rhine, called the *Seerhein*. The "Swabian Sea", with its heady combination of water, picturesque towns, Alpine scenery, balmy air, wide blue skies, and good weather always gets visitors excited, and there is the unmistakable feeling that the South starts here due to the mild climate . The lake has been popular for 4,000 years, starting with the first settlers who built houses on stilts. The pilgrimage church at Birnau sits a little higher up the surrounding slopes and the view from here is exquisite; on a clear day, you can see from the terrace in front of the Provost's Building to the island of Mainau, the hills on the other bank, and a wide Alpine panorama.

For statisticians, the lake is 64 km (40 mi) long, 14 km (9 mi) wide and 250 m (820 ft) deep, but it is usually romantics who take an interest in the "Swabian Sea", falling into raptures at the sight of St George's Church on the Wasserburg Peninsula (opposite).

This page: the broad façade of Meersburg Castle (top). The ancient city of Konstanz, with its medieval houses (middle) and High Council is the secret capital of the area around Lake Constance. Lindau owes its early flourishing in the Middle Ages to the "Lindau Messenger", a major courier and coach connection to Northern Italy.

Germany

BAMBERG

Location: South Germany (Bavaria)
Best time to travel:
throughout the year
www.bamberg.info

This town of emperors and bishops is more than 1,000 years old and cozily situated on seven hills in the valley of the river Regnitz. Unlike Nuremberg or Würzburg, the former "caput orbis" (head of the world) was only lightly damaged in World War II. There are many interesting sights to see, including the "little Venice" fishermen's quarter, and the late-Gothic cathedral with the Bamberg Horseman. The majestic Emperor's Tomb inside the cathedral was created by Tilman Riemenschneide, and contains the only papal grave in Germany, that of Clement II.

Bamberg's Town Hall was built in the middle of the Regnitz.

WÜRZBURG

Location: South Germany (Bavaria)
Best time to travel:
throughout the year
www.wuerzburg.de

In a beautiful location at the foot of Fortress Marienberg and the picturesque municipal vineyards, Würzburg extends around the market square with its late-Gothic St Mary's Chapel and the House of the Falcon with its rich rococo stucco work. Many of its treasures are hidden, for example, the small Lusam Garden behind the baroque Neumünster. The Residence (1720) is a masterpiece of the baroque built by Lukas von Hildebrandt and Johann Balthasar Neumann.

The magnificent painted ceilings above the staircase in the Residence at Würzburg are the work of Giambattista Tiepolo.

BAYREUTH

Location: South-east Germany (Bavaria, Franconia)
Best time to travel: throughout the year (July/August: Festival)
www.bayreuth.de
www.bayreuther-festspiele.de

The famous Wilhelmine von Bayreuth (1709–1758) was an enlightened margravine, an architect, philosopher, a composer and writer, as well as the favorite sister of Frederick the Great. From her privileged position she was able to influence the look of her namesake town, Bayreuth, with her style of choice, rococo. From 1736, she enlarged the Hermitage, the Old and the New Palaces and splendid palace gardens, and decided to build the beautiful baroque Opera House.

The Margraves' Opera House (1748) whose magnificence attracted Richard Wagner to Bayreuth.

ROTHENBURG OB DER TAUBER

Location: South-east Germany (Bavaria)
Best time to travel: throughout the year
www.rothenburg.de

This small town is the absolute epitome of German Romanticism, and inspired the painter Ludwig Richter to call it a "fairytale of a town". Rothenburg's unique appearance, with its red tile roofs, towers and turrets, the town hall (left), large market square with fountain, town gates, churches, half-timbered houses, and a 2-km (1.5 mi) town wall simply transports you back to another time.

Left: the fork in the road at the Untere Schmiedgasse, with the Siebers Tower in the background, which was once part of the town's fortifications.

Germany

REGENSBURG

Location: South Germany (Bavaria)
Best time to travel:
throughout the year
www.regensburg.de

Regensburg grew up in the Middle Ages from the ruins of Castra Regina, a Roman fort. Duke Arnulf of Bavaria built a wall around the western suburbs and the large grounds of the abbey of St Emmeram between 917 and 920. These were the first town fortifications to be built north of the Alps after the departure of the Romans, and although initially the artisans' quarter lay outside the walls, even this had been enclosed by the end of the 13th century. The Stone Bridge (1135–1146) was for many years the only fortified crossing over the Danube between Ulm and Vienna, ensuring Regensburg's status as a major commercial center. The number and quality of the many

NUREMBERG

Location: South Germany
(Bavaria, Franconia)
Best time to travel: throughout
the year (December: Christmas
Market)
www.nuernberg.de

The people of Nuremberg love life – their beautiful city, their beer, and their famed, bite-size sausages, either grilled with fresh sauerkraut or boiled as *saure Zipfel*. Nuremberg Lebkuchen (ginger cake) and mulled wine are also popular at the famous Christmas Market, and the people of Albrecht Dürer's home town certainly know how to indulge themselves. It may well be because this former Free Imperial City was once one of the most important cities for art and commerce in Europe. As you arrive at the main station, the first view of the city is of the medieval fortifications, the Frauentor gate, and the

Romanesque and Gothic town houses and the dynastic towers built within the complexes of merchants' houses are unmatched by any city north of the Alps. Besides all these stone buildings, Johannes Kepler's house, built around 1250, is recognised as the oldest surviving intact wooden house in Germany. The city became an important center of political power during the heyday of the Holy Roman Empire in the Middle Ages, and its considerable Romanesque and Gothic church and monastery buildings are exceptional contemporary artistic achievements. The Free Imperial City officially converted to Protestantism in 1542 and was a garrison town in the fight against Bavaria. The city has been largely spared great catastrophes.

The cathedral and the Stone Bridge (left and right) have become icons of Regensburg on the Danube river.

emperor's mighty castle (Kaiserburg). Imposing churches such as St Lawrence's, with its carvings of the *Angelic Greeting* by Veit Stoss, or the Church of St Sebald with the saint's tomb, created by Peter Vischer, not to mention the impressive town houses, are all signs of Nuremberg's great history. The bards' meeting which takes place for three days every summer is unique in Germany and has become known far and wide. The "bards" perform for free in the city's streets and squares; lutes and courtly ballads have been abandoned, however, and electric guitars and amplifiers have long been the order of the day.

Medieval Nuremberg and the beautiful backdrop of the city's half-timbered houses, such as these by the Tiergärtnertor gate beneath the imperial castle are especially picturesque in the evening light.

Germany

NEUSCHWAN-STEIN

Location: near Füssen,
South Germany (Bavaria)
Best time to travel:
throughout the year
www.neuschwanstein.de

In 1860, Ludwig II commissioned Neuschwanstein Castle. It was built in a neo-Romanesque style according to plans by theater set designer Christian Jank, to replace the ancient ruins of Vorder-Hohenschwangau. Its model was the Wartburg in Thuringia – the setting for the famous Wagner opera "Tannhäuser". Ultimately, Ludwig would only spend a few days at the castle before being arrested and deposed, partly because of the high construction costs of the castle and the resulting debts of the state.

Neuschwanstein is now one of the most visited castles in the world.

HERREN-CHIEMSEE

Location: island in Lake Chiemsee,
South Germany (Bavaria)
Best time to travel:
April–October
www.herren-chiemsee.de
www.chiemsee.de

The Federal Republic of Germany's legal code was finalized in the "Old Castle" on the lake at Herrenchiemsee in 1948. The much more famous "New Castle" was built by a fairy-tale king: Ludwig II laid the foundation stone of the building in 1878, and the façade overlooking the garden is almost identical with its model in Versailles. The project was to remain unfinished for financial reasons.

Only 20 of the planned 70 rooms could be completed, including the impressive Hall of Mirrors (right).

Germany

LINDERHOF

Location: near Oberammergau, South Germany (Bavaria)
Best time to travel: April–October
www.schlosslinderhof.de

Linderhof was an agricultural estate near Ettal that King Ludwig II knew from hunting trips with his father Maximilian II. He wished to build a copy of the palace and gardens at Versailles here, but his plans proved far too ambitious for the narrow valley where Linderhof is situated. As a result, in 1869, construction began on his father's former hunting lodge, which at the time stood on what is now the palace forecourt.

Linderhof Palace (left, the "Grotto of Venus") is the smallest of the three palaces built by King Ludwig II of Bavaria and the only one of which he lived to see completion.

WIESKIRCHE

Location: Steingaden, South Germany (Bavaria)
Best time to travel: throughout the year
www.wieskirche.de

In 1730, monks from nearby Steingaden Abbey produced an image of Christ for the Good Friday procession near Wies. Then, on June 14, 1738, the statue suddenly began to shed tears, a miracle that prompted a pilgrimage rush to see the sculpture. A cult soon developed around the Scourged Savior of Wies, resulting in the commissioning of perhaps the most exuberant rococo church in Germany. The architects were the brothers Dominikus and Johann Baptist Zimmermann.

Beautiful stucco work and ceiling frescos adorn the interior of the Wieskirche (1745–54).

Germany

MUNICH

Location: South Germany (Bavaria)
Best time to travel: throughout the year (late September: Oktoberfest)
www.muenchen.de
www.oktoberfest.de

The Residenz is the historical seat of power in Munich and it is from here that Bavaria's counts, electors and kings ruled. It was built in the 16th century to replace the Neuveste Castle, which had in turn replaced the Old Court as the ducal seat. Between 1568 to 1619, a Renaissance complex was built that was later expanded to include baroque, rococo and neoclassical styles. The Residenz now comprises ten courtyards and 130 rooms. The Court Church of All Saints as well as the former Residenz Theater (now the Cuvilliés Theater), a splendid, newly restored rococo building, are also part of the complex. The Residenz still plays an important role in Munich. It houses museums (including the Porcelain, Silver and Treasure Chambers in the Königsbau, the Cabinet of Miniatures, State Collection of Coins, and Collection of Egyptian Art) and is a prestigious venue for festive occasions and receptions. Munich's urban center is framed by the neo-Gothic New Town Hall from 1909 with its famous *Glockenspiel*, as well as the Old Town Hall from 1480. When Ludwig the Bavarian granted the market charter to Munich in 1315, he stipulated that the Marktplatz remain "free of buildings for all eternity". In 1638, Elector Maximilian I had the Marian Column erected there in gratitude for the city being spared during Swedish occupation in the Thirty Years' War. Since 1854, the center of Munich has been known as Marienplatz.

The Field Marshals' Hall inspired by the Loggia dei Lanzi of Florence, and the Theatiner Church.

Germany

ZUGSPITZE

Location: South Germany (Bavaria)
Best time to travel: April–September
www.zugspitze.de
www.tegernsee.com
www.koenigssee.com

The Alps are the largest mountain chain in Europe but the parts belonging to Germany are relatively small. Less can be more, however, and good things come in small packages. Ludwig Thoma, who lies buried at Rottach-Egern near the Tegernsee lake, once wrote "just look – everything is beautiful", and no doubt he was thinking of the huge masses of rock in the Wetterstein area which culminate in the 2,962-m (9,718-ft) Zugspitze, the "roof" of the Federal Republic, or perhaps the titanic Watzmann (2,713 m/8,901 ft) which towers over the lake at Königssee, the "most beautiful fjord in the Alps". The summit of the Zugspitze is more than 2 km (1.5 mi) higher than the largest town in the Werdenfels area, where the 1936 Winter Olympics were held. A technological marvel had entered service six years previously – Bavaria's Zugspitze railway. Some 19 km (12 mi) long, it ran from Garmisch itself to the Zugspitzplatt summit, 11.5 km (7 mi) is a funicular railway and the last 4.8 km (3 miles) runs inside the mountain. The summit of the Zugspitze now resembles a small town and on some days there are as many as 5,000 "residents". The building is a somewhat bizarre-looking construction of steel and glass. The "roof of the republic" has (almost) everything, and plenty of things that you probably didn't even know you needed. A trip to the Loisach Valley just below the Zugspitz Mountain can be inspiring.

Almost anything is possible on the Zugspitze – you can even get married against an impressive Alpine panorama.

MITTENWALD

Location: South Germany (Bavaria)
Best time to travel: throughout the year (Ski season: November–March)
www.mittenwald.de

Mittenwald began life as a settlement in a clearing in the Scharnitzwald forest and was first mentioned in a document in 1096. Situated amongst the jagged peaks of the Karwendel mountains near the Austro-German border, this climatic health resort is famed for its painted house façades and for violin-making. There is a monument to Matthias Klotz, the first luthier in Mittenwald, and instrument-making has remained one of the town's major sources of income.

The rock of the church: the parish Church of St Peter and St Paul is overlooked by the Karwendel.

BERCHTESGADEN NATIONAL PARK

Location: South Germany (Bavaria)
Best time to travel: throughout the year
www.nationalpark-berchtesgaden.bayern.de

Conservationists managed to get the area around the King's Lake recognised as an area of exceptional natural beauty in 1910, and 12 years later it became a nature reserve of some 210 sq km (81 sq mi). This little patch in the south of the area around Berchtesgaden was the first and is still the only national park in the German Alps. It was designated as a UNESCO Biosphere Reserve in 1990.

The area surrounding the lake at Königssee seems to be nothing less than a gift from a benevolent God.

SCHAFFHAUSEN

Location: Northern Switzerland
(Canton of Schaffhausen)
Best time to travel: April–October
www.schaffhauserland.ch

The Rhine Falls are Europe's largest
waterfall in terms of water volume
– although the drop in height is only 25 m (82 ft). Without the falls,

Schaffhausen would not have developed into a town as it did early
in the Middle Ages when the goods
transported along the Rhine were
offloaded onto wagons here for a
few miles. This was a practice from
which the waggoners, merchants,
aldermen, and toll keepers all
profited. The large cathedral is testi-

mony to the town's former wealth
and, dating from the 11th/12th centuries, it is a fine example of a very
pure form of the Romanesque style.
The former Benedictine All Saints
Monastery, which now houses the
comprehensive All Saints Cultural
History Museum, was added later to
the cathedral. The town's landmark

is the Munot fortress dating from
the 16th century.

**Dominated by the castle at Laufen
on the south bank of the river, the
Rhine Falls at Neuhausen are
spectacular at any time of the
year, but especially in early
summer, when the river is in spate.**

STEIN AM RHEIN

Location: Northern Switzerland (Canton of Schaffhausen)
Best time to travel: April–October
www.steinamrhein.ch

Stein am Rhein is situated where the Rhine exits the lower section of Lake Constance. Its main gem is the town hall from 1539, which boasts a variety of painted motifs depicting the history of the region. Stein's appeal comes from its meticulously maintained medieval houses. Opposite the town hall, for instance, is the late Gothic Weisser Adler (White Eagle) with its painted Renaissance façade, and the old Benedictine monastery of St George, whose buildings are now used as a museum with interesting exhibits.

Stein am Rhein rivals Murten for the title of best-preserved medieval town in Switzerland.

ST GALLEN

Location: North-eastern Switzerland (Canton of St Gallen)
Best time to travel: throughout the year
www.st.gallen-bodensee.ch

St Gallen has been an important center in the Lake Constance region since the early Middle Ages. The collegiate church and monastery were rebuilt in the mid-18th century in late baroque style – only in the crypt can remains of the 10th-century building still be seen. The monastery was founded by Abbot Otmar in the 8th century after the Irish missionary and monk Gallus had settled here as a hermit in 612. The library's inventory has been expanded continuously since the early Middle Ages.

A fitting setting for such rare and valuable works: the main hall of the monastery library.

Switzerland

ZÜRICH

Location: North Switzerland
(Canton of Zurich)
Best time to travel:
throughout the year
www.stadt-zuerich.ch
www.zuerich.com

It is a cliché, and an incorrect one at that, to assume that the country's economic metropolis on Lake Zurich, with its numerous banking headquarters, is just a boring, old-fashioned financial center. Declared a free city in 1218, the city had a monopoly on wool, silk, and leather production throughout the Middle Ages and soon became wealthy. This led to the creation of numerous architectural gems such as the mighty guild halls in the Old Town lining both banks of the Limmat. Zurich is certainly rich – it is the largest city in Switzerland (pop. 380,000) and it has both the largest gold market and

BERN

Location: Western Switzerland
(Canton of Bern)
Best time to travel:
throughout the year
www.bern.ch
www.bern-incoming.ch

Once the largest city-state north of the Alps, Bern's historic center clearly reflects the chronological order of its different periods of expansion. The stately guild and townhouses with arcades extending for a total of 6 km (4 mi) are characteristic of the city center. Construction of the late Gothic St Vincent Cathedral began in 1421 and was only completed in 1573; the magnificent main portal was designed by Erhard Küng. The late-Gothic Town Hall was erected between 1406 and 1417 and subsequently renovated in 1942. The Heiliggeistkirche (Church of the Holy Spirit), from 1729, is one of the coun-

the fourth-largest stock exchange in the world. Its wealth is obvious from the "shopping de luxe" of the Bahnhofstrasse, where it is easy to spend more on a watch than most people earn in a year. Other architectural features include the Fraumünster church in the Old Town west of the river Limmat , which has a set of five windows by Marc Chagall, and next door, the 13th-century parish church of St Peter, with Europe's largest clock face. The Grossmünster on the other side of the river, its neo-Gothic tower cupolas dominating the cityscape, entered the annals of church history as the domain of the reformer Huldrych Zwingli (1484–1531).

The twin towers of Zurich's Great Minster dominate the skyline of the "smallest metropolis on earth", which is divided by the Limmat river near the northern end of Lake Zurich.

try's most important examples of Protestant baroque architecture. Bern's landmark, however, is the Zytgloggeturm (Clock Tower) city gate. The ensemble of lovely historic residential buildings in the Gerechtigkeitsgasse stands out from the multitude of beautiful buildings in Bern, and some of them date back to the 16th century. Bern's Renaissance fountains with their lovely expressive figures are also worth seeing, three of them having been created by the Freiburg sculptor Hans Gieng.

The Old Town of Bern is a mixture of mighty city gates and arcades. Shown here are the views along the Kramgasse and the Marktgasse, with the Käfigturm und Zytgloggeturm towers in the distance (page left and right respectively). The old town boasts one of the longest covered shopping promenades in Europe.

THE BERNESE OBERLAND

Location: Western Switzerland (Canton of Bern)
Best time to travel: throughout the year (October–April: Ski season)
www.berneroberland.ch

The Bernese Oberland is the cradle of Swiss tourism. Its popularity was instigated by three famous figures: Rousseau, Haller and Goethe. They sparked an enthusiasm for nature that became a trend among high society types to escape to the mountains. The first official "Unspunnenspiele" (a festival uniting town and country) took place near Interlaken in 1805, a huge open-air event with yodelers, Fahnenschwingen (flag throwing), Steinstossen (stone throwing), and traditional costume. Visitors arrived via Lake Thun, some – like the Rothschilds for instance – with their own boats. This is still a nice way to view the spectacular scenery. The perfect way to explore the region is making a day trip by train, bus and gondola.

The legendary trio of the Eiger (3,970 m/13,025 ft), Mönch (4,099 m/13,448 ft), and Jungfrau (4,158 m/13,642 ft), shown here from left to right with the "little" 2,345-m (7,694-ft) Männlicher in the foreground, have made the Jungfrau region the premier Alpine climbing area in the Bernese Oberland.

LAKE LUCERNE

Location: Central Switzerland
Best time to travel: April–October
www.lakeluzern.ch

Surrounded by the four forested cantons of Uri, Schwyz, Obwalden, and Nidwalden, the lake is the patriotic heart of Switzerland – the Swiss Confederacy swore its oath here on the Rütli meadows in 1291, and William Tell is said to have laid low the evil reeve Gessler here too. The view from the summit of Rigi (1,797 m/ 5,896 ft), a peak which has been accessible by a funicular railway, since 1871, is perhaps the most famous in the Alps, looking far across to Titlis (3,239 m/10,627 ft), the highest mountain in the whole region. There is a cable car from the monastery village of Engelberg to the top of the glacier.

Lake Lucerne, heart of Switzerland, resembles a Norwegian fjord.

LUCERNE

Location: Central Switzerland (Canton of Lucerne)
Best time to travel: throughout the year
www.luzern.org

The oldest town in the Swiss interior (Lucerne received its town charter in 1178) is also its cultural and economic center. Watched over by Pilatus Mountain and the Rigi peak, the town is tucked into the northern end of Lake Lucerne. The Old Town of Lucerne with its picturesque squares and alleys simply compels you to take a stroll. The left bank features Franciscan and Jesuit churches, the Ritterscher Palace as well as the Culture and Congress Center, and the right has the Court Church and the Town Hall.

The Chapel Bridge crossing the Reuss is over 700 years old and is an iconic symbol of Lucerne.

ENGADIN

Location: South-eastern Switzerland (Canton of Graubünden)
Best time to travel: throughout the year (Ski season: October–April)
www.engadin.stmoritz.ch
www.stmoritz.ch
www.scuol.ch
www.bregaglia.ch

"The Upper Engadin is the nicest place on earth. I don't readily talk of happiness, but I almost think I am happy here" (Thomas Mann). The scenery of the upper Inn valley is almost without compare: there is nothing cramped or oppressive up by the treeline in the mountains, just a broad, open horizon. The lakes of the Upper Engadin, each as beautiful as the next, lie in the middle of the valley, and the pine forests, illuminated in the golden sunshine of the fall, and the white snow-capped peaks silhouetted against a deep azure sky make for the sort of Alpine picture that has been attracting nature enthusiasts here since the days of post coaches. The Lower Engadin between the Scharl and Trupchun valleys is the site of the Swiss National Park, opened on 1 August 1914, the oldest national park in Europe.

The Ice Age in the Upper Engadin: the Morteratsch Glacier (opposite) is the mightiest glacier in the Bernina Group. It is surrounded by the Piz Bernina (4,049 m/13,284 ft) and several other impressive peaks over 3,000 m (9,800 ft) high.

This page: Nietzsche spent several summers at Lake Silser (top) where he composed most of his philosophical work *Thus Spake Zarathustra*. The castle at Tarasp (middle), high on its slate cliff, has become an iconic image of the Lower Engadin. St Mortiz (bottom) cleverly markets itself as being on "top of the world".

THE ALETSCH GLACIER

Location: Bernese Alps, Southern Switzerland (Canton of Valais)
Best time to travel: throughout the year (Ski season: October–April)
www.pronatura.ch
www.jungfraualetsch.ch

The mighty flow of ice extending to the north-east between Konkordiaplatz (2,850 m/9,351 ft) near the Jungfraujoch and Riederalp (1,919 m/6,296 ft) reaches up to 1,800 m (1,968 yards) in width. What has

been evident for a long while, however, is also to be seen at the Aletsch Glacier: reduction of mass, a visible sign of climate change. While the glaciers lost about one-third of their surface area and almost half of their

total volume between the mid-19th-century and 1975, they have forfeited a further 25 per cent of their mass in the last 30 years. If the trend continues, then more than 75 per cent of the glaciers in the Alps will be gone by

2050. The ice does not only melt, it also migrates. The compacted ice moves down from the peaks and passes into the valleys, out of the so-called feeding areas and into the wear areas; a maximum of 1.5 m (5 ft) per day. A snowflake falling up on the Jungfraujoch onto the Aletsch Glacier will therefore become a drop of water again down below at the entrance to the Massa canyon after a journey probably lasting some 500 years.

The "Top of Europe", the upper end of Europe's highest rack and pinion railway on the Jungfraujoch (3,454 m/11,332 ft), has a superb view of the Great Aletsch Glacier, whose length of 24 km (15 mi) and area of some 118 sq km (46 sq mi) makes it Switzerland's largest. The whole area is part of the Jungfrau-Aletsch Protected Area, which was declared a UNESCO World Heritage site in 2001.

Switzerland

THE MATTERHORN

Location: Valais Alps, Southern Switzerland (Canton of Valais)
Best time to travel: throughout the year (Ski season: October–April)
www.zermatt.ch
www.ski-zermatt.com

What hasn't already been written about this mountain? Bombarded regularly with superlatives, the Matterhorn's incomparable shape is much vaunted, having been referred to as the "advertising mountain" due to its use in promoting just about everything. The Matterhorn adorns not only Swiss yoghurt containers and Belgian beer bottles, it has also found itself on wine labels and on Japanese confectionery, on a cigarette carton from Jamaica and even on a poster for a Rolling Stones European tour in 1976. Luis Trenker made an emotional film out of the tragic first ascent of the mountain (1865) by Edward Whymper, in which the four-man crew lost their lives, and in Zermatt the souvenir shops are full of Matterhorn kitsch. A mythical mountain and yet so much more than just pyramid-shaped rock, "Horu" (as it is called by locals) has brought great prosperity to the country village of Zermatt (1,616 m/5,302 ft). The hotel pioneer Alexander Seiler was the first to recognize the huge significance of this unique mountain backdrop for his tiny village. And indeed, the "mountain of mountains" has been captivating visitors since Whymper's time. They come from all over the world to marvel at this magnificent monument to Alpine altitudes, and some even come to climb it.

The Matterhorn with Riffel Lake in the foreground is a particularly beautiful sight. The normal route to the 4,478-m (14,692-ft) summit involves an ascent of the striking Hörnli Ridge.

Switzerland

AROUND LAKE GENEVA

Location: Western Switzerland (Canton of Geneva, Canton of Waadt)
Best time to travel: throughout the year (September/October: grape harvest on the Lavaux vineyard terraces)
www.geneve.ch
www.montreux-vevey.com
www.swissworld.org
www.lausanne.ch
www.chillon.ch

Geneva (Genève), with its Fontaine des Jet d'Eau shooting water 145 m (475 ft) into the air, lies along the banks of Lake Geneva between the Jura and the Savoy Alps. "Protestant Rome", where John Calvin propagated his rigorous notions of reform and Henri Dunant founded the Red Cross in 1864, is now a truly international city – a third of the population are foreign nationals, and more than 200 international organisations are based here, including the United Nations (UN) and the World Health Organisation (WHO). Apart from the diplomats, expensive watches, and cigars, Geneva has a number of attractions in stone: St Peter's Cathedral with its archeological sites and the adjacent Place du Bourg-de-Four, the well-stocked Museum of Art and History, the Palais des Nations, now the headquarters of the UN, and a monument to Jean-Jacques Rousseau, who was born here. Geneva is a traditional Alpine town as well, as featured in Konrad Witz's altar of St Peter of 1444, which is now in the Museum of Art. Peter's miraculous catch of fish is shown on Lake Geneva, with Mont Blanc in the background. Lausanne, the metropolis of the Waadtland area, lies on the northern shore, with its center surrounded by a series of hills covered in villas. The Cité, the Old Town, with its eye-catching Gothic cathedral, can also be reached by funicular rail-

way from the port area of Ouchy. Consecrated in 1275, the cathedral is considered the most beautiful of its time in Switzerland. The northern shore of Lake Geneva between Lausanne's eastern city limits and the Château de Chillon (immortalized by Byron in his ballad *The Prisoner of Chillon*) is a 30-km (19-mi) stretch of perhaps the finest scenery in Switzerland. Wine has been cultivated on the terraces of Lavaux for at least a millennium, and the locals maintain that three heat sources warm the grapes: the warmth of the sun, the reflection of the sunbeams from the surface of the lake, and the stored heat in the dry stone walls, which release their energy at night. The Gutedel grape grown on the shores of Lake Geneva is known locally as *Chasselas* or *Fendant*, and the modern terraces were first laid out by Benedictine and Cistercian monks in the 11th and 12th centuries. Mont Blanc can be seen from Geneva and is only an hour's drive from the city centre.

Famed for its location on a rock overlooking Lake Geneva, the Château de Chillon (opposite) is one of the most popular historic buildings in Switzerland.

Geneva (top), which lies on Lake Geneva at the mouth of the Rhône, is the second-largest city in Switzerland after Zurich.

The Château de Chillon (middle), the epitome of a romantic lakeside castle, lies about 5 km (3 mi) south-east of Montreux, a cosmopolitan resort on the north-east shore famed for its Jazz Festival and immortalized in Deep Purple's *Smoke on the Water*.

Lausanne (below), similarly located on the northern shores of Lake Geneva, is the seat of the Federal Court and the International Olympic Committee.

Switzerland

TICINO

Location: Southern Switzerland (Canton of Ticino)
Best time to travel: throughout the year
www.bellinzona.ch
www.ascona-locarno.com
www.lagomaggiore.net
www.lugano.ch

Ticino is a popular holiday region, and some may ask themselves whether this is in fact the southern part of Switzerland or the northern part of Italy. At any rate, the Alpine world here already exudes an air of Mediterranean promise. Hermann Hesse described Ticino, his adopted home, as "wonderfully rich and beautiful", and it is surely the diversity of the region that still fascinates visitors even today. The heart of Ticino beats on the Swiss side of Lake Maggiore. One of the most beautiful towns on the north shore of the lake is Locarno, not far from where the Maggia River flows into the lake from its high mountain source. Locarno has been famous since 1946 for its annual film festival. With approximately 2,300 hours of sunshine a year, the people of Locarno enjoy the mildest climate in Switzerland. The historic center of the town, first documented around the year 789, was originally directly on the lake, but over the course of the centuries, the Maggia has deposited immense amounts of sediment between Locarno and Ascona that today occupies about half the former width of the lake. In around 1900, Ascona was still a peaceful, sleepy fishing village. But then two foreigners settled here, disgruntled with their hectic lives in the city – Belgian Henri Oedenkoven, son of an industrialist, and his partner, German pianist Ida Hofmann. They called Ascona's local mountain the "Monte Verità", or "the mountain of truth", and founded a "vegetabilist cooperative" to help in their individual quests for happiness.

Light, air, and love played an important role in their mission along with nudism, theosophy, emancipation, and loads of raw foods. The days of the cooperative are long gone, but Locarno's much smaller western neighbor clearly still enjoys something of a reputation as a mecca for the avant-garde – and for art. It is also still a very good place to pursue happiness: the mountains, wonderful light and fresh air at least are guaranteed. Etruscans and Gauls had already settled on Lake Lugano long before the Romans came. The lake is around 35 km (22 mi) long, up to 3 km (2 mi) wide, and up to 288 m (945 ft) deep.

A panoramic view of the lake from one of Lugano's two mountains – Monte Bré at 925 m (3,035 ft) or Monte San Salvatore at 912 m (2,992 ft), which rises like a sugarloaf out of the water – is spectacular. The largest part of the lake, which is 217 m (712 ft) above sea level, belongs to the Swiss canton of Ticino while the smaller part belongs to the Italian provinces of Como and Varese.

The Castello Grande (top), the largest of the three castles at Bellinzona, was built on the hill within the city in the 13th century and extended by the Milanese Duke of Sforza between 1486 and 1489, to keep the Confederacy in check.

Bottom: the pilgrimage church of Madonna del Sasso (left) on the Belvedere hills has become a symbol of Locarno; Lugano (middle) alternated with Locarno and Bellinzona as the capital of Ticino for six years at a time between 1803 and 1878. It is now considered the capitale morale, the "true" capital of Ticino, and the region around Lake Lugano with its rolling hills and cypress trees is known as "the Tuscany of Switzerland".

Ascona (right), Locarno's neighbor to the west, was still a sleepy fishing village as recently as 1900.

Austria

VIENNA

Location: Eastern Austria
Best time to travel:
throughout the year
www.wien.info
www.wien.gv.at

ST CHARLES' CHURCH
St Charles' Church is the symbolic building of those euphoric centuries after the second Turkish Siege in 1683, when Vienna was transformed into the elegant metropolis that it is today. It was commissioned in 1713 by the emperor of the same name, Charles VI, at the end of a plague epidemic. Its creators, Fischer von Erlach Sr and Jr, combined the classic forms of Greek, Roman and Byzantine architecture to construct the church. A temple portico rises up under the patina-green dome, while triumphal pillars decorated with spiral reliefs and a beautiful bell tower soar up on both sides. A magnificent dome fresco by J. M. Rottmayr adorns the oval interior.

ST STEPHEN'S CATHEDRAL
St Stephen's Cathedral, Vienna's most important religious building and the city's emblem, is visible from afar and affectionately known by locals as "Steffl". It is a masterpiece of stonemasonry made from 20,000 cu m (706,293 cu ft) of sandstone. It dates back a good 750 years. Its west front still originates from the previous Romanesque building; the rest is High Gothic. The

southern spire, the third-highest in Europe, measures 137 m (449 ft) and soars gloriously towards the heavens. From its viewing deck, which is reached by climbing 343 steps, you get a panoramic view of the city.

IMPERIAL CRYPT
From the early 17th century, the Habsburg rulers and their next of kin were buried in a total of 138 metal caskets in the deep vaults here, traditionally guarded by Capuchin friars, at the foot of the rather unimposing Ordenskirche. Maria Theresa and her husband Francis Stephen of Lorraine were laid to rest here – in a double sarcophagus that was lavishly adorned with life-size figures in rococo style.

Next to them lies the reformist Emperor Joseph II in a simple copper casket much more in keeping with his humble character. Emperor Franz Joseph I also has his final resting place here, as do his wife Elisabeth of Bavaria (known more commonly as "Sissi"), his son Rudolf, his brother Maximilian, who was murdered in Mexico, and, from 1989, Austria's last empress: Zita.

St Stephen's Cathedral (top left) stands proudly in the heart of the city. The Hofburg (top right) is a remnant of the magnificence brought to the city by the emperors of the Hapsburg dynasty. The *Gloriette* in the grounds of Schönbrunn Palace gives a good idea of the size of the "Austrian Versailles".

Austria

ÖTZTAL ALPS, STUBAI ALPS

Location: Western Austria
Best time to travel: throughout the year (Ski season: October–April)
www.oetztal.com
www.stubai.at

The Ötztal valley stretches south for about 65 km (40 mi) from the Inn river at Imst to the Italian border. There are many popular resorts to visit along the gently rising valley floor before the road eventually ascends to the 2,474-m (8,117-ft) Timmelsjoch. The Alpine heart of the province of Tyrol, however, lies between the Brenner Pass and the Reschen Pass: the mountains of the Ötztal and Stubai Alps are more or less the highest peaks in the chain east of Switzerland and their northern slopes are covered with extensive glacier fields. Dark rock (gneiss, granite) and white *firn* snow dominate the scenery, and the the valleys running north to the Inn are punctuated with steep ridges.

Limestone peaks such as the 3,097-m (10,102-ft) Pflerscher Tribulaun form the kernel of the Tyrolean Mountains on the Austro-Italian border (South Tyrol).

ZILLERTAL

Location: Western Austria (Tyrol)
Best time to travel: throughout the year (ski season: October–April)
www.zillertal.at
www.tirol.at

The Zillertal valley runs down towards Italy from the Inn east of Jenbach and is considered Tyrolean scenery *par excellence*: the name is derived from the hermit's cell that St Rupert is said to have established at Zell, the main town. The valley extends more or less due south for some 30 km (19 mi), but beyond Mayrhofen it forks into four so-called "grounds". The Hintertuxer Glacier along the Tuxer valley is a great place to ski in summer, and the journey along the road linking the Zillertal summits, which reaches an elevation of 2,050 m (6,726 ft) at its highest point, has some breathtaking views.

One of the the twin peaks of the imposing Ahornspitze, a corner peak of the main Zillertal range rising to a height of 2,976 m (9,764 ft) to the south-east of Mayrhofen in the Tyrol; the northern peak is 2,960 m (9,711 ft) high.

Austria

SALZBURG

Location: Northern Austria
Best time to travel: throughout the year
www.salzburg.info
www.salzburgerland.com

Hugo von Hofmannsthal called the Salzburg state capital the "heart of the heart of Europe". This city not only produced Wolfgang Amadeus Mozart, but has also inspired artists from all over the world for centuries. The Hohensalzburg Fortress, Cathedral, Collegiate Church, residence, St Peter's and Mirabell Palace – all urban works of art on the Salzach between the hills of the Kapuzinerberg, Mönchsberg and Festungsberg, dazzle the senses with their intense baroque atmosphere. The urban gem that is the Getreidegasse largely has Archbishop Wolf Dietrich von Raitenau to thank for its present-day appearance. Around 1600, the Archbishop had half of the city's medieval center demolished and the expansive central open spaces laid out. His successor, who was just as extravagantly minded, subsequently completed the unique architectural ensemble.

The Hohensalzburg fortress stands serenely on the Mönchsberg as the Old Town of Salzburg huddles at its feet.

LAKE ATTER

Location: Northern Austria
(Upper Austria)
Best time to travel: April–October
www.attersee.at
www.salzkammergut.at

Lake Atter is about 20 km (12 mi) long, up to 3 km (2 mi) wide and about 170 m (560 ft) deep, making it the largest lake in both the Salzkammergut and the Austrian Alps. The town of the same name was an imperial residence in the 9th century, and a castle was built here for the Archbishop of Salzburg 400 years later.

Only a narrow strip of forest separates Lake Atter from Lake Mond. The fantastic panorama visible from the 1,782-m (5,846-ft) summit of the Schafberg includes both lakes and the magnificent 3,000-m (9,800-ft) peaks of the Alps.

LAKE MOND

Location: Northern Austria
(Upper Austria)
Best time to travel: April–October
www.mondsee.at

The Schafberg and Drachenwand mountains form a picturesque back-drop for Lake Mond, which is about 11 km (7 mi) long, and nearly 2 km (1 mi) wide. The town of the same name is located on the north-west-ern tip of the lake. Neolithic settlers once built huts on stilts on the south-eastern banks of the lake some 5,000 years ago, and Lake Mond cul-ture (2800–1800 BC) has become a byword for the whole period: finds from all over the Eastern Alps have been collected and displayed in the Mond Stilt Hut Museum.

Crescent-shaped Lake Mond's location at the foot of the Drachenwand mountain.

Austria

LAKE TRAUN

Location: Northern Austria
(Upper Austria)
Best time to travel: April–October
www.traunsee.at

At 12 km (7 mi) in length and up to
3 km (2 mi) in width, Lake Traun is
one of the largest lakes in the
Salzkammergut region, but with a
depth approaching 191 m (627 ft), it
is also the deepest lake in Austria. Its
main town is Gmunden on the northern shores, whose stately merchants'
houses around the Town Hall square
are a reminder of the modern spa
town's former importance as the
Salzamt ("Salt Inspectorate") of the
Salzkammergut.

**Gmunden's pretty Town Hall with its
pottery *carillon* is worth a visit, but
don't miss Ort castle by the lake,
which is accessible via a 130-m
(430-ft) jetty.**

LAKE WOLFGANG

Location: Northern Austria
Best time to travel: April–October
www.wolfgangsee.at

Also known to the locals as "Lake
Aber", the lake, which is about 11 km
(7 mi) long, nearly 2 km (1 mi) wide
and no more than 114 m (375 ft)
deep, is the "star" of the many beautiful lakes in the Salzkammergut. This
is largely due to the cult success of
Ralph Benatzky's operetta *Im
Weißen Rössl* (1930), which takes
place in St Wolfgang. The principal
attraction here is the late Gothic
parish church, with its triptych altarpiece created by Michael Pacher between 1471 and 1481. The towns of
St Gilgen and Strobl on the shores of
the lake are also worth a visit.

**Rhapsody in blue: the peaceful lake
with the sunlit mountains above.**

DACHSTEIN

Location: Northern Austria
Best time to travel: throughout the year (Ski season: October–April)
www.dachstein.at

The highest peak here – the Dachstein, at 2,995 m (9,827 ft) – towers over the extreme western end of the region of Styria. The mighty *massif* marks the point where the three states of Styria, Salzburg and Upper Austria meet. The Dachstein group (left, the Bischofsmütze or Miter) is a *karst* highland limestone plateau with several jagged peaks and the easternmost glaciers in the Alps.

The Große Bischofsmütze, or Great Miter (2,458 m/8,064 ft), and the Kleine Bischofsmütze (Lesser Miter, 2,430 m/7,972 ft) form the most striking twin peaks in the Dachstein mountains.

HALLSTATT

Location: Northern Austria (Upper Austria)
Best time to travel: throughout the year (Ski season: October–April)
www.hallstatt.net

When Johann Georg Ramsauer commenced the first excavations on the pre-history of Central Europe in the shadow of the Dachstein Mountains in 1846, he and his team unearthed upwards of ten thousand priceless discoveries documenting the transition from the European Bronze Age to the early Ice Age.

The pretty little town of Hallstatt (left) on the south-western shores of the Hallstätter See has lent its name to an entire culture; excavations between 1846 and 1849 uncovered a burial site of considerable size dating back to the Iron Age (800–500 BC).

Austria

HOHE TAUERN

Location: Central Austria
Best time to travel: throughout the year (Ski season: October–April)
www.nationalpark-hohetauern.at

There are six national parks in Austria. The one in the Hohe Tauern is by far the largest (1,836 sq km/709 sq mi) and also the highest. This region supplies the headstream of the Salzach (which flows through Salzburg) and the Isel, as well as two of the mightiest waterfalls in Europe: the 380-m (1,247-ft) high Krimmler Falls in Upper Pinzgau, and the Umbal Falls in the gorgeous Virgental valley. Some 150 years ago, mountaineering pioneer Ignaz von Kürsinger described the Hohe Tauern as a "magical world" of mountain pastures, rock and ice, "full of great, wild natural scenery and beautiful flowers".

Lying at an elevation of 2,464 m (8,084 ft) the Wangenitzsee lake (top right) provides a habitat for ibexes, marmots (top left), bearded vultures, mountain goats, and golden eagles (bottom right). Bottom left: Campion makes the park more beautiful still.

GROSSGLOCKNER

Location: Hohe Tauern, Central Austria
Best time to travel: throughout the year (Ski season: October–April)
www.grossglockner.at

The Grossglockner, Austria's highest peak, is a mighty 3,798 m (12,461 ft)

and best admired from the lookout on Kaiser Franz Josefs Höhe. The high alpine road named after it, which leads into the Salzburg Fusch Valley from Heiligenblut, winds its way through 26 hairpin turns and over 60 bridges to an altitude of 2,500 m (8,203 ft). Built in the

1930s, it has brought more than fifty million visitors closer to these exhilarating mountains since its opening in 1935. The 50-km (31-mi) stretch of road is only open from April to November, depending on the snow conditions, and features a number of museums, educational

tracks and various signposted viewing points.

The Pasterze (bottom), the largest glacier in the Eastern Alps, lies at the feet of the Grossglockner (top) on the border between Carinthia and the East Tyrol.

Austria

MELK

Location: Central Austria
(Lower Austria)
Best time to travel:
throughout the year
www.stiftmelk.at

After the tribulations of the Reformation, the Thirty Years' War, and skirmishes with the Turks and the Bohemians, Melk Abbey still stands serenely at the farthest western end of the Wachau valley, an incomparable guardian of the Danube, a masterpiece of baroque architecture, and the true epitome of monastic majesty. Its great importance is due not only to its imposing exterior (the southern façade is 362 m/1,188 ft long) but also its more than 900 years of history. Initially just a base camp for the exploration of the lands further along the Danube, in the Middle Ages the abbey attracted leading

WACHAU

Location: Central Austria
(Lower Austria)
Best time to travel: April–October
(September/Oktober: grape harvest)
www.wachau.at
www.niederoesterreich.at

The steep, narrow valley road that leads through Wachau begins in the west with the grandiose, baroque monastic residence of Melk which, with its imposing twin-spired domed church, is the "crown jewel" of this area. A number of castles, castle ruins, palaces and churches adorn the river valley between the pretty villages of Obstbauerndorf and Winzerdorf. This area is also home to the small township of Willendorf, made famous by what was the most important discovery from the Old Stone Age – the Venus of Willendorf. After the wine-growing towns of Spitz and Weissenkirchen you reach Dürn-

scholars and philosophers who published seminal theological and scientific tracts here. Modern visitors will be bowled over by the the baroque magnificence of the abbey chapel and the library, or the imperial apartments and the Marble Room. The guided tour through the museum-like rooms of the monastery will also bring the history of the Order to life. However, Melk Abbey is not just a museum – some 30 Benedictine monks still live, work, and pray here. Over the course of the years, Melk Abbey has traditionally been associated with two tasks – one is teaching and education, and the other parochial care. The two schools here are open to pupils of all faiths.

The Benedictine abbey at Melk is an outstanding guardian of the Danube valley (right, the monastery library with countless medieval manuscripts).

stein, where a hike up to the monastery beneath the castle ruins is worth the effort. The slender late-baroque tower of the monastery is one of the most elegant of its kind. The valley widens after Dürnstein, and provides a clear view as far as Krems, the medieval town with the Gothic buildings of the Gozzo-Burg, the Dominican Church and the Church of the Piarist Order. The Göttweig monastery perched ceremoniously on a hilltop marks the end of the Wachau Valley.

Dürnstein (left), with its ruined castle, Renaissance palace, baroque collegiate church, and former Poor Clares convent, has become an iconic symbol of the Wachau valley.
The wine-growing town of Weissenkirchen (right) with its imposing 14th-century fortified church lies only a short distance from Dürnstein.

Austria

LAKE NEUSIEDL

Location: Eastern Austria
(Burgenland)/Hungary
Best time to travel: April–October
www.neusiedlersee.com
www.neusiedlamsee.at

The area around Lake Neusiedl on the Austro-Hungarian border is a unique biosphere reserve with a long cultural history. The Neusiedler See/Seewinkel National Parks on the Austrian and Fert-Hanság Park and Fertöd Castle on the Hungarian side were combined in 2001 to form a cross-border UNESCO World Heritage Site. The lake is known as the "Sea of the Viennese", as it offers ample opportunities for sailing and windsurfing.

The idylls of nature beside Lake Neusiedl: some huts protected by a thick banks of reeds on Ruster Bay (large image), a great egret and some marsh orchids.

GRAZ

Location: South-eastern Austria
(Styria)
Best time to travel:
throughout the year
www.graztourismus.at
www.steiermark.com

This historic city on the Mur is Austria's second-largest. The Herrengasse lies in one of the best-preserved Old Towns in Central Europe – an exemplary series of winding residential streets, bourgeois mansions and aristocratic palaces from the Renaissance and baroque periods. Surrounding the clocktower, the main icon of Graz located on the castle mound, there is an extremely vibrant cultural city of universities, theaters, museums, and festivals.

The *Muschelinsel* ("Mussel Island") in the Mur is a piece by the New York artist Vito Acconci.

Austria

LAKE MILLSTATT, NOCKBERGE MOUNTAINS

Location: Southern Austria (Carinthia)
Best time to travel: April–October
www.millstaettersee.at
www.nockberge.at

A famous monastery, an ancient Roman settlement, and diverse fauna await visitors on the shores of Lake Millstatt. Nearby Spittal an der Drau can lay claim to the most beautiful Renaissance building in the country: Porcia Castle. A matchless ambience welcomes those seeking rest and relaxation in the Nockberge mountains (above), whose highlight is the Schi-estlnock region at 2,206 m (7,238 ft), largely unsettled grassy mountains reminiscent of Scotland. The region is strictly protected in a national park covering 185 sq km (71 sq mi). Conversely, high alpine scenery characterizes the backdrop of the Malta Valley, which leads westward from Gmünd, the region's capital, into a world of thundering waterfalls and majestic ice-capped peaks towering up to heights of 3,000 m (10,000 ft).

Idyllically beautiful: the view from Döbriach towards Seeboden.

KLAGENFURT, LAKE WÖRTH

Location: Southern Austria (Carinthia)
Best time to travel: April–October
www.klagenfurt-tourismus.at
www.woerthersee.com

Klagenfurt is the region's cultural and political center. Its historic town center has been lovingly renovated and exudes an almost Latin ambience during the summer. The city's most recognizable icon is the Lindworm at Neuer Platz square and the "Wappensaal" in the regional parliament building. Near Klagenfurt, large stretches of Lake Wörth (Wörthersee) shoreline radiate sophistication. The highlight and main cultural-historic attraction on the southern shore is the predominantly late-Gothic former collegiate church – today parish church – of Maria Wörth. The Madonna on the high altar at this popular pilgrimage site is an exquisite piece from 1420.

Top: a view across Lake Wörth to the parish church of Maria Wörth in the morning light.
Bottom: the heraldry room in the Carinthian Provincial Hall in Klagenfurt, the capital city of Carinthia. All the sights have a demonstrative southern flair.

Slovenia

JULIAN AND STEINER ALPS

Location: North-western Slovenia/Italy/Austria
Best time to travel: throughout the year (Ski season: October–April)
www.julijske-alpe.com
www.slovenia.info

The arduous journey through the passes on the Carinthian border is suddenly interrupted by the Julian and Steiner Alps. Almost every path here will quite literally lead you away into the wilderness – the Triglav National Park includes almost all of the Julian Alps. Parts of the Steiner Alps (Grintovec, 2,558 m/8,392 ft) to the north of the Slovenian regional capital of Ljubljana have also recently been placed under protection.

The highest peak in the Julian Alps is the Triglav ("Triple-headed"), at 2,865 m (9,400 ft).

BLED

Location: North-western Slovenia
Best time to travel: April–October
www.bled.si
www.slovenia.info

The 8-km (5-mi) long Karawanken Tunnel ensures a comfortable journey from Carinthia into Slovenia. The spa town of Bled on the lake of the same name is definitely worth a visit, and the little island here has been a popular pilgrimage site for more than 1,000 years. Bled's most interesting attraction by far is the castle on its high rock – many sections of its Romanesque walls have survived the centuries unscathed. There is a comprehensive regional museum in the baroque section of the castle. A trip round the lake and a passage across to the island in a wooden pletna is also recommended.

St Mary's Church on its island has become an iconic symbol of Bled.

ŠKOCJAN

Location: East Slovenia
Best time to travel:
June–September
www.park-skocjanske-jame.si

The waters of the Reka River disappear underground at skocjan, only emerging again eight days later near the Adriatic coast. The intervening stretch of the Reka has carved a series of beautiful *karst* caves with all the typical features left in limestone by thousands of years of erosion: fissures, gorges, chimneys, collapsed funnels, chasms, lakes, waterfalls, narrow crevices, and "chambers". Water levels can rise rapidly here as the snow melts.

The almost 6-km (4-mi) long cave system to the east of Trieste in the Slovenian karst is one of the most important caves in the world.

LJUBLJANA

Location: Central Slovenia
Best time to travel:
throughout the year
www.visitljubljana.si
www.ljubljana-calling.com

Although it has a population of less than 300,000, Slovenia's capital has all the trappings of state sovereignty: embassies, a parliament, a national museum, gallery, and library. It also has a vibrant cultural life, but most of all it has an abundance of grace and charm. Just as in Salzburg, the historic Old Town is dominated by a castle, and from here the viceroy of the emperor in Vienna ruled the dukedom of Krain for centuries.

The view from Ljubljana's western riverbanks towards the Three Bridges and the Old Marketplace is especially atmospheric.

ROME

Location: Central Italy (Lazio)
Best time to travel:
throughout the year
http://en.turismoroma.it

The center of the present-day metropolis of Rome – located at a bend in the Tiber River – was first settled around 3,000 years ago. The people who settled here left traces of their civilizations from the very start, providing Rome with tremendous appeal for anyone interested in art, architectural and cultural history. The presence of the city's mythical founders, Romulus and Remus, can be felt during a walk through its fascinatig streets just as much as that of the other well-known Roman emperors and popes who resided in this, the capital city of Christianity, during the Renaissance and baroque periods. More than any other city, Rome is testimony to the advanced development of European culture and it is here that some of the deepest roots of western civilization are to be found. In ancient times, there was a temple on the Capitoline Hill that was dedicated to Jupiter, king of the gods. It was reached by a winding path leading south-east from the Forum. Today you climb the hill from the west on a flight of stairs designed by Michelangelo. At the top is a piazza, also designed by Michelangelo, and which is paved with a geometric pattern. The bronze equestrian sculpture of Marcus Aurelius in the

center of the square is the only one of its kind to have escaped being melted down in the Middle Ages because the rider was thought to be Constantine I, defender of Christianity. The Palazzo Senatorio on the piazza is the seat of the mayor of Rome. Located between the Palatine Hill and the Capitoline Hill, the Roman Forum and the other build-

ings dating from the 6th century BC were the site of religious ceremonies and political gatherings. The fall of the Roman Empire saw the deterioration of Forum buildings such as the triumphal arch of Septimius Severus, the Temple of Saturn, and the Temple of Vespasian in front of the baroque Santi Luca e Martina Church, which then fell into disuse.

Protection of the historic legacy of the city of Rome (opposite: the Via Appia Antika, commonly said to be the "queen of the long roads", which once connected Rome to Brindisi, Apulia, in southeast Italy, and, below, the famous Colosseum of Rome. This page, main picture: the Forum Romanorum, located between the Palatine Hill and the

Capitoline Hill and the Pantheon (bottom, left), and the Spanish Steps (right) was a matter of concern even in late antiquity. The Western Roman emperor Majorian decreed in 458 that "everything contributing to the glory of the city should be kept in good order through the diligence of the citizenry".

THE VATICAN

Location: Rome, Central Italy
Best time to travel:
throughout the year
www.vatican.va
www.vaticanstate.va

Laid out in 1937, the Via della Conciliazione is not just a literal connection between Rome and the Vatican, it is also a symbol that the Papacy, which had had to relinquish its position as a secular ruler after the unification of Italy in 1870, had, with the Lateran Pacts of 1929, agreed to a reconciliation (conciliazione) between state and church. The head of

the Church at least managed to retain the title of the "Sovereign of the State of the Vatican City". Facing St Peter's Square is the mighty façade of St Peter's Basilica, officially known as San Pietro in Vaticano and which was built in the 16th century on the site of the apostle Peter's crucifixion. The present-day building is some 45 m (148 ft) high and 115 m (377 ft) wide. The height of the lantern crowning the dome is 132 m (433 ft) and the interior covers an area of 15,000 sq m (16,145 sq ft). It can accommodate around 60,000 worshippers, and with this building the Papa-

cy sought to provide a foundation for its claim to be the one true representative of God on earth. The square in front of the church was designed by Bernini and built between 1656 and 1667, the elliptical area is 240 m (790 ft) long and surrounded by a 17-m (56-ft) wide colonnade of 284 pillars topped with the statues of 140 saints. Naturally, the most famous artists of the age were involved in its construction: architects Bramante and Sangallo, sculptors Bernini and Maderno, and master painters Michelangelo and Raphael (both of whom were employed as ar-

chitects as well). St Peter's grave is said to be located in the so-called "grotto" beneath the church. The Sistine Chapel, commissioned in 1477 by Pope Sixtus IV, was not just a place of worship but also a fortress with walls that are 3 m (10 ft) thick. It continues to serve as the venue for the papal conclave, in which the College of Cardinals elects a new pope. Upon the completion of construction work in 1480, Lorenzo de' Medici, the "ruler" of Florence, sent a number of his city's leading artists to Rome to decorate the interior of the chapel with frescoes. The artists included Pietro Perugino, Sandro Botticelli and Domenico Ghirlandaio. It was only later (from 1508 to 1512) that it was painted over by Michelangelo to include his famous frescos of the Creation and the Fall of Man.

St Peter's Square and Basilica compete with the Sistine Chapel and its frescos by Michelangelo. The latter is famous for its architecture, evocative of Solomon's Temple of the Old Testament. The Vatican is watched over by the Papal Swiss Guard. It was founded in 1506.

GRAN PARADISO NATIONAL PARK

Location: North-western Italy (Val d'Aosta/Piedmont)
Best time to travel: throughout the year
www.parks.it
www.pngp.it

There are 700 sq km (270 sq mi) of national park surrounding the Gran Paradiso (4,061 m/13,323 ft) in the southern Val d'Aosta, and the Parc National de la Vanoise is a natural continuation of the protected area on the French side. The national park, which boasts 40 sq km (15 sq mi) of glaciers, can be accessed via the Val di Rhêmes, Val Savarenche, and Val di Cogne, all of which branch off to the south from the val d'Aosta, but the most impressive way in is via the road leading across the 2,612-m (8,570-ft) high Colle del Nivolet to the south-west of the park; this is reached by driving west from Ivrea up to Cuorgnè and from here into the Valle di Locana. You will soon see Alpine scenery as you drive along beside the wild waters of the Orco, and the pass itself has an idyllically beautiful view of the Gran Paradiso and its magnificent glaciers. If you are patient and a little fortunate, you may also see marmots, mountain goats, and eagles from the pass.

Viktor Emanuel II (1820–1878), passionate sportsman, declared the Gran Paradiso massif a royal hunting ground, thus paradoxically ensuring the survival of the mountain goat (right) with its powerful horns. The Parco Nazionale del Gran Paradiso (above) was declared Italy's first national park in 1922.

Italy

LAKE GARDA

Location: Northern Italy
Best time to travel:
April–September
www.lagodigarda.it
www.gardatrentino.it

The Upper Italian lakes, include Lake Garda, Lake Como, much of Lake Maggiore, Lake Orta, and a few others. Lake Garda was known as *Lacus benacus* in antiquity, after the Neptune-like divinity Benacus. The lake, 54 km (33 mi) long and up to 346 m (1,135 ft) deep, is fed by the Sarca, Ponale and Campione rivers. It has long been a popular holiday destination and is particularly popular among windsurfers.

A place to yearn for: Gardone on Lake Garda. The tower of the Grand Hotel Gardone, which was built on the lake shore in 1884, can be seen in the middle of the image.

LAKE COMO

Location: Northern Italy
Best time to travel: April–September
www.lagodicomo.com
www.turismo.como.it

Lake Como is 51 km (32 mi) long and 4 km (2.5 mi) at its widest point and is situated between the Lugarno and Bergamo Alps. The lake is also known as Lario in Italian. Bellagio is the loveliest town on this stunning body of water, carved into the narrow valley by the Adda glacier and still fed by the Adda River. Comer divides into the Como and Lecco arms to the south. The resort town of Varenna lies on the widest section of the lake, and from here there is a ferry connection to Bellaggio and Menaggio.

The picturesque town of Bellaggio is known as the "Pearl of Lake Lario".

SOUTH TYROL

Location: Northern Italy
(South Tyrol)
Best time to travel:
throughout the year
www.suedtirolerland.it
www.schlosstirol.it
www.kloster-neustift.it
www.brixen.org
www.bolzano-bozen.it
www.meran.eu
www.visittrentino.it

BRESSANONE

At the confluence of the Rienza and Isarco rivers, the Isarco Valley widens to form a broad natural caldera that is home to the town of Bressanone, a bishop's see since 990, as well as the oldest and second-largest settlement in the South Tyrol. Bressanone remained the bishop's seat for nearly 1,000 years until 1964, when Bolzano took over for the then newly created diocese of Bolzano-Bressanone. Its historic center, which has been at least partially transformed into a pedestrian zone, is a perfect example of well-preserved alpine city architecture.

NEUSTIFT MONASTERY

Legend has it that the founding of Neustift Monastery can be traced back to the fate of bereaved parents: when their four-year-old son died, Reginbert and Christine of Sabiona are said to have given up all hope of earthly fortune and bequeathed their belongings to Bressanone's Bishop Hartmann, who founded an Augustinian choral monastery in front of the gates of the city in 1492. Since then, people have lived there according to the "Rule of St Augustine", which dates back to the Church Father, Augustine of Hippo (354–430), and states: "First and foremost, you shall dwell together in unity, and be of one mind and one heart in God". As a popular resting stop for pilgrims on the way to Rome or the Holy Land, the monastery quickly became an im-

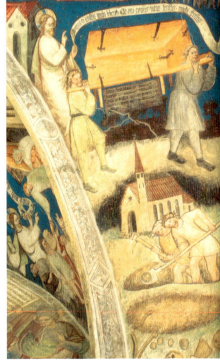

portant point of reference in European spiritual life. The "Wunderbrunnen" (miracle fountain) in the monastery courtyard testifies to the confidence and humor of the Order, and its frieze not only depicts the seven ancient wonders of the world, but includes the Neustift Monastery – as the eighth.

BOLZANO

The main square in the capital of South Tyrol (Bozen, in German) is named after German minnesinger Walther von der Vogelweide, who has been looking out over Waltherplatz from his pedestal since 1889. Bolzano subsequently developed into a big city. In the Mussolini era, it was given a more Italian look, with imperial features and heroic monuments around the Piazza Vittoria,and a growing industrial district.

MERANO

Merano is a popular health resort town in the Adige Valley, with a mild climate, cozy loggias, elegant promenades, tiny alleyways, and the Tyrol Castle towering majestically over the city. The Adige has its source somewhat above Lago di Resia, which was dammed in 1950, and for which 163 houses in the villages of Curon and Resia had to be sacrificed. Today, only the tip of one church spire can be seen poking up out of the water. Italy's second-longest river, the Adige, flows through Merano, Bolzano, Trento and Verona before reaching the Adriatic.

Page left: Tyrol Castle (top) on a once-glaciated hill on the northern outskirts of Merano. The current appearance of the triple-naved collegiate church of Neustift Monastery (bottom left) dates back to 1753. The transept of Brixen Cathedral with domestic Gothic frescoes (bottom right). This page, top to bottom: the Waltherplatz in Bolzano, the spa building in Merano, and the cathedral square in Trento.

Italy

THE DOLOMITES

Location: Southern Alps, Northern Italy
Best time to travel: throughout the year (Ski season: October–April)
www.infodolomiti.it
dolomiti.discover-eu.com

The Tethys Ocean is said to have once covered the area where the towering Dolomites now stand. The Dolomites have a total area of about 1,419 sq km (548 sq mi) and the Marmolada (3,343 m/10,968 ft) is the highest peak. The "Three Peaks" or the Rosengartenspitze are probably best known for their charming appearance, although the Kesselkogel, the highest peak in the Rosengarten group, is 3,004 m (9,812 ft) high. The Dolomites is a region of opposites, with lush Alpine meadows alternating with jagged rocky peaks, and plains filled with moraine. Such variation is explained by the different ways these local landscapes were created: some are fossilized and elevated coral reefs, others are volcanic rock. There are plenty of glaciated surfaces to be found in the Dolomites as well as the *karst* scenery typical of limestone areas, and the Dolomites are an excellent example of a landscape whose genesis can be documented by the geology and the fossil record. This genesis is still ongoing and evident in every flood, mud slide, rockfall, and avalanche which re-shapes the surface.

Top: the most famous peaks in the Dolomites lie in the far eastern reaches of the chain. Although they are known as the "Three Peaks" there are actually five of them. Bottom: "The most beautiful mountain range in the world? The Dolomites!" – according to Le Corbusier. The area enclosed by the Eisack, Marmolada, the Puster Valley and Feltre is full of beautiful natural spectacles.

Italy

VERONA

Location: Northern Italy (Veneto)
Best time to travel:
throughout the year
www.tourism.verona.it

Verona became popular thanks to William Shakespeare, before whom, admittedly, half-dozen other authors had already told the melodramatic story of Romeo and Juliet – although none had done it so touchingly as the Englishman. Many visitors still come to Verona's Casa Giulietta to stroke the right breast of the bronze figure of Juliet in the hope of finding luck in love. Thousands also come for the Opera Festival in the ancient arena, which of course goes well with Shakespeare: opera is often a feast of fantasy, frequently melodramatic, and very rarely without heartbreak.

An ancient venue for opera: the Arena di Verona on the Piazza Bra.

MANTUA

Location: Northern Italy (Lombardy)
Best time to travel:
throughout the year
www.turismo.mantova.it
turismo.comune.mantova.it

The heart of Manuta is the Piazza Mantegna, with the Basilica di Sant'Andrea, whose construction started in 1472, at the Piazza dell'Erbe. Rising up at the Piazza Sordello is the Palazzo Ducale – a residence of the Gonzaga family. Its ornate rooms, lavishly decorated with frescoes and paintings, are now home to an antiques collection and a collection of paintings. The Castello San Giorgio, the oldest part of the palace, dates back to the 14th century.

The Piazza Sordello is flanked by the baroque façade of the cathedral, the Romanesque *campanile*, and the Palazzo Ducale.

VICENZA

Location: Northern Italy (Veneto)
Best time to travel:
throughout the year
www.vicenzae.org

Vicenza was founded back in Roman times and rose to architectural fame when it joined together with the Republic of San Marco – Venice, that is – in 1404. Gothic residences and Renaissance buildings have been lovingly preserved in the Old Town, in particular the works of Antonio Palladio, who was born in Padua in 1508. The artworks in the Museo Civico (in one of Palladio's former palaces) and the palaces along the Corso Andrea Palladio are also worth seeing. His design for the town hall (also known as the "Basilica") surrounded the two levels of the building with rows of arcades, and the window that was later called the "Palladio motif". An extreme rarity is the Teatro Olimpico, Palladio's last work and a fascinating attempt at reconstructing a building from Classical antiquity.

Palladio's Teatro Olimpico in Vicenza is a building of the utmost rarity.

PADUA

Location: Northern Italy (Veneto)
Best time to travel:
throughout the year
www.turismopadova.it
www.padovaincoming.it

In ancient times, Patavium was one of the wealthiest cities in northern Italy.

After being totally destroyed by the Lombards in the early 7th century, Padua quickly recovered and in 1222, became one of the first university cities in Europe. The Giotto frescoes in the Arena Chapel depict the life of Mary and Christ, as well as the Last Judgment and allegories of virtue and vice – a realistic, religious cosmos created by the artist born near Florence in 1266. Following a fire, the Palazzo della Ragione, the medieval town hall, was reconstructed with the giant, almost 80-m (262-ft) long and 27-m (89-ft) high hall on the first floor – an architectural feat so impressive that the entire building has been called "Il Salone" ever since.

The Arena Chapel was painted by Giotto at the turn of the 14th century. The strikingly three-dimensional representation was an innovation for the period.

Italy

VENICE

Location: North-eastern Italy (Veneto)
Best time to travel: throughout the year (February: Carnival)
www.turismovenezia.it
www.comune.venezia.it

Make way for a city about which the writer Harold Brodkey said it is "a country in itself … a city of independ-

ent will". Two pillars – a third collapsed into the sea as it was being erected – form a monumental entrance to the Piazzetta opening onto the lagoon. Originally looted from the Phoenician city of Tyre, they were installed in the first year of his reign by the Doge Sebastiano Ziani, a diplomat and merchant who had become rich by assiduously collecting interest

payments. From the Piazzetta at the Doge's Palace it is easy to see the San Giorgio Maggiore Church situated on a small island in the Canale della Giudecca – one of more than 100 islands in Venice. The relics of St Stephanus of Constantinople are said to have been brought here in 1109, the result being that the church and monastery adjacent to the grave of

the apostle Mark subsequently became an important pilgrimage site in the lagoon city. In 1223, the monastery was destroyed by an earthquake, but its buildings were rebuilt between the 15th and 17th centuries and those are what you see today. St Mark's cathedral features five mosaic portal niches that form the eastern end of St Mark's

Square. The square is the site of a number of the principal tourist attractions in the city, including the Palazzo Ducale, the campanile, the Torre dell'Orologico (clock tower), and the Quadri and Florian cafés. The close connections with the Byzantine Empire meant that Venice's main church, built between 976 and 1094, had the stylistic influences of that re-

gion. Starting in 9th century, the Doge's Palace was the residence of the Venetian head of state and the seat of the Venetian government. The present day appearance of this marble and stone masterpiece dates from the 14th and 15th centuries. The Canale Grande is roughly 4 km (2.4 mi) long and lined with magnificent palaces built and owned by

nearly five centuries of merchants and nobility. It is the main traffic artery in Venice upon which a throng of gondolas and *vaporetti* make their way. The end of the canal is marked on the right bank by the baroque Santa Maria della Salute Church with its wonderful dome. The roofed Rialto Bridge (above) spans the canal at about its halfway point.

Originally a wooden bridge, between 1588 and 1592 it was built of stone with its present design-

Opposite, from top: looking between the gondolas towards the Giudecca San Giorgio Maggiore, the Piazzetta (middle), and the Rialto Bridge (bottom). This page: the Basilica di San Marco.

MILAN

Location: Northern Italy (Lombardy)
Best time to travel:
throughout the year
www.turismo.milano.it

During Late antiquity the Roman Empire was at times ruled from Milan, and the city became one of the focal points of the new Italy in the Middle Ages. Its greatest sightseeing attraction is the cathedral (left), a masterpiece of Italian Gothic 157 m (515 ft) in length and 92 m (302 ft) wide. It is one of the world's largest Gothic churches and the marble façade is decorated with no less than 2,245 statues.

The Piazza del Duomo forms the heart of Milan and is linked to the Piazza della Scala by the Galleria Vittorio Emanuele II, which has been an exemplary model for many modern shopping centers. The Teatro alla Scala is Milan's famous opera house. The High Gothic church of Santa Maria delle Grazie was built between 1465 and 1482. Leonardo da Vinci completed his fresco of the Last Supper on the abbey's refectory wall in 1497.

The cathedral of Milano (opposite), La Scala Opera House (middle); and Leonardo's Last Supper (bottom)

Italy

GENOA

Location: North-western Italy (Liguria)
Best time to travel: throughout the year
www.genova-turismo.it

Genoa, which forms the southern corner of the Milan-Turin-Genoa industrial triangle of north-west Italy, is one of the country's major economic centres. Thanks to its natural harbor and the surrounding mountains which afford it protection, Genoa was able to become a major sea power, experiencing its first heyday in the 16th century under Andrea Doria, Charles V's First Admiral. You cannot escape the name Christopher Columbus here, although it is by no means certain that the legendary seafarer was born in the city. Columbus' father is nonetheless documented in the city records and Columbus is said to have claimed he was born in Genoa. By the 16th century, the powers-that-be had become unhappy with the tangle of streets in the Old Town and wished to create housing appropriate for the well-off families now living in this financial and commercial metropolis. For the first time ever in the history of European town planning, a fixed construction plan was drawn up and the authorities determined the allocation of land. The Strada Nuova ("New Street") laid out as part of this plan was 7 m (23 ft) wide and thus nearly twice the size of the average street in the Old Town. The modern Via Garibaldi is flanked by imposing Renaissance palaces and baroque villas. The district was extended at the turn of the 17th century to include more "new streets" and the ensuing palaces were used both as dwellings and for ceremonial purposes – a decree of 1576 ordained that the owners were obliged to receive dignitaries on state visits. The so-called *rolli* ("lists") recorded which families had been chosen by lottery to accommodate state visitors, thus ascribing their name to the palaces.

Genoa is known by locals as *La Superba* ("the Proud"), and this pride is inspired by the second-largest port in the Mediterranean (after Marseilles) and the historic Old Town (right: the Piazza San Matteo and the church of the same name). The Palazzo Spinola, once the seat of the Grimaldi family, gives a good idea of the lifestyle of the Genoese aristocracy.

Italy

Italy

CINQUE TERRE

Location: North-western Italy (Liguria)
Best time to travel: April–October
www.cinqueterre.it
www.cinqueterre.com

The five villages (Cinque Terre) of Monterosso, Vernazza, Corniglia, Manarola, and Riomaggiore are simply striking, clinging to the cliffs and bays of the steep Ligurian coast between Levanto and Portovenere. Though hard to believe, there is still no direct road along the coast that connects the five sleepy hamlets – but perhaps it is for the better. In the past the impassable coastline was accessed using footpaths and steps. The Via dell'Amore, which seems to hug the craggy rocks, links Riomaggiore, the most eastern Cinque Terre village, with Manarola, where the Natività di Maria Vergine Church boasts a Carrara marble rose window on its façade. Corniglia is the only one of the five villages to lie at an elevation, being more than 100 m (328 ft) above the sea. It took many centuries for the steep slopes to be turned into terraced fields where grapes could be cultivated, but these yielded a good wine that was exported as far as England in the late Middle Ages. No one got too rich from this, however; the ports of the Cinque Terre were too small for intensive fishing or trade, and working the steep fields was too arduous for the farmers to make anything other than a subsistence living and a little wine.

Adjoining the port in Vernazza there is a small piazza with brightly painted houses and the Romanesque church of Santa Maria di Antiochia (1318). Parts of the Genoese fortifications have survived to the present day.

Italy

BOLOGNA

Location: Northern Italy
(Emilia-Romagna)
Best time to travel:
throughout the year
http://iat.comune.bologna.it
www.provincia.bologna.it

The capital of Emilia-Romagna is a major traffic node at the foot of the Apennines. The city was ruled by the citizens themselves between the 13th and the 16th centuries, a period in which it flourished magnificently: city walls, towers, palaces, and churches were built to outdo one another, and the university was free to develop unhindered – there were some 10,000 students in 13th-century Bologna.

The Piazza Maggiore is the heart of Bologna; arcades such as those in the image right, on the Piazza Santo Stefano, are a typical feature of the city.

FERRARA

Location: Northern Italy
(Emilia-Romagna)
Best time to travel:
throughout the year
www.ferraraterraeacqua.it
www.ferraraturismo.it

The Este, one of the oldest aristocratic families in Italy, ruled Ferrara from the 13th to the 16th century, and under them, Ferrara attracted such leading artists as Antonio Pisanello. The Palazzo Comunale opposite the cathedral (built 1135–1485) is connected to the Castello Estense by a gallery whose rooms are adorned with precious frescos. *Maestri* from the Ferrara school created an exceptional cycle of frescos in the Palazzo Schifanoia, one of the Este's town houses.

Ferrara's cathedral of San Giorgio has an impressive marble façade.

MODENA

Location: Northern Italy (Emilia-Romagna)
Best time to travel:
throughout the year
http://turismo.comune.modena.it

After the collapse of a building which had held the relics of San Geminiano since the 8th century, construction of a cathedral was begun on the same site by the Lombard master mason Lanfranco in 1099; the church was not to be consecrated until 1184. The ornate carvings on the portals and in the interior are the work of Master Wilgelmus and his pupils. The marble and blind arcades of the gabled façade draw attention to the main portal with its pillars supported by lions, and rose window.

The cathedral of San Geminiano dominates the Piazza Grande in the center of town.

RAVENNA

Location: North-eastern Italy (Emilia-Romagna)
Best time to travel:
throughout the year
www.turismo.ra.it
www.turismo.ravenna.it

Ravenna was once the capital of the Western Roman Empire, later becoming the center of power of the Goths, before developing into the focus of the Byzantine part of Italy until it was conquered by the Lombards in 751. Several buildings from that era survive in nearly original form, and feature fascinating mosaics. They are among the most important remnants of early Christianity.

San Vitale Church was built close to the old city wall between 525 and 547 and closely modeled on the Hagia Sophia in Constantinople (now Istanbul).

Italy

PISA

Location: North-western Italy (Tuscany)
Best time to travel: throughout the year
www.comune.pisa.it
www.pisaunicaterra.it

In 1063, a site just beyond the city walls of the time saw work begin on a cathedral that had been designed by the architect Buscheto. Its magnificent, 35-m (116-ft) long façade was designed by Rainaldo and the bronze doors of the Porta di San Ranieri were created by Bonanno Pisano in 1180. The ornately decorated coffered ceiling in the vaulting of the nave dates back to the 16th century and the free-standing, cylindrical *campanile* was begun by Bonanno in 1174 but began to lean in 1185, at which point only the first three floors had been completed. One hundred years would pass before any efforts were made to counter the leaning by creating a significant slant in the op-posite direction, and it was feared for many centuries that the tower would collapse. It has since been underpinned with new foundations. The decoration of the baptistery (1152–1358) is a good example of the transition phase between the Romanesque and the Gothic periods. The cathedral features the characteristic light and dark stone stripes of the Pisan style. The most eye-catching feature of the interior is the mosaic by Francesco di Simone and Cimabue in the apse depicting the seated Christ, flanked by Mary and John. The use of white Carrara marble and the common architectonic elements (such as arcades and colonnades) allow all the buildings on the cathedral square to blend together in a cohesive whole.

Right: the cathedral, the Leaning Tower, and the Fontana dei Putti. Above top, the Piazza by night; bottom, a view of the nave.

Italy

FLORENCE

Location: Northern Italy (Tuscany)
Best time to travel:
throughout the year
www.firenzeturismo.it
www.firenze-tourism.com

The Tuscan capital on the Arno River is considered to be the birthplace of the Renaissance and of humanism, which began around 600 years ago and is of paramount importance for the history of European art. The elevated Piazzale Michelangelo provides a stunning view of the city including the mighty red dome of Santa Maria del Fiore built by Filippo Brunelleschi between 1420 and 1436. Upon seeing the baptistery Michelangelo is purported to have said that, "only the gates of paradise could be so wonderful". The church, which dates back to the 4th century and is the location of Dante's baptism, is among the oldest buildings in the city. Magnificent 13th-century mosaics adorn the cupola above the baptismal font. The baptistery is also renowned for its splendid portals depicting scenes from the Old and New Testaments. Construction of the Santa Maria del Fiore Cathedral began in 1296. Consecrated in 1436, Florence's most famous landmark is 153 m (502 ft) long, 90 m (295 ft) wide in the transept and, with the lantern on the octagonal dome, 116 m (381 ft) high, making it the fourth largest church in the Occident after the cathedrals in Rome, London and Milan. Construction of the free-standing bell tower, almost 85 m (279 ft) in height and clad in marble of different hues, was begun by Giotto in 1334. The secular center of Florence is the Piazza della Signoria, home to the Loggia dei Lanzi, with its priceless sculptures, and the Palazzo Vecchio, the seat of the mighty Medici government, which was completed in 1322. The Medici family determined the city's fate for generations. Their rise began with

Giovanni (1360–1429), who was able to increase his fortune through banking, the Pope being his best customer. The Uffizi, begun in 1560, was initially used as administrative buildings for the Medicis. Only goldsmiths used to be permitted to ply their trade on this world-famous bridge with its tiny shops. In Roman times a wooden bridge spanned the Arno here. The Palazzo Pitti was begun in 1457 for the banker Luca Pitti and completed in 1819.

It combines several styles due to its centuries of building phases. In 1550, the Medicis made the palace their main residence. The adjacent Boboli Garden from 1590 is a gem of Italian garden design. Today the palace and garden are home to seven museums and galleries, including the world famous Galleria Palatina. This Dominican church was built in the 13th century and is famous for the many frescos in its choir chapel. San Lorenzo is one of the oldest churches in Florence.

The first structure was consecrated in 393; the second was built in 1059; and Brunelleschi renovated the church in 1419. This majestic complex is the final resting place of the many members of the Medici family. It includes the Cappella dei Principi, designed in 1604, and its crypt, as well as the Sagrestia Nuova, the new sacristy.

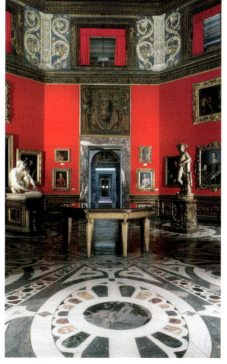

There is a magnificent view of Florence from the Piazzale Michelangelo. The city skyline includes the giant dome of the cathedral, the Palazzo Vecchio and their respective bell towers. Below from left: the original of Michelangelo's monumental sculpture of David can now be admired in the Galleria dell'Accademia. The Hall of Five Hundred on the first floor of the Palazzo Vecchio is adorned with city views and battle scenes by Vasari and his pupils.

Italy

VOLTERRA

Location: North-western Italy (Tuscany)
Best time to travel:
throughout the year
www.comune.volterra.pi.it
www.volterratur.it

The former Etruscan town of Volterra is situated about 45 km (30 mi) from the coast on a cliff amidst the Tuscan hills. Excavations indicate that the town was extremely prosperous during the 4th century BC. A 7-km (4-mi) long wall encompassing fields and pastures surrounded Volterra at the time, meaning the residents were able to fend for themselves when under siege.

Volterra has a magnificent location overlooking the Cecina Valley. The picturesque *balze* – rocky clefts and scree slopes – are the result of centuries of erosion.

SAN GIMIGNANO

Location: Northern Italy (Tuscany)
Best time to travel:
throughout the year
www.sangimignano.com
www.turismo.intoscana.it

Seen from afar, San Gimignano looks like a hedgehog and you could be forgiven for assuming that the many fortifications were intended to deter outside enemies. In fact, they are much more related to the internal rivalries between aristocratic dynasties; these families built the tower houses in order to outdo one another.

Only 15 of San Gimignano's 72 original towers are still standing. They stand guard over the Piazza della Cisterna in the center of the Old Town, giving San Gimignano its characteristic skyline.

PIENZA

Location: Northern Italy (Tuscany)
Best time to travel:
throughout the year
www.pienza.info
www.ufficioturisticodipienza.it

Situated between Montepulciano and Montalcino in the Val d'Orcia, the little town of Corsignano, birthplace of Pope Pius II (reigned 1458–1464), was re-designed by Bernardo Rossellino as an "ideal Renaissance town" on the orders of the Vatican, and renamed Pienza in honor of the pontiff. The focal point of the historic center is the Piazza Pio II, which is lined with a number of impressive buildings.

The view between the colonnades of the Palazzo Civico of the cathedral. The Piazza Pio II is bordered to the left and right by the Palazzi Vescovile and Piccolomini.

LUCCA

Location: North-western Italy (Tuscany)
Best time to travel:
throughout the year
www.luccatourist.it
www.luccaportal.it

Lucca originally developed on a tiny island in the marshes of Serchio. Situated on the Via Francigena, Lucca enjoyed economic importance even as a Roman colony. The fortifications of the town began in 1544, and anyone wanting to reach the city center today has to pass through one of the 11 fortified gates. The city wall, which is 4 km (2.4 mi) in length and up to 30 m (98 ft) thick, has trees growing on it.

The buildings surrounding the Piazza del Mercato were constructed around the site of the former Roman amphitheater.

Italy

SIENA

Location: Northern Italy (Tuscany)
Best time to travel: throughout the year (July/August: Palio di Siena)
www.terresiena.it
www.comune.siena.it

Siena was originally an Etruscan settlement, later became a Roman colony (Saena Iulia), and eventually sided with the Ghibellines in the Middle Ages, thus becoming Florence's arch rival. The city reached the height of its political power in the 13th century, after which it was ruled by a council of nine merchants between 1287 and 1355. Siena was conquered by the Spanish in 1555, who then ceded it to the Grand Duchy of Tuscany. The historic city, which has survived almost entirely intact, is dominated by the Gothic cathedral. The marble floor was created between 1369 and 1547 by a team of over 40 artists and is just one of the many beautiful art treasures to be found inside. The Piazza del Campo has been the venue of the biannual Palio since the Middle Ages, a horse race that always takes place on July 2 and August 16. Siena's opposing city districts compete against one another in the race, and the residents don historic costumes.

The Piazza del Campo (above) with its Palazzo Pubblico und Torre del Mangia is the heart of the city, although the cathedral overlooks all (left). Very top: the colossal dome of the cathedral.

CHIANTI, MAREMMA, MASSA MARITTIMA

Location: Northern Italy (Tuscany)
Best time to travel: April–October
(September/October: grape harvest)
www.chiantiturismo.it
www.maremmaturismo.com
www.massamarittima.info

CHIANTI
The center of the Chianti region lies north of Siena. Extensive vineyards, wine estates and attractive cypress and pine alleys characterize the scenery. And yes, Chianti Classico wine estates with their Gallo Nero – black cockerel – emblem as a quality guarantee are everywhere, tucked into misty valleys down narrow country roads. The turning point for the region came in 1841, when Bettino Ricasoli developed his idea of an "original" chianti at Brolio Castle, and it was he who established the best blend of grapes.

MAREMMA, MASSA MARITTIMA
Maremma, the coastal region between Livorno and Monte Argentario, has been settled since Etruscan times. The Romans were also able to cultivate the area, although their drainage systems later fell into disrepair and were forgotten.

The rolling hills of typical Chianti scenery in the morning light at sunrise (top). Massa Marittima (bottom) became a bishop's see in the 12th or 13th century, and a few medieval buildings are still standing here.

CRETE, VAL D'ORCIA, MONTEPULCIANO

Location: Northern Italy (Tuscany)
Best time to travel: April–October
(September/October: grape harvest)
www.turismo.intoscana.it
www.valdorcia.it
www.montepulciano.com

CRETE
"Crete", not to be confused with the island, is an area to the south-east of Siena, between Vescona and Asciano. It lures with its unique and at times lunar landscape, known as the Crete Senesi. The grey and yellow boulders, a result of erosion, are still a beautiful feature of this surrealist lunar landscape. Here – and a little further south in the Val d'Orcia in particular – was where the first landscape artists found inspiration for their frescoes.

VAL D'ORCIA
The Val d'Orcia – roughly 50 km (31 mi) south of Siena – embodies a Renaissance landscape. Over the centuries, graphic depictions of this area had a major influence in the history of European art.

MONTEPULCIANO
Situated on top of a picturesque hill between Valdichiana and the Val d'Orcia, Montepulciano at 605 m (1,985 ft) is one of the highest towns in Tuscany.

Cypresses, lonely farmhouses, and a little church on a hill add up to typical Tuscan scenery (top, Crete; middle, Val d'Orcia). San Biagio (bottom) near Montepulciano.

Italy

URBINO

Location: Central eastern Italy (Marche)
Best time to travel: throughout the year
www.turismo.pesarourbino.it
www.isairon.it

Perched upon two hills in the Marche, Urbino enjoyed its heyday back in the 15th century, when important Renaissance artists and scholars made it Italy's center of culture and science. Under the Montefeltro dynasty the artists of the age created an architectural ensemble of Renaissance buildings, the homogeneity of which is unique.

The town's major building is the Palazzo Ducale (now in use as an art gallery), which was transformed from an old fortress into a extensive Renaissance palace starting in 1444.

ORVIETO

Location: Central Italy (Umbria)
Best time to travel: throughout the year
www.orvietoturismo.it
www.orvietoturismo.com

Orvieto's origins go back to Etruscan times when the town was settled above the Paglia Valley. During the course of some 3,000 years of human activity here, a labyrinth of caves both large and small has developed within the depths of the underlying mountain, interconnected via stairs and passages. The town's inhabitants also dug into the soft rock to remove "pozzolan", which can be mixed with water to make a cement-like material.

Orvieto cathedral is considered one of the most beautiful in Italy. It took 500 years to build and was not completed until the end of the 17th century.

ASSISI

Location: Central Italy (Umbria)
Best time to travel:
throughout the year
www.assisionline.com
www.bellaumbria.net

St Francis of Assisi was born here in 1182 and founded the mendicant Franciscan order in 1210. He was canonized in 1228, two years after his death, the same year that work began on the construction of the Basilica di San Francesco where he was buried in 1230. The church, which consists of an upper and lower basilica, is decorated with magnificent frescoes – it is considered to be Italy's largest church of artworks.

Situated on a rocky promontory beneath the summit of Monte Subasio, Assisi, Italy's principal pilgrimage site, can be seen from all around.

PERUGIA

Location: Central Italy (Umbria)
Best time to travel:
throughout the year
turismo.comune.perugia.it
www.bellaumbria.net

Perugia, the capital of Umbria, is situated on a range of hills between the Tiber Valley and Lake Trasimeno. It was an important town even in Etruscan times and remains so today, a fact evidenced by its university and the historical buildings that give Perugia's Old Town its very special atmosphere, with narrow, often covered alleyways, and splendid squares.

The Piazza IV Novembre and the Palazzo dei Priori lie at the heart of the Old Town. The Fontana Maggiore was built in 1278, and the fountain is still fed with water from the hills around the town.

Italy

CERVETERI, TARQUINIA

Location: Central western Italy (Lazio)
Best time to travel:
April–October
www.comune.cerveteri.rm.it
www.ufficioturistico.
comunetarquinia.it

The Etruscans created one of the most advanced civilizations in the western world, building roads, bridges, and irrigations systems, and gaining fame as potters, metalworkers and goldsmiths. They taught the Romans the secret of writing and bequeathed to them their alphabet. Their origins are uncertain – areas of modern-day Tuscany, Umbria, and Lazio were settled around 1000 BC, but the Etruscan language, the oldest surviving works of art, and recent genetic research suggest that it was actually immigrants from Lydia in Asia Minor (modern-day Izmir on the Turkish coast) who mixed with the local population to form Etruscan culture. The highpoint of the culture, around 600 BC, is evident from the multitude of first-class art objects which have been discovered in the region of Tuscany. The Etruscans controlled the whole of central Italy by this time but had no centralized polity, instead forming a federation of city states ruled by the aristocracy. One of the principal pillars of Etruscan wealth was the mining and refining of metal ore in Tuscany and the island of Elba, and the other was seafaring. Initially productive sea trade with the Greeks soon gave way to military campaigns, however, and the Etruscan fleets were defeated. Skirmishes with the Celts, the Gauls, and the Romans further weakened the Etruscans, who finally made peace with the Roman Empire, which assimilated their culture in about 100 BC. The rich archeological finds in

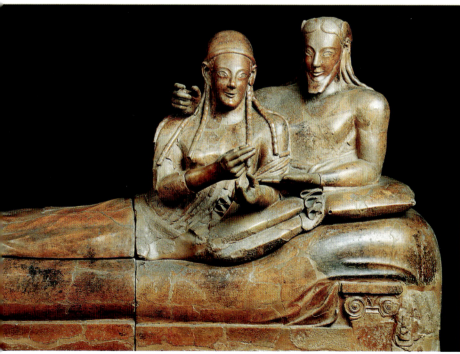

their *necropoleis* are particularly informative about their culture. The Etruscan "cities of the dead" of Cerveteri and Tarquinia in the provinces of Rome and Viterbo are not only evidence of the widely varying burial practices of the earliest civilization in the northern Mediterranean, but also an insight into their everyday lives. There are several varying kinds of tomb: burial chambers carved out of the tuff and covered with mounds of earth or tuff rubble known as tumuli, passage graves, simple burials, and rock tombs. The common factor with all these burial sites is the attempt to make the grave look like a dwelling – the masons have carved columns, tables, beds, and benches out of the rock, which is decorated with reliefs, and occasionally even paintings. The graves are a real insight into Etruscan life. The extensive cemeteries almost resemble an underground city with streets and courtyards and monuments. Tarquinia's frescos, many of which have still survived, are a highlight, with more than 200 painted grave sites having been uncovered so far; these often depict the relaxed and privileged life of the Etruscan aristocracy.

Painted in 530, the frescos in the "Priest's Tomb" are among the most impressive finds in the Etruscan necropolis at Tarquinia (top).

Trade with the Greeks brought the Etruscans Corinthian ceramics with black figures painted on the vessels, and these influenced the style of their domestic creations (far left, a Greek amphora unearthed in Cerveteri). Other popular motifs included everyday scenes and representations of myths.
Left: an Etruscan sarcophagus lid from Cerveteri depicting a married couple.

Italy

NAPLES

Location: South-western Italy (Campania)
Best time to travel: throughout the year
www.inaples.it
www.comune.napoli.it

The historic center of Naples, capital of the province of the same name, dates back to the Greek settlement of Partenope, whose Old Town was eventually expanded with a new town ("Neapolis"). Numerous Mediterranean cultures – from the Greeks to the Normans and the Spanish Bourbons – have all made their mark here. Time seems to have stood still in some parts of the city, and the fact that it dates back to a Greek settlement from the 5th century BC can be seen in the remains of a market from ancient Neapolis, the ruins of which were found under the Gothic San Lorenzo Maggiore Church. Next to the Chapel of St Januarius is the 6th-century Santa Restituta Basilica, a proud testament to the early prevalence of paleo-Christianity belief in the region. Located inside the San Gennaro Church, the basilica features ancient columns and a baptistry from the 4th century. San Gennaro also has important catacombs. The Castel Nuovo, residence of the Neapolitan kings and viceroys, dates back to the 13th century. The city councilors today meet in the castle's Sala dei Baroni, with its ornate star vault. The Palazzo Reale was built between 1600 and 1602 based on designs by Domenico Fontana.

"Old Naples" is to be found down by the port, with busy sellers racing through the narrow lanes on mopeds and storekeepers displaying a variety of wares. The crib scenes, presepi in Italian, from the stores on the Via San Gregorio Armeno are extremely popular.

Italy

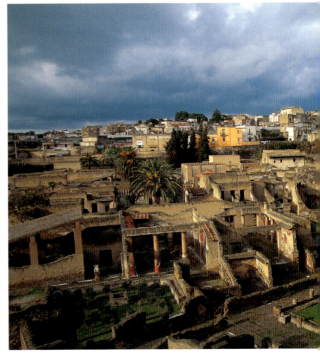

POMPEII

Location: South-western Italy (Campania)
Best time to travel: throughout the year
www.pompeiturismo.it

Vesuvius erupted on August 24 of the year AD 79, completely covering the Roman town of Pompeii under a layer of ash within roughly six hours. The neighboring town of Herculaneum was also smothered under glowing lava. After the eruption, the towns were not rebuilt and were eventually forgotten. However, Pliny the Younger (ca. AD 61–113), whose uncle and adopted father were killed by the eruption, had described the event, which pointed archaeologists in the right direction. The first excavations began in 1748, and today the resulting finds provide an invaluable impression of life in antiquity. The remains of shops and the painted walls of splendid villas were still left standing; even petrified bread was found in the bakeries. Other discoveries included a mill, a latrine, and some "graffiti" on the walls. The stepping stones that enabled passers-by to cross the street without getting their feet wet are even still visible. The dead are the most impressive, however, their bodies forming hollows of volcanic ash. Filled with plaster, the human figures are now visible again as sadly authentic and silent witnesses of the eruption.

Vesuvius (top), the only remaining active volcano in mainland Europe, lies only 15 km (9 mi) from Pompeii. Excavations in the layer of lava and ash have been unearthing finds from the settlement since the 18h century (below, middle). This representation of two gods (far left) or the double portrait of Paquius Proculus and his wife (left) are just two of the treasures which have been discovered.

Italy

AMALFI COAST, CAPRI

Location: South-western Italy (Campania)
Best time to travel: throughout the year
www.amalfitouristoffice.it
www.aziendaturismopositano.it
www.turismoinsalerno.it
www.capritourism.com
www.capri.it

The small town of Amalfi on the Gulf of Salerno was once one of Italy's leading seafaring republics. Today the name is associated with one of the loveliest stretches of Mediterranean coastline. Cut straight into the cliffs in places, the Amalfitana coastal road connects the villages between Nerano and Salerno. It follows winding stretches of the shoreline for around 45 km (30 mi), continually providing spectacular views of the azure-blue ocean and the Costiera Amalfitana. The view from the garden of the Villa Cimbrone is especially lovely, as is that from the Villa Rufulo, both in Ravello. The villages are strung together like pearls with lemon groves and vineyards scattered between them. The world's oldest maritime law – the Tavole Amalfitane – has its origins in Amalfi, the most important town along this stretch of coast. The 9th-century cathedral, which can be reached by a magnificent flight of steps from the Piazza Duomo, is a source of local pride. "I have the feeling", wrote John Steinbeck of this town founded in the Middle Ages, "that the world is vertical in Positano. An unimaginably blue and green ocean washes up on the fine pebble beach in the bay". There are crossings to the island of Capri from this splendid town.

Amalfi (right) is the largest town along the coast here. Far right from top: the view from Ravello. Cosmopolitan Positano and Capri.

Italy

MATERA

Location: South-eastern Italy (Basilicata)
Best time to travel: March–October
www.materaturismo.it

The labyrinthine caves of Matera were still occupied until the 1950s, forming one of the largest slum areas in Italy whose inhabitants lived without electricity and water. An article about the unacceptable and unhygienic conditions here by Carlo Levi, the author of *Christ Stopped At Eboli*, forced the authorities to re-house the slum residents. The cave city was left to rot until the Italian government later stepped in with a program to save this unusual settlement in the mid-1980s.

The cathedral (built 1230–1270) looks out over the picturesque Old Town clinging to the hill.

ALBEROBELLO

Location: South-eastern Italy (Apulia)
Best time to travel: March–October
www.tuttoalberobello.it

As you travel through Apulia you will occasionally see tiny cottages for farmworkers and shepherds that have a domed roof made of slabs of limestone that have been joined without mortar. Alberobello, about 60 km (37 miles) from Bari on the Adriatic coast, is a town entirely composed of such *trulli*: white, cylindrical houses with dome-like stone roofs and a single room beneath. The walls are also made of gathered stones joined together without mortar. The *trulli* have a square floor plan inside.

Known as *trulli*, the roundhouses seem exotic and yet archaic.

CASTEL DEL MONTE

Location: South-eastern Italy (Apulia)
Best time to travel: March–October
www.turismo.regione.puglia.it

Built by the emperor Frederick II, who ruled over southern Italy as King of Sicily, this octagonal fortress is surrounded by tales of mystical numerology, and unites various elements of Classical, Islamic, and Gothic architecture. The Staufer emperor's castle was completed in 1250 and lies near Andria in Apulia's Terra di Bari. It consists of a regular octagon with eight equal octagonal towers surrounding an octagonal courtyard. The deep purple portal beneath its ancient gable is decorated with Arabic ornamentation. The alabaster and marble columns in the interior are a hint of its former glory, and some precious mosaic floors have survived. There is a striking lack of Christian symbols, and whether the emperor actually ever lived here is still unclear. It is not even known for sure for what purpose the castle was used; it may have been an imperial hunting lodge, but the unusual form of the structure has given rise to all kinds of speculation, much of which is based on numerology. The number eight was of magical importance in ancient Oriental and Arabic cultures, and Frederick may have been influenced in his design choice by the Islamic scholars with whom he came into contact, although the octagonal chapel within Aachen Cathedral is another possible inspiration.

The Castel del Monte – the "Crown of Apulia" symbolizes the might of the Staufer emperors. Each point of the octagonal structure, which combines ancient Islamic architecture with Gothic stylings, terminates in an octagonal tower.

AEOLIAN ISLANDS

Location: Southern Italy (Sicily)
Best time to travel:
March–October
www.isolelipari.it
www.lipari.com

This archipelago composed of solidified lava and volcanic tuff rock is the mythical kingdom of the Aeolus, the god of the winds and the inventor of sea travel, who once received the erring Odysseus. The Aeolian Islands, sometimes known as the Lipari Islands after their principal land mass, comprise Lipari, Vulcano, Alicudi, Filicudi, Salina, Panarea, and Stromboli. The islands came into being when the Tyrrhenian sea was created during the Pliocene, and the most spectacular of all is Stromboli, with its volcano of the same name. The volcano juts 1,000 m (3,300 ft) out of the sea; volcanic activity began here with older volcanoes about 40,000 years ago, and the crater floor is still covered with fissures from which small amounts of lava and red-hot ash are expelled, accompanied by the occasional violent explosion. Thousands of holiday-makers visit the Aeolian Islands each year seeking a road-free idyll and a close-up view of volcanic fireworks.

Italy is where the African and Eurasian tectonic plates meet, causing earthquakes and volcanic activity. The volcano on Stromboli, also known as the Isola di Fuoco, "Fire Island", is one of the most active volcanoes on earth (right). Far right: Filicudi (top) consists of three volcanic cones, none of which is active. The idyllic island of Salina (middle) lies to the northwest of Lipari. The quays of the Marina Corte in Lipari (below) are visited by speedboats which connect Lipari with the other Aeolian Islands and Sicily.

Italy

PALERMO, MONREALE

Location: Southern Italy (Sicily)
Best time to travel:
throughout the year
www.palermotourism.com

Palermo was the main base for the Carthaginian fleet in the First Punic War and went on to enjoy exceptional periods of prosperity under the Moors, Normans and the Hohenstaufens of Germany. Thankfully, a tremendous number of historic buildings have survived from all of these epochs. In the Old Town, Byzantine churches stand next to Moorish mosques, and baroque and Catalan palaces are juxtaposed with classical barracks and Arabian-style pleasure palaces. Highlights here include the splendid cathedral (top, right); the Norman Palace with the mosaic-embellished Cappella Palatina (top, far right), and the 16th-century Piazza Pretoria with the mannerism-style Fontana Pretoria. The San Cataldo, La Martorana and San Giovanni degli Eremiti churches, the La Zisa Palace, the Teatro Massimo, the catacombs of the Capuchin monastery, the National Gallery, and the Archaeological Museum are all worth seeing as well. The lively Vucciria market on the Piazza Caracciolo is nicknamed the "belly of Palermo". The kiosks and shops selling fish, meat, fruits, and vegetables are all strung together like an oriental souk along the narrow alleyways. Situated around 8 km (5 mi) from Palermo is the small episcopal town of Monreale. Monte Caputo provides fabulous views of the Sicilian capital.

Bottom, right: the Piazza Pretoria with its Fontana Pretoria was laid out in the 16th century. **Far right:** the mosaics in the cathedral at Monreale are a magnificent display of Bible stories over a total area of about 6,300 sq m (67,800 sq ft).

Italy

VALLE DEI TEMPLI, SELINUNT

Location: Agrigento, Southern Italy (Sicily)
Best time to travel: throughout the year
www.lavalledeitempli.it
www.provinciatrapani.com
www.sicilytourist.net

The Greeks began settling in Sicily in the 8th century BC, founding settlements such as Naxos, Messina, Catania, Syracuse, Gela, and Agrigento; the island quickly became the western epicenter of Greek culture. The Valli dei Templi, located close to the modern city of Agrigento on the southern coast of Sicily, contains the impressive ruins of Akragas, one of the major Greek colonies and trading hubs in the Mediterranean. The ancient Greek minstrel and composer of lyrical odes Pindar called the city the "fairest of the mortals". The archeological site of the Valley of the Temples now stretches along the still-visible ancient city walls. Founded in the 7th century BC by the Dorians, Selinunt was one of the most important Greek towns on Sicily and was sacked by the Carthaginians in 250 BC. Several impressive buildings on the gigantic ruin site have at least in part survived many earthquakes and the permanent use of the site as a stone quarry.

The Valli dei Templi (top) contains a whole series of ruined Doric temples as evidence of the heyday of the Greek colony of Akragas in the 5th century BC.

The Temple of Hercules with its eight reconstructed columns (far right) was built around 500 BC. No less than nine temple complexes have been unearthed on the acropolis and two other hills at Selinunt.

Italy

MOUNT ETNA, TAORMINA

Location: Southern Italy (Sicily)
Best time to travel:
April–October
turismo.provincia.ct.it
www.vulcanoetna.com
www.taormina-sicily.it
www.taorminanetwork.it

Unlike the highly explosive Vesuvius near Naples, Mt Etna is a "good mountain": it erupts consistently and calmly instead of unexpectedly and intensely, and its lava contains little in the way of gases, making the volcano less explosive. The fertile volcanic soils support extensive agriculture, with vineyards and orchards spread across the lower slopes of the mountain and the broad Plain of Catania to the south. Provided one sticks to the signposted paths, it is safe to make an excursion up to the 3,000 m (9,843 ft) peak – an unforgettable experience. Anyone looking to keep more of a distance can enjoy a wonderful hike around its lower slopes. The whole east coast of Sicily is dominated by the silhouette of Etna, and the town of Taormina, the most frequently visited settlement on the island. Its idyllic location on a cliff high above the ocean and its ancient amphitheater ensured that Taormina was to become a popular destination as far back as the 19th century. Founded in the 4th century BC, Taormina was Greek for more than 200 years before ultimately falling to Rome in 215 BC.

Right: Etna looms over Siciliy's entire east coast (top). There are good views to be had from the terraces of Taormina's Piazza IX Aprile, 200 m (660 ft) above the sea (middle), and from the Teatro Greco, one of the most beautiful settings for a theater in the world (bottom). Opposite: Etna is just as fiery thankfully not as explosive as Vesuvius.

Italy

VAL DI NOTO, SYRACUSE

Location: Southern Italy (Sicily)
Best time to travel:
throughout the year
www.valdinoto.com
www.costierabarocca.it

A violent earthquake in 1693, which cost the lives of almost 100,000 people, caused the eight towns of the Val di Noto – the provincial capital of Catania and Caltagirone, Militello Val di Catania, Modica, Noto, Palazzolo Acreidi, Ragusa, and Scicli – to begin an extensive building program, creating an unusual concentration of late baroque architecture. Despite considerable dilapidation, the eight towns still display much of the creative inspiration that gave rise to their buildings, and the splendor of European baroque has been brought to life once again. At first glance it is difficult to imagine that 2,300 years ago, the provincial capital of Syracuse had a population of more than a million and was one of the mightiest Greek towns in southern Italy, functioning both as a commercial hub and as a center of philosophy and science. However, a stroll through the ruins of Old Town, the historic heart of Syracuse, will be enough to reveal its early magnificence.

Top: the semi-circular Piazza Duomo in Syracuse, the most important city in ancient Sicily, is lined with baroque *palazzi* and the early Christian cathedral of Santa Maria delle Colonne. Bottom: the Elephant Fountain on the Piazza del Duomo (left) is the heraldic symbol of Catania. The most important building in the Upper Town of Ragusa is the Duomo San Giovanno (1706–1760, middle). The Palazzo Ducezio (1746) in Noto is now the Town Hall (far right).

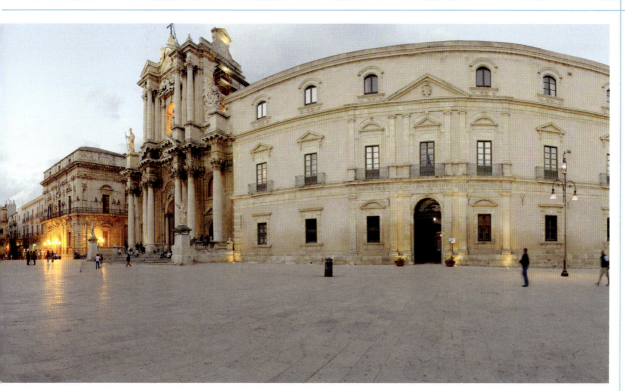

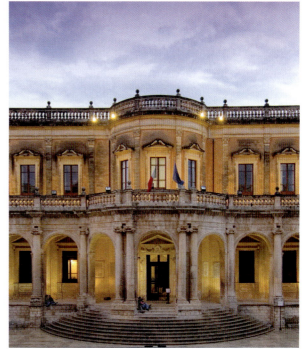

SARDINIA

Location: Island off western Italy
Best time to travel:
April–October
www.sardegnaturismo.it
www.marenostrum.it

Sardinia is the second-largest island in the Mediterranean after Sicily and has a tremendous cultural heritage to match its magnificent natural splendor. Over thousands of years, the Phoenicians, Romans, Vandals, Byzantines, Moors, Pisans, Genoese, Aragonese, Spanish, and mainland Italians have all left their mark here. Nevertheless, Sardinia was able to maintain its own language and culture. The north is the most popular region with magnificent diving, various watersports, and sailing. It features quaint villages with ancient, labyrinthine town centers, good infrastructure, and a romantic landscape with granite cliffs and dark maquis shrub land in the interior. The "Costa Smeralda", the Emerald Coast where the Aga Khan created an exclusive holiday resort in the early 1960s, is of course legendary. Archaeological sites include the Li Muri "Tomba dei Giganti" (Giants' Grave). The Capo d'Orso rock formations are one of the landmarks of the Costa Smeralda, with its clear blue bays and idyllic landscape. Just a few miles wide, the Bocca di Bonifacio separates the Capo Testa from the bizarre rock formations of the island of Corsica to the north. This group of tiny islands belong to the Parco Nazionale dell'Arcipélago de la Maddalena to the north-east of Sardinia. There are 62 in total. The Capo Caccia is Sardinia's westernmost point. The Grotta di Nettuno can be reached via the Escala del Cabirol with its 656 steps.

Capo Caccia is the westernmost point of Sardinia. The north-western coast of Sardinia is well-known for its coral.

Malta

VALLETTA

Location: Malta
Best time to travel: April–October
www.visitmalta.com
www.cityofvalletta.org

Surrounded by the sea on three sides, Valletta is situated on a 60-m (200-ft) high cliff on the northern coast of Malta. Control over the town of Valletta changed hands many times over the centuries starting with the Phoenicians and moving on to the Greeks, the Carthaginians, the Romans, Byzantium, and the Moors un- til it was finally handed over to the Order of St John following the Turk- ish siege of 1565. Their leader Jean Parisot de la Vallette founded the town anew after the siege was lifted and Valletta was named after him. It then grew into a fortified town, characteristic of the 16th century, and was extended between 1566 and 1571 to designs by the archi- tects Girolamo Casar and Francesco Laparelli, one of the Medici's military designers and a pupil of Michelangelo. The Order of St John

proceeded to construct a series of Renaissance and baroque palaces, churches and hospices within its walls, the Order's newly-found confidence and wealth being expressed in the magnificent décor of the Grand Master's palace and its two courtyards. The baroque church of Our Lady of Victory was built as a sign of gratitude for having survived the siege of 1567. St John's Co-Cathedral, built between 1573 and 1578 as a burial place for the knights of the Order, was decorated with ceiling frescoes and magnificent side chapels. The library founded by the order in 1555 houses valuable manuscripts. The Manoel Theatre dating from 1731 can be found within the labyrinth of alleys and steps and is one of the oldest stages in Europe. Stage productions are also in English.

The principal church in the Maltese capital of Valletta is the imposing St. John's Co-Cathedral, with its ornate interior and magnificent side chapels (left; right, a rather lovely depiction of the Madonna).

MEGALITHIC TEMPLES

Location: Malta
Best time to travel: April–October
www.heritagemalta.org

Malta's coral limestone monuments are older than the Egyptian pyramids and no less mysterious – their exact meaning is still disputed, but they are assumed to have been shrines dedicated to the *magna mater*, a mother goddess. The monuments were thought to be of Phoenician origin until well into the 20th century, when modern dating methods revealed the true age of what are the oldest stone temples in the world. Of the seven great temple complexes, the one at Gigantija on the island of Gozo is the oldest. Surrounded by a wall, the two temples consist of a series of horseshoe-shaped chambers arranged like a cloverleaf around a central courtyard. The temples on the main island of Malta follow a similar pattern. The façades of the structures at Hagar Qim are 12 m (39 ft) high and were probably completed around 2000 BC. Excavations have unearthed numerous religious sculptures, of which the most famous is probably the Venus of Malta. The façades of the religious site at Mnajdra are covered with ornate reliefs of a particular beauty surpassed only by the temples discovered at Tarxienin 1914.

Mysterious megalithic temples on the south-eastern coast of Malta

HYPOGEUM HAL SAFLIENI

Location: Malta
Best time to travel:
April–October
www.heritagemalta.org

Construction work at Paola near Valletta in 1902 revealed a gigantic underground chamber complex of several levels in which the remains of more than 7,000 people had

been laid to rest. A shrine at ground level had once marked the entrance to this *hypogeum* ("that which lies under the earth"), a subterranean labyrinth of many passageways, chambers, and niches reaching down more than 10 m (33 ft) below ground and covering a total surface area of about 500 sq m (5,400 sq ft). It has since been es-

tablished that the oldest parts of the *hypogeum* were dug out around the year 3000 BC using simple Neolithic tools such as animal horns and stone adzes, and extended over a period of about 1,300 years. The *hypogeum* was used both as a cemetery and as a religious site. The center of the necropolis also houses a sanctuary, and this may

have been used for initiation rites rather than devoted to public worship or religious observance.

The *hypogeum* at Hal Saflieni on Malta is an underground temple complex and one of the oldest Neolithic burial grounds and religious sites in the world.

Poland

WARSAW

Location: Central Poland
Best time to travel:
throughout the year
www.e-warsaw.pl
www.warsaw-hotel-guide.net

Rise, occupation, and reconstruction – the changing fortunes of the Polish capital reflect the turbulent history of the the whole country: the first phase of prosperity was ushered in when King Sigismund III moved his court from Krakow to Warsaw in 1600, but this was swiftly followed by the depredations of the Swedes and then a Renaissance at the hands of the Wettins, a dynasty of princes from Saxony. The Russians gained control of the city after the division of Poland in 1815, and it was completely destroyed by the Germans during World War II. It took the Communists less than ten years to rebuild the city completely – reconstructing the Old Town using the original plans, although the rest of the city was rebuilt according to the precepts of Socialist Functionalism. The city's skyline is still dominated by the 230-m (755-ft) high Palace of Culture (top) which was built between 1952 and 1955.

According to legend, Warsaw was founded by Wars and his sister Zawa at the command of a water sprite, a myth commemorated by the statue of the naiad Syrenka on the market place (above right; left, the Knights' Hall in the castle.

GDANSK

Location: Northern Poland
Best time to travel:
throughout the year
www.en.gdansk.gda.pl

Gdansk has a history going back more than 1,000 years. It maintained close trade relations with Flanders, Russia and Byzantium, and this continued well into the 12th and 13th centuries. Danzig, as it was known, was a member of the Hanseatic League from 1361 and was assigned to the Polish crown in 1466. With ninety-five percent of the city in ruins at the end of World War II, Gdansk has since become a model of reconstruction work. The most important attractions are naturally in the city center. St Mary's Church, for example, is the largest medieval brick church in Europe, its most striking feature being the 82-m (269-ft) high bell tower. The city's Old Town comprises Long Street and the streets adjoining it. Influential patricians built magnificent palaces for themselves in the heart of the Old Town. The 15th-century Arthur's Court is among the finest examples of late-Gothic architecture in Northern Europe; the town hall, the Golden House and the Torture House are also worth seeing.

The Crane Gate on the Motlawa in Gdansk was a city gate during the Middle Ages and was later converted for use as a loading crane.

Poland

MALBORK

Location: Northern Poland
Best time to travel:
throughout the year
www.polish-online.com
www.visitmalbork.pl

A white cloak with a black cross was the uniform of the Teutonic Knights, an order of knights that formed in the Holy Land during the Third Crusade (1189–1192). The knights turned their attention to Europe just a few decades later and Prussia, along with Livonia and Courland, were subordinated and Christianized in the name of the black cross. Given sovereign powers as landlords by the emperor, the order founded towns, built castles, brought in German farmers as colonists, and promoted the arts and science. At the head of the order was the Grand Master, who was elected for life and whose seat and main fortress after 1309 was here in Malbork Castle on

FROMBORK

Location: Northern Poland
Best time to travel:
throughout the year
www.frombork.pl
www.frombork.art.pl

The small town of Frombork in Warmia is culturally the most interesting town in the region with its historic complex located on the cathedral hill. The museum next to the cathedral is dedicated to the important work of the astronomer Nicolaus Copernicus. He developed his theory of a heliocentric solar system, which displaced the Earth from the center of the universe, here in the 16th century. The water tower provides lovely views of the Vistula Lagoon and the port.

Nicolaus Copernicus, the dean of Frauenburg Cathedral (14th century).

the Nogat River. It was here that all of the threads of the order's states came together, its territories extending far into the Baltic States as well as into southern and central Germany. The costly Battle of Tannenberg in 1410 against the more superior Poles and Lithuanians is seen to represent the beginning of their decline. Held with some effort until 1457, Malbork Castle finally fell into Polish hands in 1466 with the Peace of Torun. The story of the holy state came to a definitive end in 1525 when it became the secular Duchy of Prussia with Albrecht von Brandenburg-Ansbach as its first duke. It later became a hereditary duchy under Polish sovereignty during the Reformation.

The castle precincts of Malbork, the official residence of the leader of the Teutonic Knights between 1309 and 1457, are surrounded by mighty walls and towers.

TORUN

Location: Northern Poland
Best time to travel: throughout the year
www.torun.pl

The knights of the Teutonic Order built a castle here, and a commercial center developed around it in the 14th century. The town even maintained its own merchant fleet for the purposes of trading with the Netherlands. The First and the Second Peace of Torun were concluded here in 1411 and 1466 between the Teutonic Order and Poland. In 1454 the Teutonic Order castle was burnt down by the citizens of Torun (only remnants survive to this day) and the town became an independent city-state under the sovereignty of the Polish king.

The 14th-century Church of St Mary's is just one of the imposing churches in the city.

THE MASURIAN LAKE DISTRICT

Location: Northern Poland
Best time to travel:
April–October
www.visitpoland.org
www.poland.travel

There is no denying the magic of this district. Hikers, cyclists, and canoeists alike can all enjoy the thoroughly fascinating water landscape here. More than 3,000 lakes are linked via rivers and canals, all mingling with wonderful forests. Gnarled trees shade cobblestone alleys that are still traveled by horse-drawn carts, while storks build their nests in the tops of the steeples. A visit to Masuria is like taking a journey back in time to the early 20th century. Olsztyn is the main center of the Masuria region as well as the perfect starting point for excursions to a number of different sightseeing attractions, including Lidzbark Warminskj with its mighty castle that used to be the seat of the Warmia bishops. Reszel Castle nearby dates back to the 13th century. The powerful Teutonic Knights built a castle in Ketrzyn in 1329. Beyond Ketrzyn there is a sign pointing to the north-east indicating the *Wolfsschanze* ("Wolf's Lair"), which Hitler built in 1939, as his headquarters. The pilgrimage church of Swieta Lipka is a baroque gem.

The natural paradise of the Masurian Lakes: more than 350 species of bird have found a habitat here.

BIALOWIEZA

Location: North-eastern Poland
Best time to travel: April–Oktober
www.bpn.com.pl
www.bialowieza-info.eu

Despite the extreme temperatures here, which often sink well below freezing point in winter, this cross-border national park possesses an astounding level of biodiversity.

There are some 3,000 types of mushrooms and more than a dozen species of orchids. The heavily protected central zone of the park is home to the highest trees in all of Europe: 55-m (180-ft) high spruces and 40-m (131-ft) high ash trees. The Polish government began using zoo animals to breed European bison in the 1920s, with a scheduled program

of reintroducing them into the wild in 1952. Hunting had made these primeval oxen almost extinct by the end of the 19th century, but today there are around 300 of them wandering the vast forest areas again. They are the largest species of big game in Europe. The wild horses that used to be found throughout Eurasia and which no longer exist in the wild

have also found a refuge in this protected haven. In addition to rare mammals such as bears, moose, lynxes and wolves, the area is also home to more than 220 different bird species.

Bison have been released into the wild to live in the national park.

Poland

JAWOR, SWIDNICA

Location: Western Poland
Best time to travel: throughout the year
www.jawor.pl
www.pl-info.net

The Peace of Westphalia sealed the end of the Thirty Years' War in 1648 and after this point, Protestants in Hapsburg-ruled Silesia were allowed to build churches only under certain conditions: they had to stand outside the city walls and could be built only of wood, clay, sand, and straw. Bell towers were also forbidden. The newer belief abided by the rules, but decorated the inside of their churches all the more magnificently. The Evangelical Church of Peace in Swidnica, a UNESCO Heritage site, was built from 1656–57, and the plain façade of the church conceals a wealth of ornate ceiling frescos from the late 17th century. The magnificent church also houses a large organ, and a baroque high altar was added in 1752. With several storeys of galleries and boxes for the aristocratic families, more than 7,500 people could be accommodated in the church's interior. Jawor's Peace Church has a similarly magnificent interior. Both buildings were, until recently, in a rather desolate state but a number of German-Polish cross-border initiatives have begun a program of painstaking restoration.

The Protestant Peace Churches in Jawor and Swidnica are the largest half-timbered churches in Europe and certainly belong among the most beautiful churches in Silesia. The paintings in the galleries in the Peace Church at Jawor (right) depict scenes from the Old and New Testament. The ornate pulpit (opposite) in the Peace Church at Swidnica was built by Gottfried August Hoffmann in 1729.

Poland

KRAKOW

Location: Southern Poland
Best time to travel:
throughout the year
www.krakow-poland.com
www.krakow.pl

Krakow was the capital of the Polish kings until 1596, and their coronation venue from the 11th to the 18th centuries. Wawel Hill with its royal castle and cathedral remains a striking testimony to this bygone era. The Old Town here was designed by master builders and artists from throughout Europe, from the 12th to the 17th centuries. The market square, one of Europe's largest medieval town squares, is the site of the textile halls and the Gothic St Mary's Church, converted in the 14th century. The famous high altar by Veit Stoss who created his most important works in Krakow between 1477 and 1496, can be found here. Pivotal medieval intellectuals taught at the university, founded in the 14th century. A number of Gothic, Renaissance and baroque buildings also demonstrate the city's rich history. The Kazimierz Quarter was once home to a thriving Jewish community where the Old Synagogue is worthy of special mention.

The Drapers' Halls in the middle of the market square (Rynek) were built in the 13th century. Above: the choir of St Mary's Church is dominated by Veit Stoss' High Altar (completed 1477 to 1489).

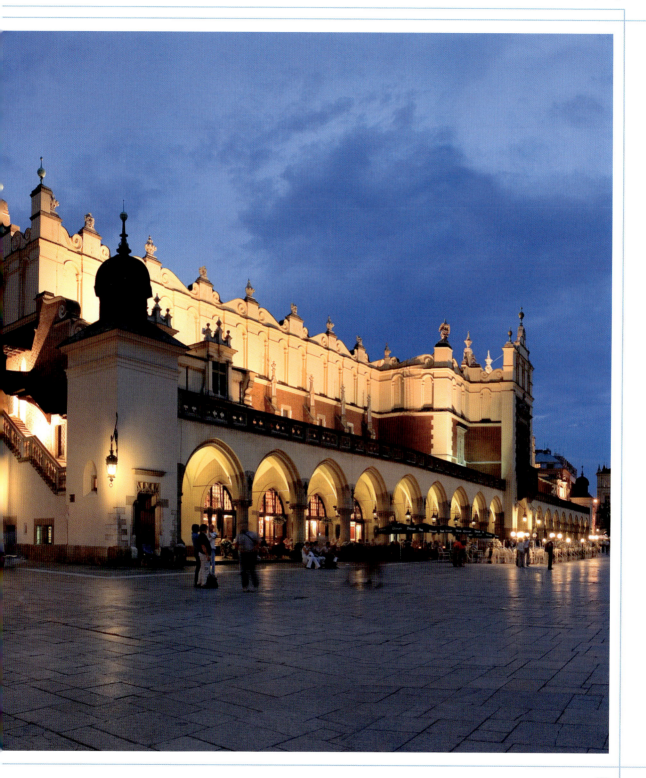

Poland

ZAMOŚĆ

Location: South-east Poland
Best time to travel:
throughout the year
www.zamosc.pl

Every aspect of life was thought of during the planning of the town of Zamość in the province of Lublin: two market squares form the heart of a city which was to be settled by Armenians, Jews, Greeks, Italians, and Germans, creating a vibrant multi-national community. The town houses built around the squares are decorated with impressive arcades and ornate façades. The Town Hall was built between 1639 and 1651, although the monumental baroque steps are an 18th-century addition. St Thomas' Church of the Resurrection, built between 1587 and 1598, is perhaps the most beautiful church of the late Polish Renaissance. Built between 1610 and 1620, the interior of the former synagogue is an explosion of masterfully executed stucco work. The town's fortifications were completed in 1587 and survived until 1866, when they were demolished. Rosa Luxemburg, the well-known Marxist theorist, philosopher, economist, and activist was born on the market place at Zamość and her birth house can be seen to this day.

Zamość Town Hall has a magnificent set of swung steps and is topped with a 52-m (170-ft) octagonal tower. It is surrounded by charming Renaissance houses, with their ornate parapets, which were once occupied by Armenian merchants.

WOODEN CHURCHES OF SOUTHERN LITTLE POLAND

Location: Southern Poland
Best time to travel: April–October
www.wrotamalopolski.pl
www.visit.malopolska.pl

The wooden churches of Little Poland are rectangular buildings constructed from horizontally stacked tree trunks. This technique was widespread in eastern Europe but is less well-known in Roman Catholic Churches. The wooden churches were commissioned by aristocratic families in the villages of Binarowa, Blizne, Debno, Haczow, Lachowice, Lipnica Murowana, Orawka, Sekowa, and Szalowaim in southern Little Poland. With one exception, they were all completed in the 15th and 16th centuries, and the best artisans and artists of the period were involved in their construction. The churches are complicated structures with ornate painted interiors and are very well preserved. The churches initially had no towers; these are later additions, intended to reflect the status of the commissioning families. The churches have been constantly extended since their construction, with the interiors especially being adapted to the taste of the day.

The traditional wooden churches all have very different architectural styles, and they were acknowledged by UNESCO in 2003. Although rather modest from the outside, the churches are extremely ornate inside, such as this one at Haczow. Inside, valuable figural wall paintings dating from 1494 can be s. It is believed to be the biggest Gothic wooden church in Europe.

Czech Republic

PRAGUE

Location: Central Czech Republic
Best time to travel:
throughout the year
www.prague-tourist.com

The unique beauty of the historic buildings in the "Golden City", combined with centuries as a European intellectual and cultural capital have made Prague a truly wonderful place to visit. Despite having been spared much of the destruction of World War II, the ravages of time have nevertheless left a definite mark on the city. Thankfully, however, renovations have seen this more than 1,000-year-old city on the banks of the Vltava River restored to its former glory. Indeed, the Czechs have every reason to be proud of their lovely capital, which was formerly a grand residence of the Bohemian kings and seat of the Hapsburg emperors. Their former place of residence, the Vysehrad, also provides the best views of this marvel of historical urban development.

Construction of the Charles Bridge (right) in Prague was begun under Charles IV in 1357. The master builder Peter Parler took his inspiration from the stone bridge in Regensburg.

Far right: the Old Town Square is about 9,000 sq m (97,000 sq ft) in size. It was originally a central market place for merchants, but was also used as a stopping point for the coronation processions of Bohemian kings, and as a place of execution. The houses of the Golden Lane (middle) were built beside the castle walls in the 16th century to provide accommodation for guards and artisans. Franz Kafka lived in one for a number of years. The Old New Synagogue in Prague (bottom) is the only synagogue of its age on European soil where Jewish services are still held.

Czech Republic

FRANTISKOVY LAZNE

Location: Western Czech Republic
Best time to travel: throughout the year
www.franzensbad.cz
www.czechtourism.com

People have been enjoying the healing power of the waters at Frantiskovy Lazne since the 15th century. The springs are some 5 km (3 mi) north of the town of Cheb (or Eger) which was the Bohemian regional capital and a fortress town. In 1661, the first filling house was built at the mineral water source, and a bathhouse was later added in 1694. A town was officially founded in 1793 and was initially named "Kaiser Franzendorf" after the Austrian Emperor Franz II (1768–1835).

Frantiskovy Lazne, home of one of the first mud baths in Europe.

KARLOVY VARY

Location: Western Czech Republic
Best time to travel: throughout the year
www.karlovy-vary.cz
www.karlsbad.cz

Emperor Charles IV (1316–1378) was allegedly the first to discover the salt springs here in Karlovy Vary, formerly called Carlsbad, while out on a stag hunt. Some 500 years later, Bohemia's most extravagant health resort had developed around the site and the political, artistic, and social elite of Europe began meeting here. In 1989, after fifty years of decline, the resort experienced a dazzling rebirth and most of the grandiose Wilhelminian buildings are resplendent once again.

Karlovy Vary, one of the most famous spa towns in the world, is located at the confluence of the Tepla and the Eger rivers.

MARIANSKE LAZNU

Location: Western Czech Republic
Best time to travel:
throughout the year
www.marianskelazne.cz
www.marienbad.com

Marianske Laznu is a spa resort town surrounded by green mountains, parks, and mansions. It is also where Goethe wrote his Marienbad Elegy, a pained farewell by the poet to his "last love", Ulrike von Levetzow, after their final breakup. The baths have been completely restored, with pretty stucco façades painted in the "emperor's yellow" color of Vienna's Schönbrunn castle. Particularly magnificent is the 120-m (394-ft) long colonnade made out of cast iron.

Nove Laznu Spa Hotel where the customer is king, and where kings are often customers.

Czech Republic

CESKY KRUMLOV

Location: South-western
Czech Republic
Best time to travel:
throughout the year
www.ckrumlov.info

The location of this town is simply enchanting, situated as it is on both sides of a narrow bend in the Vltava River. The Old Town's labyrinthine alleyways like those in the Latran quarter, with its lovely shingled-roof houses, could hardly be more picturesque. The Gothic St Veit's Church and the Schiele Center form the highlights of any tour. The main attraction, however, is the glorious castle, Bohemia's second-largest after the Vysehrad in Prague. The collection of Flemish tapestries and the art gallery are especially worth seeing.

The iconic castle and tower (1257)

HOLASOVICE

Location: South-western
Czech Republic
Best time to travel:
throughout the year
www.czechtourism.com
www.holasovice.eu

The Bohemian King Wenceslas II donated several villages to the Abbey of Vyssí Brod in 1292, including the small village of Holasovice, which retained a close link with the monastery for over five centuries. It was only at the beginning of the 19th century that the first stone buildings were built on the site of this medieval village, and it was between 1840 and 1880 that the buildings acquired their present-day appearance.

The houses of Holasovice with their decorated gables ends are among the loveliest examples of simple peasant architecture.

TELC

Location: Southern Czech Republic
Best time to travel:
throughout the year
www.telc-etc.cz

The town of Telc was founded in Moravia in the 12th century, but was soon destroyed in a great fire. Its modern appearance is due to the efforts of Prince Zachariah of Rosenberg-Neuhaus, a great fan of the Renaissance, who converted the Gothic castle into a magnificent palace. Further Renaissance buildings were added and the local bourgeoisie who had grown rich through trade had their Gothic houses similarly adorned with ornamental gables and *trompe-l'oeil* paintings, or simply demolished them and built new ones.

Both sides of the market place at Telc are lined with a unique ensemble of historic town houses.

TREBIC

Location: Southern Czech Republic
Best time to travel:
throughout the year
www.trebic.cz
www.visittrebic.eu

Benedictine monks founded a monastery on the northern banks of the Jihlava river in 1101 and a market soon grew up around it, attracting many merchants, some of whom were Jewish; thus began the history of the town of Trebíc. The Basilica of St Procopus was built in the middle of the 13th century; it is mostly a Romanesque and Gothic structure, with baroque additions. The basilica survived the decline of the monastery and is considered one of the finest buildings of its period.

The baroque vaulting in the Basilica of St Procopus was added in the 18th century.

Czech Republic

LEDNICE-VALTICE

Location: Southern Czech Republic
Best time to travel:
May-September
www.lednicko-valticky-areal.cz
www.lednice.cz

A castle was built in Lednice in the mid-18th century to house a valuable art collection. A tree-lined boulevard was also laid out from here to Valtice, where a mighty castle had been built in the 17th century. Both castles are surrounded by 200 sq km (77 sq mi) of grounds containing pavillions, forests, lakes, and parks.

The first designs for the castle at Valtice (left) were drawn up by Giovanni Giacomo Tencalla. The modern appearance of the castle at Lednice (right) is the result of alterations carried out between 1846 and 1858.

OLOMOUC

Location: Eastern Czech Republic
Best time to travel:
throughout the year
www.olomouc-tourism.cz
www.discoverczech.com

The imposing Pillar of the Holy Trinity, standing in front of the Town Hall on Peace Square at the center of town was dedicated in the presence of the Empress Maria Theresia in 1754. The mason Wenzel Reder and the sculptor Andreas Zahner, who was born in Franconia, are just some of the famous artists associated with Olomouc. The goldsmith Simon Forstner created the gilt sculpture of the Holy Trinity located at the top of the pillar.

The Pillar of the Holy Trinity in Olomouc was the largest of this kind of column monument to be built in the 18th century.

KUTNÁ HORA

Location: Central Czech Republic
Best time to travel:
throughout the year
www.kutnahora.info
www.pragueexperience.com

In 1300, King Wenceslaus II commanded Florentine coin-makers to strike the "Prague Penny" at the Welsche Hof palace. This was just the beginning of Kutna Hora's rise to its status as one of the richest towns in Bohemia. The Welsche Hof was also used as a royal residence and underwent considerable alterations and restorations until the 19th century.

The Gothic St Jacob's Church (left), which now houses many art treasures. Frantisek Rint created a rather idiosyncratic interior for the Sedlec Ossuary out of the bones of 40,000 people (below).

Slovakia

SPIS CASTLE

Location: North-eastern Slovakia
Best time to travel:
May–September
www.spisskyhrad.sk
www.spisskyhrad.com

Medieval Spis Castle, one of the largest of its kind in Central Europe, was built on the site of an earlier Slavic fortress in Spis, a scenic region and historic administrative district in the foothills of the High Tatras. Following its sudden collapse, the 13th century tower house was subsequently replaced by a two-storey Romanesque palace with a new round tower. The castle chapel also dates back to the 13th century, when the castle survived an attack from the Mongolians almost without damage. Another fortress was built beneath the castle in the 15th century and both complexes underwent a Renaissance makeover in 1540. Spis Castle

CARPATHIANS

Location: North-eastern Slovakia and several other states
Best time to travel: throughout the year (Ski season: October–April)
www.carpathianparks.org

The Primeval Beech Forests of the Carpathians (a UNESCO world heritage site), are an outstanding example of undisturbed, complex temperate forests. They contain an invaluable genetic reservoir of beech and many species associated with, and dependent on, these forest habitats. They are also an outstanding example of the recolonization and development of terrestrial ecosystems and communities after the last Ice Age, a process which is still ongoing.

Pure beech woods and forests which are found in the Ukrainian and Slovakian Carpathians.

declined in importance after its capture by Hapsburg troops in 1710. Spisska Podhrahie and the Spisska Kapitula are located just a few miles away. Spisska Kapitula is today a municipal cultural reservation. The St Martin Cathedral is the dominant cultural monument in the village. It was built in 1245–1273, in the late Roman style with two towers. The cathedral has particularly valuable interior, including Gothic altars, statues, tomb stones, chalices, and bells. Inside the cathedral you will also find the oldest known Roman-style sculpture in Slovakia – Leo Albus. The early-Gothic Church of the Holy Spirit in lehra is also worth a visit.

After a fire in 1780, the castle lay in ruins for several centuries before being partially rebuilt in the 20th century. It now attracts many thousands of visitors every year.

BARDEJOV

Location: Eastern Slovakia
Best time to travel: throughout the year
www.e-bardejov.sk
www.slovakia.travel

Bardejov was founded on an old trade route into Poland in the 14th century, but its cultural heyday came in the 15th and 16th centuries, when the first library in the country was founded. No less than two printing presses were established, and a humanist grammar school also opened its doors here. The town's golden age ended in the 16th century, when several wars, pandemics, and other disasters plagued the country.

The market square at Bardejov is also the site of the Town Hall. Originally Gothic in style, it was later altered in a Renaissance style.

BUDAPEST

Location: Northern Hungary
Best time to travel: throughout the year
www.budapestinfo.hu
www.budapest.com

Buda, Óbuda (Old Buda) and Pest were all joined in 1872 to form "BudaPest," the new capital of the former Kingdom of Hungary. The royal castle town of Buda has largely retained its medieval character, with numerous Gothic and baroque buildings lining the narrow streets. Trinity Square lies at the center of the castle hill, which has been a municipality since the 17th century, and is dominated by the Church of Our Lady. Originally built in 1250, the church underwent a neo-Gothic conversion in the 19th century. The royal castle, built on the site of a structure that was destroyed in the great siege of 1686, was begun in 1749 and is located just to the south of the castle hill. The excavation sites of the Roman settlement of Aquincum, with its large amphitheater that accommodated some 13,000 spectators, can be found in Óbuda. The monumental, classical-style synagogue was erected in 1820 and is also worth visiting. Pest, which lies on the other side of the Danube, was a commercial hub and a center of intellectual life for the *haute bourgeoisie* of the 19th century. The parliament building, which architecturally has much in common with the Palace of Westminster in London, has a magnificent staircase and was built between 1885 and 1904 to plans by Imre Steidl. The Hungarian parliament has sat here since 1989. Built in the Secessionist (*Art Nouveau*) style and opened in 1918, the Gellért Hotel and the Gellért Baths are the most famous in Budapest. The men's baths, the outdoor pools, and the thermal and steam baths for women are opulent in their design and decorated with lovely mosaics.

The Danube is Budapest's principal artery. Nine bridges (left, the Elizabeth Bridge in the foreground, with the Chain Bridge behind it) connect the two parts of the city, Buda and Pest. The Fisherman's Bastion (top) was built between 1895 and 1902 on the site of the old fish market at Buda. The architect Frigyes Schulek, who was also responsible for the neo-Gothic restyling of St Matthew's Church, designed the strange towers of the structure to be reminiscent of the tents of the Magyar people.

ESTERHÁZY

Location: near Fertod, Western Hungary
Best time to travel: April–October
www.esterhazy.net
www.hungarytourism.hu

Esterházy Castle is located just a few miles south of Lake Neusiedl on the outskirts of the small town of Fertod, where it forms part of the Fertod-Hanság National Park. It was originally built at the beginning of the 18th century as a small hunting lodge and later expanded by Prince Nicholas I who took his inspiration from a visit to Versailles. In 1764 he commissioned the royal Viennese builders Ferdinand Mödlhammer and Melchior Hefele with the con-version, which was to take almost half a century. Esterhazy is also famous for having been the home of composer Joseph Haydn for several years. In fact, his famous Symphony No. 45 in F sharp minor was performed in the concert hall of the rococo castle for the first time in 1772. It is his legendary "Farewell Symphony", at the end of which the musicians leave the stage one by one. Today the middle wing of the castle is a public museum, and one of the side wings is now home to various schools.

Esterhazy, one of the most beautiful rococo palaces in the country, has been described as the "Hungarian Versailles".

PANNONHALMA

Location: Western Hungary
Best time to travel:
April–September
www.bences.hu

The former Benedictine abbey of St Martins in Pannonhalma, roughly 30 km (19 mi) south-east of Gyor, is still inhabited by monks today. The monastery was founded by Prince Géza (940–997), became an arch-abbey under King Stephen I, and has been the center of the Benedictine Order in Hungary ever since then. The oldest part of this sizable monastery is the collegiate church, consecrated in 1225 and constructed on the site of two previous buildings. With its strictly configured architecture, the complex remains impressive despite a number of extensive conversions. The crypt under the elevated choir was probably built on the foundations of the original church. In addition to lovely baroque stucco work and other classical elements, the collegiate church also houses a number of Romanesque and Gothic artworks. The 55-m (180-ft) high west tower was only built in 1830 during the classical conversion of the complex. A particular gem from this era is the ceremonial room of the Classical Library, built between 1824 and 1832.

King Stephen I is commemorated with a statue in the library. The monastery church has numerous late Romanesque and early Gothic touches.

HORTOBÁGY

Location: Eastern Hungary
Best time to travel:
April–September
national-park.hungaryguide.info

The landscape known as *puszta* ("desolate, remote area") was once forested before the Mongols and later the Turks burnt down all the villages and trees. The re- introduction of cattle rearing in the ares brought over-grazing and salti- fication, resulting in the landscape which can be seen today. The Horto- bágy National Park was founded in 1973 to promote traditional forms of agriculture. It was the first nation- al park in Hungary. Older domestic species such as Hungarian steppe cattle and water buffalo, which are now protected, are bred here to save them from extinction. Besides the cattle, the national park has an enormous wealth of local flora and fauna: dry and wet habitats alter- nate in close proximity with one an- other, creating ecological niches for many plants and animals, such as marsh and steppe flowers, birds, in- sects, and mammals.

The Hortobágy *puszta* with its draw-wells (top) is the largest contiguous natural grass steppe in Europe, and this protected environment has become a habitat for ancient Hungarian domestic species such as the racka sheep (left). Many bird species have also found a home here, including the barn swallow (right).

TOKAJI WINE REGION

Location: Eastern Hungary
Best time to travel: April–October (September/October: grape harvest)
www.tokaji.hu
www.tokaj.com

The Tokaj-Hegyalja wine region is situated in the northern reaches of the *puszta* near the Slovakian border with the Ukraine. It includes a total of 26 domains, of which the largest is the pretty little town of Tokaj on the banks of the Tisza. The town is named after the wine, which the Sun King Louis XIV said was *vinum regum, rex vinorum* ("the wine of kings, and the king of wines"). Tokaji, which is made from the furmint grape variety, is indeed one of the oldest and most fa-

mous of wines, and this little area in northern Hungary about 200 km (125 mi) east of Budapest, the capital, is its home. The entire Tokaji region is given over to the traditions and infrastructure of viticulture, creating a cultural landscape where people live from the vine. The quality of Tokaji vintages has been rigorously controlled for three centuries.

The area surrounding the historic Old Town of Tokaj, which is worth seeing in its own right, is crisscrossed with a warren of tunnels, cellars, casemates, and catacombs where the wine is stored. Since 2007, only authorised regional wine producers are able to use the Tokaj brand name. The name Tokay came to be used in the Alsace region.

Croatia

TROGIR

Location: Southern Croatia (Dalmatia)
Best time to travel:
April–September
www.trogir.hr
www.trogir-online.com

Trogir's beach promenade and Old Town are dominated by the St Nicholas tower of the Benedictine monastery and the clock tower of the St Laurence Cathedral. The Dalmatian port dates back to a Greek colony founded in 385 BC. The town, built on an island, fell under Byzantine control in the 6th century, after which the Croats, Bosnians, Hungarians, and Venetians disputed its possession, with the Republic of Venice ultimately gaining the upper hand from 1420 to 1797. The Benedictine monastery is home to reliefs and inscriptions dating from the 3rd to 1st centuries BC. The St Laurence Cathe-

POREČ

Location: North-western Croatia (Istria)
Best time to travel:
April–September
www.porec.hr
www.istra.hr

There have been Christians in Poreč since the 3rd century, and a chapel was built here in the 4th century to house the relics of St Maurus, the first bishop and a martyr. Little was left of him, and still less remains of the chapel today. The first large basilica was erected here in the 5th century, and was given its present appearance under Bishop Euphrasios in the 6th century.

The marble columns lining the interior of the Euphrasian Basilica, came from the island of Prokonnesos near ancient Constantinople (Istanbul).

dral, a Romanesque-Gothic work, houses masterpieces of medieval painting and its West portal, built in around 1240 by master builder Radovan from Trogir, is one of the most important stone works in Croatia. The town hall and the loggia with the clock tower date from the 15th century. Camerlengo Castle and the Markus Tower are part of the Venetian fortifications from the 15th and 16th centuries. Numerous Late Gothic as well as Renaissance and Baroque palaces and town houses have also been preserved. The main street running north-south in the center of town has been named the *Ulica Kohl-Genschera* in honor of the German chancellor and minister who campaigned for Croatian independence.

The spire of St Nicholas' Church and the bell tower of St Laurence's Cathedral overlook the marina promenade and the Old Town.

ROVINJ

Location: North-western Croatia (Istria)
Best time to travel: April–September
www.rovinj.com
www.rovinj.hr

For those in the know, this resort with its Venetian bell towers, brightly painted houses, enchanted lanes, and countless bathing beaches is one of the most beautiful towns on the coast. This rocky island has been inhabited since ancient times, and under Venetian rule, Rovinj was a flourishing center for fishing and commerce. Rovinj's heart lies in the magnificent late Renaissance clock tower on Trg Tita Square, which opens out onto the marina promenade with its cozy cafés, and the town museum.

Guaranteed good views: Rovinj's promenade.

Croatia

THE PLITVICE LAKES

Location: Central Croatia
Best time to travel: throughout the year (Ski season: October–April)
www.tzplitvice.hr

The 16 lakes of Plitvice Lakes National Park, close to the border with Bosnia-Herzegovina, are connected by terraces, cascades, and waterfalls and are testimony to the constantly changing yet pristine natural panorama of Croatian limestone. The chain of lakes extends over about 7 km (4 mi) and owes its existence to calcification and sinkholes. Over several thousand years the limestone sinter has formed barriers and dams behind which the water pools up: algae and mosses are the reason for the shimmering blue and green hues of the 12 larger lakes. The most impressive waterfalls, with drops of up to 76 m (249 ft), are near the four lower lakes. The lime-enriched water plunges over numerous terraces, themselves constantly collapsing and reforming, into tiny ponds. The Korana is the end of the lakes where the Plitvica flows out. The region at the foot of the mountain range known as the Small Kapela was declared a national park in 1949 and boasts rich flora and fauna. The dense forests are home to about 120 bird species as well as to deer, wolves and brown bears.

Natural barriers of travertine limestone divide the lakes, forming terraces which are constantly shifting as they erode, and these can generally be reached by visitors along a series of gangplanks, jetties, bridges, and catwalks, although some are only accessible by boat. Limestone caves are present as well and wait to be discovered.

Croatia

KORCULA

Location: Island off southern Croatia (Dalmatia)
Best time to travel: April–September
www.korculainfo.com
www.korcula.ca

The capital of the island of the same name is proud of the fact that it is Marco Polo's birthplace. The late-Gothic St Mark cathedral boasts modern sculptures that contrast with the Gothic tracery. Renaissance and baroque palaces line the alleyways of the Old Town, and Marco Polo House documents the life of the legendary sea voyager.

The beautiful Old Town of Korcula is surrounded by walls, and the streets are arranged in a herringbone pattern allowing free circulation of air but protecting against strong winds.

SPLIT

Location: Southern Croatia (Dalmatia)
Best time to travel: throughout the year
www.visitsplit.com

The Roman Emperor Diocletian had a palace built for the period following his abdication in 305. His retirement home near the Roman town of Salona covers an area of about 215 by 180 m (705 by 591 ft) and was fortified with battlement walls. Following the Avar and Slav incursion (615) some of the residents of Salona fled into the ruins of the ancient Roman palace, the grounds of which came to form the core of what is now Split.

The imperial apartments in the palace are accessed via an anteroom (right). The Riva marina promenade has a Mediterranean atmosphere (opposite).

Croatia

DUBROVNIK

Location: Southern Croatia (Dalmatia)
Best time to travel: throughout the year
www.dubrovnik-online.com
www.tzdubrovnik.hr

Dubrovnik was one of the most important centers of trade with the Eastern Mediterranean (the Levant) during the Middle Ages. Known at the time as Ragusa – Dubrovnik being its official name only since 1919 – the town successfully fended off claims in the 14th century by the Venetians and the Hungarians. Officially under Turkish rule as of 1525, it determined its own fate as a free republic up until the annexation of Dalmatia by Napoleon in 1809. Its mighty fortresses, with walls up to 6 m (20 ft) thick and 25 m (82 ft) high remain a testimony to its strength. Ragusa was a bastion of Humanism in its time and had a tremendous influence on Slavic literature and painting. It was here that Croatian developed as a literary language between the 15th and 17th centuries. The town was almost entirely destroyed by an earthquake in 1667, but large medieval buildings such as the Rector's Palace and the monastery have been renovated. Most of the structure and some of the interior decor of the cathedral were rebuilt in the baroque style.

With its old port and the fortress of Sveti Ivan, Dubrovnik (top) presents a breathtaking panorama. A stroll through the Old Town is especially atmospheric; left, a view of the pillared portico of the Sponza Palace on St Vlaho; right, lined with cafés, Lula Square is also the site of both the 31-m (103-ft) high clock tower, built in 1444, and the baroque church of St Blasius, Dubrovnik's patron saint, which was built between 1706 and 1715 to a design by Marino Gropelli.

Croatia

HVAR

Location: Island off southern Croatia (Dalmatia)
Best time to travel:
April–September
www.hvar.hr
www.hvarinfo.com

This long, narrow island is a sight to behold in the summer, in particular when the lavender is in bloom. The main road leads to Hvar, a truly romantic town with a main square lined with Venetian and Classical buildings. The 16th-century Croatian poet Petar Hektorovic lived in an attractive Renaissance castle in Stari Grad, the island's second town. This "old castle", is the main attraction in the peaceful little hamlet.

The Classical and Venetian designs of the loggia, cathedral, and arsenal in the town of Hvar lend it a romantic feel.

SIBENIK

Location: South-western Croatia (Dalmatia)
Best time to travel:
April–September
www.sibenik-tourism.hr
www.htz.hr

This attractive port is dominated by St Jacob's Cathedral. The architects who succeeded one another in the construction of the Cathedral – Francesco di Giacomo, Georgius Mathei Dalmaticus and Niccolò di Giovanni Fiorentino – developed a structure built entirely from stone and using unique construction techniques for the vaulting and the dome of the Cathedral: a technical masterpiece at the time. Construction was completed in 1505 by Bartolomeo and Giacomo dal Mestre.

The Cathedral of St James, the most important building in Sibenik.

MOSTAR

Location: Bosnia and Herzegovina (Herzegovina)
Best time to travel:
throughout the year
www.visitmostar.net

The capital of Herzegovina is an extraordinary example of multi-cultural urban life – but mainly as a result of the conflicts that this can cause. Mostar ("guardian of the bridge") derives its name from an old wooden bridge over the Neretva which was replaced in 1566 by a single-span bridge on the orders of the Sultan. Even today, most of the city's Christians live on the western side and the Muslims live on the eastern side, a division which was only cemented during the war which raged in Bosnia between 1992 and 1995. The Croats and Muslims initially joined forces against the Serbs at the beginning of the 1990s, governing the city jointly for about six months before declaring war on one another (1993–4). Bosnian Croat forces began shelling the bridge, and it collapsed in 1993; many other old buildings on the eastern, Bosnian side of the city were also badly damaged or destroyed. The reconstruction of the city was not to begin for another five years, supported by an huge international aid program which started in 1998.

Christianity and Islam face one another in Mostar in the form of the spire of the Franciscan church in the west and the minaret of a mosque on the eastern banks of the Neretva (top).
The Old Bridge over the Neretva (above) which was destroyed in 1993 was ceremonially reopened on 23 July 2004. It is particularly picturesque when it is illuminated at night.

Montenegro

BUDVA

Location: Montenegro
Best time to travel:
April–October
www.budva.com
www.discover-montenegro.com

According to Greek legend, Budva was founded more than 2,500 years ago by Kadmos – son of the Phoenician King Agenor and brother of Europa. Budva was destroyed in an earthquake in 1979, but has since been rebuilt in its original form. The oldest church in the town is the triple-naved Church of John the Baptist, which was founded in the 9th century.

Originally situated on an island, Budva is now connected to the mainland via a causeway. The picturesque historic Old Town is surrounded by impressive fortifications.

KOTOR

Location: Montenegro
Best time to travel:
April–October
www.discover-montenegro.com
www.visit-montenegro.com

Founded by ancient Greek colonists, Kotor and its large natural harbor once equaled Venice as a seafaring and trading town in the 13th and 14th centuries. With its seven islands, the bay sharing the town's name extends about 30 km (19 mi) inland and is considered to be one of the most beautiful along the Adriatic coast. Today, the town is still enclosed by an imposing, 5-km (3-mi) long wall with covered battlements that extend as far as the ruins of the Sveti Ivan fortress 250 m (820 ft) above the historic town center. The Romanesque Cathedral of St Tryphon (Sveti Tripun) was built in the 12th century but its twin tow-

SVETI STEFAN

Location: Island off Budva (Montenegro)
Best time to travel: April–October
www.montenegro.com
www.svetistefan.biz

Sveti Stefan lies in the middle section of the Budvanska Riviera. Dating back to the 15th century and initially built on an island to afford protection against pirates, this medieval fishing village is now a comfortable hotel town with around 250 beds. Its facilities also include a casino, and Sveti Stefan has often been called the "Monaco of the Adriatic".

Good things come in small packages (1.46 ha/4 acres). Much like Budva, Sveti Stefan is linked to the mainland by a short causeway; this luxury holiday resort has become the destination of choice for well-heeled visitors.

er façade was not completed until 1681. The Church of St Lucas (1195) is an early example of a religious building in the medieval Serbian Razka style. A number of palatial residences and patrician houses date from the Renaissance and baroque era in particular. Kotor's Old Town was destroyed in a devastating earthquake in 1979 and has since been reconstructed.

The beautiful bay at Kotor resembles a Norwegian fjord as it cuts deep into the Montenegrin coast. The limestone mountains here rise to a height of almost 2,000 m (6,600 ft) above sea level. The ancient seafaring town of Perast (left, the spire of St Nicholas' Church) stands on a narrow spit of land in the bay. A joyful pilgrimage by boat is conducted every July to the island of Gospa od Skrpjela (opposite).

Serbia / Kosovo

MEDIEVAL MONUMENTS IN KOSOVO, STUDENICA, SOPOÇANI

Location: Serbia/Kosovo
Best time to travel:
throughout the year
www.kosovo.net
www.serbiatouristguide.com
www.studenica.org
www.peja-komuna.org

Medieval Serbian art and architecture experienced its highpoint in the 14th century, but it grew up at the meeting-place of two cultures: Byzantium in the east and the Latin empire to the west. Many architectural gems from the period were built in the historic *Kosovo polje*, the "field of blackbirds", the largest of which is the five-naved, Romanesque and Gothic Pantokrator Basilica (1327–1335) in Visoki

Deaani Monastery. The place of the Palaiologan Renaissance, named after the Palaiologoi, the last dynasty of Byzantine emperors who reigned from 1259–1453), was established in Serbian painting by Michael Astrapas and Eutychios, the two court painters employed by Stephan Uro II Milutin; their masterpieces include the frescos in the monastery church at Gracanica. Studenica, lying hidden in a wood south-west of Kraljevo, was the scene of the first flourishing of the medieval Serbian "Raska" style of architecture. Only three of the original ten churches have survived, and of these, the single-naved Church of the Mother of God is the largest and the oldest (1183–1196). Its portals, windows, and mouldings

were carved by Benedictine monks and are largely Romanesque in style. The 12-sided crossing cupola is the work of Byzantine master craftsmen. The frescos, which were created between 1208 and 1209, are also of Byzantine origin, although further scenes were added in 1568. Few monuments now remain in the capital of the ancient Serbian homeland of Raska to the south of the modern town of Novi Pazar; Sopoçani Monastery to the west of Novi Pazar was dedicated as the burial place of King Stephan Uro I (reigned 1243–1276). The image of the death of St Mary painted here between 1263 and 1268 is one of the most artistically important frescos in churches built in the Raska style.

There are many representations of Mary the Mother of God in 14th-century Serbian and Byzantine iconography, including this one at Gracanica (left). Studenica was founded by the Serbian king Stephan Nemanja and was to become the largest Serbian Orthodox monastery complex. Its magnificent frescos include this Crucifixion of Christ (top right) on the west wall of the Church of the Mother of God. The church of the Holy Trinity in Sopoçani Monastery was destroyed at the end of the 17th century and restored after World War I. The largest fresco depicts the death and ascension of the Mother of God.

OHRID

Location: South-western Macedonia
Best time to travel:
April–September
www.ohrid.gov.mk
www.exploringmacedonia.com

Founded by the Illyrians as Lychnidos, the Romans were also quick to recognize the strategic position of the town that later would be called Ohrid. Situated on the Via Egnatia, the main arterial road between Byzantium and the Adriatic, the town quickly developed into an important staging post. The town became a Greek Orthodox bishop's see at the end of the 10th century as well as the imperial capital of the Bulgarian Czar Samuil for a spell. Subsequent Serbian rule under the auspices of Dushan was ended by the Ottomans in 1394, who then remained in Ohrid until 1913. The Church of St Sophia was built by Archbishop Leo in the 11th century. It was converted to a mosque by the Ottomans and lost its dome, bell tower, and interior galleries. The Church of St Clement houses the region's most valuable collection of icons. The historically protected Old Town boasts numerous Macedonian-style buildings of particular appeal.

The rather unusual fresco in a side cupola of the church in Naum monastery in Ohrid in Macedonia appears to show Jesus as the ruler of the world holding a child in his arms.

THE CHURCHES IN MOLDOVA

Location: Northern Romania
Best time to travel:
throughout the year
www.romanianmonasteries.org
www.manastiri-bucovina.go.ro

During the 15th and 16th centuries, Moldovan Prince Stephen III (Stephen the Great, 1457–1504), his successors and other high-ranking dignitaries founded some forty monasteries and churches in the north of the country around the capital Suceava. The exterior walls of the religious buildings in Humor, Voronet, Moldovita, Sucevita, and Arbore were painted up to their overhanging eaves. The tradition came to an end with the ornamental painting in Sucevita in around 1600. The probable intention was to provide an object of worship for the faithful for whom there was no room in the church. The images included legends of the saints, scenes from the Bible such as The Last Judgment, the genealogy of Jesus, and the Hymn to the Mother of God. There are also references to political events such as the siege of Constantinople by the "non-believers". The paintings in the church in Arbore date back to 1541 and are of particular artistic value.

The paintings in the churches (top, Voronet) brought the Christian content to ordinary people, who may not have understand the official Slavic language of the church.

Romania

THE DANUBE DELTA

Location: Eastern Romania
Best time to travel:
April–September
www.romaniatourism.com
www.visit-romania.ro

One of the highlights of a trip to Romania is an excursion through the Danube Delta. This mighty river divides into three main arms close to Tulcea, over 2,800 km (1,740 mi) from its source in Germany and almost 80 km (50 mi) before its estuary on the Black Sea coast. The three broad waterways encompass a wetland of around 4,500 sq km (1,737 sq mi), a unique ecosystem that is home to the world's largest cohesive reed cluster (over 800 sq km/309 sq mi). This vast network of waterways, backwaters, canals, lakes, islands, floodplain forests, and marshes is also home to a huge diversity of animals and plants. The mighty forests of oaks, willows and poplars are overgrown with lianas and creepers, an especially impressive sight. Water lilies and floating reed islands (Plaurs) cover vast expanses of the water. The diversity of the bird life is also particularly striking, with huge flocks of pelicans and cormorants, for example, and fish eagles and egrets – so rare elsewhere. Gliding slowly through the narrow channels in a boat or crossing one of the lakes is a wonderful experience. Only seldom do you get a glimpse of the reed-covered huts, which serve as seasonal homes for the fishermen, beekeepers, and reed cutters. A fishing village will occasionally crop up, typically inhabited by Romanians as well as Ukrainians and Lipovans, the descendants of 17th-century Russian immigrants.

The area surrounding the Danube delta as it flows into the Black Sea regularly floods with heavy rainfalls in spring.

Romania

BIERTAN

Location: Central Romania
(Transylvania)
Best time to travel:
April–September
www.biertan.ro

The Kirchenburgen fortress which
stands on a hill in the middle of
town here was the most impressive
building to be built in Transylvanian
Saxon territory at that time. It was
intended to protect the villagers
from any attack attempted by the
Turks, whose raiding parties were
advancing as far as Transylvania.
The fortified churches were built between the 14th and the 16th centuries and those in Biertan are particularly worth seeing.

**Biertan's fortified curtain walls,
towers, and particularly robust
church buildings are extremely
impressive.**

SIBIU

Location: Central Romania
(Transylvania)
Best time to travel:
throughout the year
www.turism.sibiu.ro
www.sibiu.ro

The fame of the venerable town of
Sibiu is due to its location at the
crossing-point of two long-distance
trade routes between the Banat and
Braflov, and Wallachia and northern
Transylvania. German colonists settled here in the 12th century, attracted by the fame of Gesa II, the king of
Hungary. Four km (2.4 mi) of triple
curtain wall fortified with five bas-
tions, four gatehouses, and 39 turrets
ensured that the town was never tak-
en by an enemy.

**The Romans settled at Sibiu, which
lies just beyond the confluence of
the Zibin and Olt rivers.**

SIGHISOARA

Location: Central Romania (Transylvania)
Best time to travel: throughout the year
www.sighisoara.com
www.romaniatourism.com

The old Saxon settlement of Schassburg, once an important trade and manufacturing center, was known as the "Pearl of Transylvania". The Old Town is one of the best-preserved architectural complexes in Romania. Sighisoara, which had been founded by immigrant German artisans and merchants, became the sixth of the seven seats of power in 12th-century Transylvania, and Schassburg is first documented as *Castrum Sex* in 1280. This flourishing commercial center in the Kokel valley was first incorporated as a town in 1367. The Old Town consists of about 150 well-preserved town houses, most of which date back to the 16th and 17th centuries. The landmark of the city is the Clock Tower, built in 1556. It is today a museum of history. Count Dracula, the world's most famous vampire, is said to have been born in Sighisoara. The inspiration for Bram Stoker's – purely fictitious – novel character was Vlad III, Prince of Wallachia (c. 1430–1476 or 1477), who received the nickname *Draculea* ("son of Dracul"). "Dracula's birth house" was built in the 17th century, but this should not detract unduly from the fame of the bloodthirsty count, whose impersonators have maintained a huge presence in films, television, and books to the present day.

The mighty clock tower of Sighisoara has become an iconic image of the town and was once part of the medieval defences of the Upper Town. The clockwork mechanism includes large 17th-century figures representing the seven days of the week.

Bulgaria

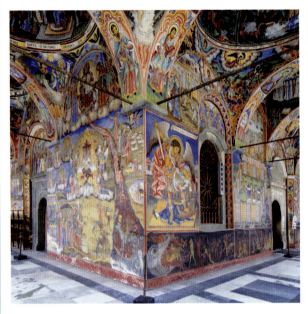

RILA

Location: South-western Bulgaria
Best time to travel:
throughout the year
www.rilanationalpark.org
www.bulgarianmonastery.com

It is traditionally thought that the monastery was founded by the hermit St. Ivan of Rila, whose name it bears, during the rule of Tsar Peter I (927–968). The hermit actually lived in a cave without any material possessions not far from the monastery's location, while the complex was built by his students, who came to the mountains to receive their education. Ever since its creation, the Rila Monastery has been supported and respected by the Bulgarian rulers. Large donations were made by almost every tsar of the Second Bulgarian Empire up until the Ottoman Conquest, making the monastery a cultural and spiritual centre of Bulgarian national consciousness that reached its apogee from the 12th to the 14th century. The Rila monastery fell into disrepair following Bulgaria's conquest by the Ottoman Empire. After being restored to its former glory between 1816 and 1862, it again became a cultural center and a "national sanctuary". The multi-storey monastery buildings surround an inner arcaded courtyard of 3,000 sq m (32,300 sq ft) and are overlooked by the five-storey Chreljo Tower (1335). The pride of the complex is the Nativity of the Virgin Church, a domed basilica with three naves, surrounded by an open colonnade. Both the exterior and the interior of the church are almost completely covered with frescos. The iconostasis is covered with carvings and icons of breathtaking beauty.

Pavel Ivonovitch, the builder of the monastery church (1834–1837) allowed himself the indulgence of alternating shades of stonework and a reversal of the usual order of the five cupolas. The Church of the Nativity of the Virgin, a triple-naved basilica with a crossing cupola, is surrounded by an open arcade.

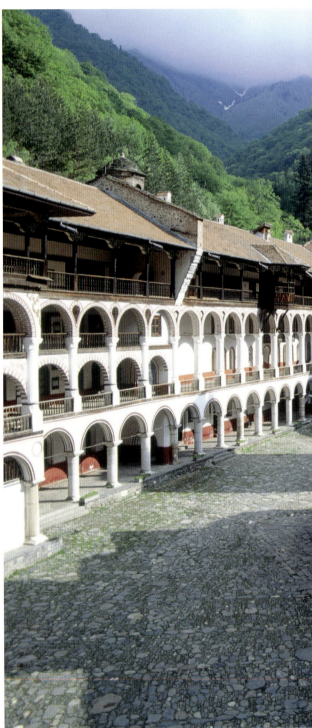

Bulgaria

PIRIN

Location: South-western Bulgaria/Northern Greece
Best time to travel: throughout the year (Ski season: October–April)
www.bulgariaski.com
www.visitbulgaria.net

The craggy landscape of the Pirin Mountains, which boasts 45 peaks above the 2,600 m (8,531 ft) mark, includes the national park of the same name. The park is dominated by Wichren, the third-highest mountain on the Balkan Peninsula at 2,914 m (9,561 ft). Characteristic of this limestone soil region are the approximately seventy glacial lakes – remnants of the last ice age – as well as the many waterfalls and caves. The diverse flora includes coniferous forests and many rare plant species, some of which, such as the Rumelian pine, are endemic. This pristine landscape is also home to endangered wolves and rare bird species.

The Pirin National Park has an area of about 270 sq km (104 sq mi) and an impressive variety of scenery. The national park encloses a number of different vegetation zones from beech forests to treeless meadows. The European brown bear has also found a habitat in this unspoilt landscape.

Bulgaria

NESSEBAR

Location: Eastern Bulgaria
Best time to travel:
throughout the year
www.nesebarinfo.com
www.nessebar.net

This ancient commercial center located on a narrow peninsula on the Black Sea coast is one of the oldest settlements in Europe. Thracian walls, a Greek town layout with an acropolis agora, various temples, and the ruins of medieval churches are all evidence of Nessebar's 3,000 years of history. Conquering Greeks in the 6th century BC took over Mesembria, which had been founded by the Thracians, and built fortifications here. In the shelter of these walls a flourishing trading center was to develop and attract the interest of a number of foreign powers; the city eventually fell to the Ottomans in 1371. There are still remnants of Greek, Roman, and Byzantine fortifications to be seen along the coast and near the port. Of the many churches built since the 5th century on the peninsula, which only measures 850 by 300 m (2,800 by 1,000 ft), only ten remain and most of these are ruins.

A number of houses from the 18th and 19th centuries have survived in Nessebar (top, a view of the port; right, the alternating courses of stone of the church of St John Aleiturgetos). The impressive frescos in the church of St Stephen (the New Metropolitan Church, above) cover an area of 600 sq m (6,500 sq ft). They date back to the 13th century.

Greece

ATHENS

Location: South-eastern Greece
(Attica)
Best time to travel:
throughout the year
www.cityofathens.gr
www.athensguide.org

Settlement on the fortress hill in
Athens can be traced back to the
New Stone Age. The former royal
fort was converted into a religious
site as far back as the 6th century
BC. After being destroyed by the Persians, the sanctuaries were quickly
rebuilt in the second half of the 5th
century BC. The image of Athens'
Acropolis is now dominated by the
Parthenon. This temple, built between 447 and 422 BC, was dedicated to the goddess of the city, Pallas
Athene. The structure is flanked by a
series of mighty columns with eight
across the ends and 17 along the
sides. The cult image of Athena once
adorned the interior of the temple,
the so-called Cella. The inside and
outside of the building were decorated with elaborate, three-dimensional marble statues, of which only
parts still exist today. The gable reliefs in the west, for example, depict
Athena's birth, while those in the
east illustrate her epic battle with
Poseidon. The Erechtheion, named
after the mythical king of Athens,
was built between 421 and 406 BC.
It is home to several religious sites,
which explains the unusual layout of
the complex. The structure is surrounded by three large porches; the
roof of the Caryatid Porch is supported by columns in the shape of
young women. The Propylaea are
the monumental gate complexes of
the walls surrounding the Acropolis.
They are considered the masterpiece
of architect Mnesikles and were
built between 437 and 432 BC. The
variety of column arrangements
here are remarkable. While the entire façade is Doric, slender Ionic
columns form a contrast in the cen-

tral passage. Kallikrates' temple of Athena Nike was built between 425 and 421 BC, and is one of the oldest remaining buildings in Ionic style. The small but elegant temple has porches on both the eastern and western side. The "Dimotikí Agora" market is over 100 years old and still the best address for fresh meat and fish. Although the products are now displayed in glass freezers and include everything from hen and sheep tongues to cow hearts and lamb cutlets, they are always artistically organized on their various shelves. Cheese, nut and olive dealers have their stalls outside while fruit, vegetable, sausages, and stockfish are traded on the opposite side of the road. Athens' most beautiful historic quarter is the Plaka, right below the Acropolis. You'll find eateries, small hotels and of course a slew of souvenir stores here among the stately neoclassical villas from the 19th century. Folklore is the focus in the music taverns of the steep "Odos Mnisikleous" alleyway. The merchant and handicrafts quarter, Psirrí, has become the hip place to be, but many artisans and merchants still pursue their trade here during the day.

The Parthenon (top) lies at the heart of the Acropolis in Athens and was designed by the famous sculptor Phydias at the command of the Athenian statesman and general Pericles. The main temple of the complex stands on a plateau created out of the piled-up rubble from a demolished Temple of Athene.
Far left: The Athenians worshiped a number of gods and heroes in the maze of the Erechtheion. The roof of the Caryatid Porch to the south is supported by six female figures. Left: The market halls of the Dimotiki Agora are open 24 hours a day and have become a hangout for night owls and early risers.

Greece

MT ATHOS

Location: North-eastern Greece (Chalkidikí Peninsula)
Best time to travel: throughout the year
www.mountathos.gr
www.inathos.gr

The first monastery was built on Mt Athos in 963, a holy mountain at the southern tip of the Chalcidice Peninsula. The monks' republic proclaimed here was declared autonomous as early as Byzantine times. Men under the age of 21 and women are still forbidden from entering. The monastery's quarters are currently inhabited by some 1,400 monks. Athos has been an important center of Orthodox Christianity since 1054. Over the centuries, its scope of activities also included some 3,000 farmers working for the monastery in the 14th century; at its height, the republic's estate covered around 20,000 hectares (49,420 acres). The Athos school of icon painting had a significant influence on Orthodox art history, and the typical monastery architecture left its mark in regions as far away as Russia. Each of the 20 main monasteries – 17 Greek, one Russian, one Serbian and one Bulgarian – has a Greek cross plan church in the center of the courtyard, with apses on three arms of the cross. Other buildings as well as the residential cells are located around the courtyard.

The fortress-like monastery of Moní Esfigmenou (opposite) is located on the very edge of the north-eastern coast of the Athos Peninsula. A miraculous icon is kept in the monastery chapel. This page: There are 20 large monasteries (top, Vatopediou, bottom, Hilandari) and 22 sketes (monastic communities) make up the monastic republic of Athos. The monastery church of the Romanian skete is particularly beautifully painted.

THESSALONIKI

Location: North-eastern Greece (Macedonia)
Best time to travel: throughout the year
www.thessaloniki.gr

Thessaloniki was founded by king Cassander of Macedon on the Thermaic Gulf, an inlet of the Aegean Sea, and the city has had a turbulent history. Macedonians, Romans, Byzantines, Ottomans, and Venetians have taken it in turns to rule here and all have left their architectural mark. The largest community of Sephardic Jews in Europe also lived here until their deportation in 1941. Christianity soon spread from Thessaloniki, as did the fame of the city's redoubtable early Christian and Byzantine fortifications. The late 5th-century mosaics in the Church of St Demetrius are one of the masterpieces of early Christian art, and those in the church of St David are of a similar quality. The dome of the Church of St Sophia which was rebuilt some time after 700, rests on a tambour (circular wall) featuring a row of windows. The Church of the Apostles was built between 1312 and 1315 and is also worth a visit.

A church was soon built on the site where St Demitrius was martyred by the Romans in 305 (opposite). This was replaced in the 5th century by a 55-m (180-ft) long basilica. After several fires, the church was rebuilt in 1917. This page: the Church of St Demetrius, one of the largest in Greece, is also a major pilgrimage site. The pilgrims come to see the Virgin Mary, who is depicted as the Mother of God in an icon which is decorated and brought out on special occasions (top). The markets have slightly more worldly preoccupations (middle and bottom).

METEORA

Location: Northern Greece (Macedonia)
Best time to travel: April–October
www.meteora-greece.com
www.gnto.gr

The name Meteora means "floating", which is a good description of the location where these monasteries are perched. The seemingly impossible Meteora formations soar out of the glacial valley of the Pinios like bizarre bowling pins. Hermits settled on the pillars in the 11th century, and a monk from Mount Athos founded the first of these rock monasteries in the 14th century. A total of 24 were eventually built. The Megalo Meteoro was founded by St Athanasios, Bishop of Alexandria, around 1360 and is the highest. The other monasteries were

subordinate to it after 1490. The walls of the St Nikolas Anapavsas Monastery, founded around 1388, rise up on one of the other high cliffs. The Varlaam Monastery, named after the hermit who had built a church here back in the 14th century, was completed in 1517. The Roussanou Monastery has recently been re-inhabited by nuns and looks like a smaller version of Varlaam with its octagonal church. Agia Triada, or Holy Trinity, was established as early as 1438 and is accessed via 130 steps.

At one time, the monasteries at Meteora could only be reached using rope ladders or pulleys. Steps and bridges have now been carved in the rock to make access easier.

Greece

SOUNION

Location: South-eastern Greece
(Attica)
Best time to travel: March–October
www.greeklandscapes.com
www.athensinfoguide.com

The Temple of Poseidon in Sounion, has 16 remaining Doric marble columns which still support the epistyle on which the temple's roof once rested. The location marks the southern border of Attika, which starts in the north near Egosthena at the Corinthian Gulf and Skala Oropou at the Southern Euboean Gulf. In ancient times, Attica was basically the bread basket of Athens' agricultural hinterland. Slaves labored and largely contributed to lay the foundations for Athens' wealth in the silver mines of Lavrio near Sounion. In the Demeter Sanctuary of the present-day industrial city of Elefsina, free citizens demanded better conditions for the afterlife by participating in a mysterious cult. In ancient times, the crews of Athenian war and trading ships thanked the temperamental god of the sea for their safe return at the Temple of Poseidon, which was partly decorated in gaudy colors. People hoped to be healed of illnesses, while pregnant women made pilgrimages to Brauron to ask for assistance from the Goddess Artemis.

The Temple of Poseidon built between 444 and 440 BC on Cape Sounion at the tip of the Attic Peninsula can be seen for miles around. Poseidon, Zeus' brother, was god of the sea and thus of great interest to adventurous seafarers, but his other siblings were also venerated in the Olympic pantheon: Hades ruled the underworld and the realm of the dead and sacrifices were made to the earth goddess Demeter to ensure a good harvest.

Greece

DELPHI

Location: Central Greece
Best time to travel:
March–October
www.greecetravel.com

Delphi is both an archaeological site and a modern town in Greece on the south-western spur of Mount Parnassus in the valley of Phocis. From the 8th century BC, Delphi was one of the most important shrines of ancient times. In the center of the holy district was a temple for Apollo where Pythia, a divine priestess, presided over the famous Oracle of Delphi. The Pythic Games took place every four years, with the musical and literary competitions held in the now well-preserved theater, and the athletic disciplines held in the stadium, located at the highest part of the sanctuary perched above the Corinthian Gulf. A large monastery was built east of Delphi in the 10th century. Its church is one of three places of worship in Greece whose magnificent mosaic decorations are largely preserved from that time, around the year 1100. Excavations of the ruins of the Temple of Apollo and the surrounding area began in 1892. The "Holy Road", which in ancient times would have been lined with precious votive offerings and treasure houses donated by the Greek city states, begins to the south-east of the shrine. The Road reaches a large ceremonial square beside the Hall of the Athenians before ending at the square in front of the Temple of Apollo in the middle of the complex.

Three of the Doric columns in the round temple of the 4th-century shrine to Athena Pronaia have been reconstructed.

EPIDAURUS

Location: Southern Greece (Peloponnese)
Best time to travel: March–October
www.ediakopto.gr

The complex of Epidaurus, located in a narrow valley in the far eastern expanses of the Peloponnese, spans several levels. It was of key importance to the cult of Asklepios, which spread throughout all of Greece in the 5th century BC. In Greek mythology, the god of medicine was the son of Apollo, whose powers of healing were also channeled through him. Epidaurus was an important religious town and a health resort at that time. The complex included a spa, clinic and even hospitals. Aside from the Temple of Asklepios, the most important monuments are the Temple of Artemis, the Tholos, the Enkoimeterion, and the Propylaea.

The most impressive example of classic Greek architecture in Epidaurus is the theater, dating back to the early 3rd century BC. It is the best-preserved building of its kind in Greece. The theater is marveled for its exceptional acoustics, which permit almost perfect intelligibility of unamplified spoken word from the proscenium to all 15,000 spectators, regardless of their location in the audience.

The seats are arranged around the circular *orchestra*, where the choir would have stood in performances in Antiquity. Only ruins remain of the stage buildings beyond, where the actors once stood to perform both tragedies and comedies. As is usual for Greek theaters, the view of the lush landscape is an integral part of the theater itself and was not to be obscured.

Greece

MYCENAE

Location: Southern Greece (Peloponnese)
Best time to travel: March–October
www.gnto.org

The Mycenaean culture, which dominated the entire eastern Mediterranean from the 15th to the 12th centuries BC, played an invaluable role in the development of classical Greece. Its name was taken from the Bronze Age fort, Mycenae, in the eastern Peloponnese. The region had been settled since 4,000 BC, but greater development did not start until the late Bronze Age. Most of the ruins of Mycenae uncovered by Heinrich Schliemann after 1874 date back to the 13th century BC and the mighty walls were built in three stages. Only the south-eastern aspect was deprived of a fortified wall as this side of the city had a

OLYMPIA

Location: Southern Greece (Peloponnese)
Best time to travel: March–October
www.gnto.org
www.greecetravel.com

An ancient document registers the name of the first winner of a track race in the Sanctuary of Zeus in Olympia in the year 776 BC, a date that has since been considered the date of the first Olympic Games. They were held every four years for over 1,350 years until a Byzantine emperor forbade them as heathen practices. Near the village of Olimbía, German archaeologists have been excavating the stately remains of this ancient cult district, including its sporting sites, for more than 100 years; the Olympic flame for the modern Olympic Games is always lit here at the Temple of Hera. Human occupation of Olympia

deep gorge as a natural defence. According to Greek tradition, the ancestral seat of the Atrides family was established by Perseus, son of the god Zeus. The main gate, commonly known as the "Lion's Gate", is impressive with a relief of two mighty – but now headless – lions and enormous blocks of stone forming the frame. Just behind that is the royal burial area where German archaeologist Heinrich Schliemann found the gold funeral mask of Agamemnon, who led the Greeks against Troy. The acropolis was excavated in 1902, and the surrounding hills have been methodically investigated by subsequent excavations.

The "Lion's Gate" (left) forms the entrance to the fortified section of Mycenae, the location where the archeologist Heinrich Schliemann discovered what is thought to be the death-mask of Agamemnon, the king of Mycenae (far left).

goes back to the 3rd century BC and there was a shrine dedicated to Pelops, the son of Tantalus, from the end of the 2nd century. The first excavations in Olympia were undertaken in 1875 and the religious sites here have revealed one of the greatest concentrations of art treasures ever discovered.

Olympia was first settled in prehistoric times and by the 10th century BC it had become a major religious center and the venue for the Games which were to bear its name. The Palaestra, a 3rd-century hall marked out by semi-fluted columns (far left), was a training area where athletes learnt wrestling, boxing, and jumping. There are three museums exhibiting masterpieces of ancient art and dealing with the sporting aspects of the Olympic Games in antiquity and the modern period. There is also the Nike of Paionios to admire (left).

Greece

ZÁKINTHOS

Location: Ionian island off western Greece.
Best time to travel: March–October
www.zakynthos.gr

The southernmost of the Ionic islands was once called "the Flower of the Levant" by the Venetians. With its cobbled streets and squares, arcades, and the free-standing church spires, the island capital still bears clear Venetian traces, although it had to be completely rebuilt after a severe earthquake in 1953. The wide Bay of Laganas, where giant sea turtles lay their eggs on the beaches, has been declared a marine national park. Liquid pitch, which was used to caulk boats until very recently, still wells up from the ground near Kerí.

Shipwreck Beach near Anafonitria can only be reached by boat.

CORFU

Location: Ionian island off western Greece.
Best time to travel: March–October
www.corfu.gr

Corfu, with more than 100,000 inhabitants, is the most densely populated island of the Ionic Archipelago. The villages have managed to retain much of their charm, and the island's capital is considered one of the most beautiful towns in Greece. Its Old Town quarter is towered over by the Old Fort and the spire of the Spyridon Church (far right). On the eastern side of Corfu, facing the Albanian and Greek mainland, the beaches are long, narrow, and pebbly. Sandy beaches line the northern coast of the island.

Rolling hills and beautiful coasts (right, Cape Drástis) are typical of Corfu.

Greece

MÁNI

Location: Southern Greece (Peloponnese)
Best time to travel: March–October
www.mani.org.gr

Lying amongst the foothills of the Taigetos mountains, Mani is one of the most contrasting areas of Greece; its northern half, still part of Messenia, is full of wide and beautiful olive groves with gnarled trees, and yet the southern half, in Laconia, is barren and inhospitable. The Ottomans had little interest in this "inner Mani" and local Greek culture was able to continue here relatively undisturbed in the Middle Ages. The many small chapels, often decorated with frescos, are indicative of the deep piety of the local population, and the fortified villages are signs of their warlike temperament and the tradition of "blood vengeance", which has carried through even into the 20th century. The only good beaches are at Kardamili in the "outer Mani" and the most arresting natural spectacle is the limestone cave at Spileon Dirou where you can take a boat trip on an underground river.

Vathia in the far south of the barren Mani is almost like a model village with its many stone towers. The houses were occupied up until a few decades ago, but Vathia's fortresses-like homes now lie abandonned.

MONEMVASSIA

Location: Southern Greece (Peloponnese)
Best time to travel: March–October
www.thereareplaces.com
www.goldacreestatesgreece.com

The island mountain of Monemvassia once belonged to the mainland but was separated from it by an earth-quake in 375. Its 100-m (330-ft) high cliffs now tower over the bay beyond the ancient trading port of Epidauros Limera. The cliffs are steep and forbidding and the island is connected to the mainland only by a bridge (Greek: mone embasis, "only access"); it was probably used as a place of retreat in the 6th century. The Venetians exported a fortified wine from here, which was known as Malvasia in Europe and Malmsey in England. Although the Old Town is overrun with tourists during the summer (as is its sister town of Gefyra on the mainland), the unique charms of this Greek island with its countless souvenir shops, a host of Byzantine churches, and a considerable number of good tavernas lining the little streets have also attracted the attention of the Athens scene, which stops here on its regular excursions to the Peloponnese.

The church of Agia Sofia has an incomparable location on the edge of a steep cliff and is not quite as ostentatious as its Turkish sister.

DAFNI, HOSIOS LUKAS, NEA MONI

Location: Central and southern Greece, island of Chios
Best time to travel: March–October
www.sacred-destinations.com
www.distomo.gr
www.chiosonline.gr

The church at Dafni near Athens is somewhat smaller than many churches and also has no galleries.

The walls are its most charming feature, with exquisite, well-preserved 11th-century mosaics. There are two churches at the monastery of Hosios Loukas near Delphi. The Theotokos, the smaller and older of these, was built around 1000, and the Katholicon – with its cross-shaped floor plan, crypt, and galleries – dates back to the early 11th century. The ornamental features of the interior – marble floor, mosaics, and frescos – have remained almost completely unharmed. Most of the precious mosaics depict monks and ascetics or depictions of the life of Christ. The monastery of Nea Moni on the island of Chios is also an 11th-century foundation, but the only original buildings remaining are the cistern, the refectory – which has been altered several times since – and a square tower to the south-east. Be sure not to miss the beautiful mosaics in evidence here.

Although the three Byzantine monasteries are separated by considerable distances, they are very similar in their construction. The mosaics are especially fascinating (above, Jesus as Ruler of the World at Dafni).

PATMOS

Location: Dodecanese island (eastern Aegean)
Best time to travel: March–October
www.patmos.com

The Monastery of St John the Theologian situated high above the Old Town of Patmos dates back to the early 11th-century. Although its current buildings were constructed in the 17th century, a Temple of Artemis once stood on the site in Classical antiquity. The inner courtyard with its well-preserved frescos, the library, and the items from the treasury exhibited in the monastery museum are all worth seeing. The treasured items on display include the 2-m (6.5-ft) long deeds of foundation of the Monastery of St John from 1088. The monastery was a pilgrimage site from that date on, forming the heart of a monastic state until the Turks took control of the island in the mid-16th century. The religious ceremonies held here have changed little since the time of the early Christians. The cave where St John is said to have written the Book of Revelation has been enlarged to form a church and the impressive frescos within it date back to the 12th century.

The Monastery Church of St John on Patmos lies just beyond a hall whose walls are decorated with 17th to 19th-century frescos. The paintings in the inner narthex date back to the 16th century (above, left and right). It was here St. John had his vision and this is why Patmos is sometimes called "The Jerusalem of the Aegean".

Greece

SANTORINI

Location: Island in the southern Aegean
Best time to travel:
March–October
www.santorini.gr
www.santorin.gr

Delicate bell towers and blue church domes are as much a feature of this island's scenery as its windmills and the cats that roam every street. Until some 3,600 years ago, a mighty volcano soared out of the sea here. When it erupted, only the edges of the island remained. The Aegean branched into the resulting crater and eventually people built quaint whitewashed villages on the more than 300-m (984-ft) high crater rim. The hamlets stretch far down the steep lava wall and use all available space for small terraces. Anyone who spends a few days here, or even just enjoys a sunset, will be spending time between heaven and earth. Santorini was already settled before the volcano erupted, and the island was circular and known as Strongili ("the round one"). The first settlers of any influence were the Minoans, who arrived here from Crete and whose civilization reached its climax some time around 2000 to 1600 BC. Merchants and sailors, who had their houses decorated with artistic murals, lived in a city near present-day Akrotiri. In 1967, archaeologists discovered it under a thick layer of ash and lava, and it is thought that the volcanic eruption could well have been responsible for putting an end to Minoan culture. The well preserved ruins are often compared to the spectacular ruins at Pompeii in Italy.

All of Santorini's towns and villages are located on the lip of the crater created by a volcanic eruption about 3,600 years ago. The Aegean flowed into the chasm created to form the archipelago.

Greece

DELOS

Location: Cyclades, Aegean Sea
Best time to travel:
March–October
http://you.travel/Cyclades

The island of Delos, near Mykonos, is one of the most important mythological, historical and archaeological sites in Greece. Settled since the 3rd century BC, the island first appeared in historical texts in the 14th century BC. It then became an important cult center and pilgrimage destination in the 7th century BC as the "birthplace" of the god Apollo. In the 5th century BC, the island was the focal point of the First Delian League, and later became an important trading site deemed useful by the Romans in the 2nd century BC. The emergence of new trading centers, pirate raids, and attacks by the soldiers of Mithridates of Pontos in the 1st century BC finally resulted in Delos' collapse. Excava-

tion work since has unearthed the ruins of numerous houses whose inhabitants had laid mosaics in their interior courtyards depicting different images such as dolphins, tigers and a variety of religious idols. The three temples of Apollo, reached via the Holy Road, are probably the simplest of all the sanctuaries dedicated to this god. To the west is the Artemision, the temple to Apollo's sister.

Above: the marble lions guarding Apollo's mythical birthplace have become an iconic image of Delos. Both the statues illustrated are to be found in Cleopatra's house.
Right: the House of Dionysus is a luxurious 2nd century private house on the island of Delos. This mosaic depicts Dionysus, the Greek god of wine, intoxication, and fertility, riding on a leopard whose collar is adorned with a wreath.

Greece

MYKONOS

Location: Cyclades, Aegean Sea
Best time to travel:
March–October
www.mykonos.gr
www.mykonos-web.com

One hundred years ago, admirers of Greek antiquities stayed on the Cyclades island of Mykonos and visited the sites of Apollo's cult on nearby Delos. They were also drawn here by the attractive hamlet of Chora, with its Old Town quarter. Artists and bohemians soon moved in. For fifty years now, the rich and beautiful of Europe have been frequenting Mykonos and, although the long beaches near town as well as those on the southern and south-eastern coast are often quite crowded, the largely treeless coasts and bays still boast long sections where you can still find yourself all alone. There are at least four museums worth visiting

CHIOS

Location: East Aegean island
Best time to travel: March–October
www.fragrant-chios.com
www.chiosonline.gr

The northern part of this island is the location of much of Greece's shipping industry, and many of the locals find jobs on the boats which sail from here. The south has been a source of the mastic tree for a thousand years; the resin from this tree is extremely valuable and is used in perfumes, incense, the production of lacquer, and even as chewing gum, as well as a flavouring for spirits and toothpastes. The Genoese were aware of the value of the product and built impregnable walls round the mastic farmers' villages.

In the lee of history: the blind poet Homer is said to have been born on Chios.

here as well: the Nautiko Moussio (which deals with seafaring since Minoan times), the Archaeological Museum, the Folklore Museum, and the House of Lena (with exhibits illustrating civilian life in the 19th century). The most unusual architectural gem on Mykonos is the Panagia Paraportiani church, which is situated behind the quay where the ferries to Delos dock, not far from the Venetian-style suburb of Chora. Additions have been made since the Middle Ages, merging oddly with one another under a multi-layered coat of whitewash.

"Cyclades" derives from *kyklos*, the Ancient Greek word for "ring" and means "ring islands"; the largest island in the chain is Naxos, which has also become a smart destination for the jet set (right, a view of the island's capital of the same name) in the morning light over the calm bay.

NAXOS

Location: Cyclades, Aegean Sea
Best time to travel: March–October
www.naxos.gr

The Portara, a monumental marble gate on the Palateia Peninsula north of the port, is the only remains of a giant temple project that had been planned to honor the god Apollo in the 6th century BC. Also revered in Naxos is a mountain grotto beneath Mt Zas ("Zas" is Modern Greek for Zeus), where Crete-born Zeus is said to have grown up. The Bronze Age culture of the Cyclades in the 3rd millennium BC saw the emergence of a special form of marble idols. The slender, usually female and often abstract figures range in scale from a few centimeters to life-size.

The Portara, which has become the symbol of Naxos, can be seen for miles around.

Greece

RHODES

Location: Dodecanese island
(Eastern Aegean)
Best time to travel: March–October
www.rhodos-info.de
www.rhodos-travel.com

The main island of the Dodecanese group, and Greece's fourth-largest island, has seen many a ruler come and go. The island fell under Macedonian hegemony during the time of Alexander the Great, before a spell of independence, and later rule by Byzantium. From 1310, Rhodes fell under the rule of the Order of St John, and then in 1523 under Ottoman control. The Turkish rule lasted until 1912, when Italy conquered the island and held on to it until 1943. It was not until 1948 that the island became part of Greece.

Rhodes was considered the property of the sun god Helios.

KARPATHOS

Location: Dodecanese island
(south-eastern Aegean)
Best time to travel: March–October
www.karpathos.org

The second-largest island of the Dodecanese is still very unspoilt. The whitewashed and pastel-colored houses, churches, and windmills of what is arguably Greece's most beautiful mountain village are nestled tightly onto a steep slope. The town of Olympos was founded in 1420 by inhabitants of the now orphaned neighboring island of Saria, and the ancient Vrykos, who sought protection from pirates in the mountains. Nowhere else in Greece has retained so much of its original culture thanks to the isolation of the island and its villages. The houses are built in the traditional style, the ancient Doric dialect is still spoken here, and the women still wear their tra-

SAMOS

Location: Sporades islands
Best time to travel:
March–October
www.greekisland.co.uk

Samos is the ninth most populous
Greek island. Samian wine was well-
known in antiquity, and is still
produced on the island. The tyrant
Polykrates built a temple to Hera on
the island in the 6th century BC –
legend has it that the wife (and sister) of Zeus, the father of the gods,
was born here. Another legendary
figure to hail from the island was the
famous mathematician and philosopher Pythagoras (c. 570 BC to after
510 BC). Samos has ferry connections to the Dodecanese, the Cyclades, and several other islands
nearby.

**Pythagorio is located on the south-
east coast of the island of Samos.**

ditional costume on an every-day
basis, not just for the traditional festivals. Bread is still baked in collec-
tive stone ovens, and centuries-old
customs live on. Naturally, tourism
helps to maintain these traditions
as visitors expect to experience this
rustic ambience. Indeed, the main
source of income today apart from
cattle breeding is tourism. All the
same, the festivals in Olympos are
colorful and celebrated with
real gusto, particularly the traditional Easter festival.

**From its remote position
Karpathos has preserved many
peculiarities of dress, customs
and dialect, the last resembling
those of Crete and Cyprus. No
other island in the Dodecanese
celebrates Easter in with as much
enthusiasm and attention to
traditional detail as the villagers
of Olympos, with their brightly
colored costumes.**

Greece

CRETE

Location: Crete (southern Aegean)
Best time to travel: March–October
www.culture.gr
www.crete-region.gr
www.explorecrete.com

Crete is roughly 260 km (162 mi) long and 60 km (37 mi) wide and situated between the Aegean and the Libyan Sea. Three mighty mountains, each of them over 2,000 m (6,562 ft), cut through the island and represent a continuation of the mountain range of the Peloponnese towards Asia Minor. Surrounded by a large wine-growing area, Heraklion, the vibrant capital, is home to a quarter of the island's population. It has long since expanded beyond the Old Town, whose ancient Venetian and Turkish walls have survived into the modern period; the marina, airport, industrial estates, administrative district, and university here ensure it is the undisputed center of the Cretan economy. German bombing during World War II and random attempts at regeneration have destroyed much of the city's ancient appearance. However, a few lone buildings, such as Venetian churches and fountains, are occasional evidence at least of its long history, and a fortress and some Venetian shipyards have been preserved down by the docks. Nikos Kazantzakis, the author of *Zorba the Greek* and probably Crete's most famous literary son, lies buried in the Martinengo Bastion in the city walls. This was where Europe's first civilization was created 4,000 years ago. The enigmatic Minoans were, for over 500 years, able to pacify the eastern Mediterranean and operate a flourishing trade with Egypt and the kingdoms of the Middle East. From 1900 to 1941, English archaeologist Sir Arthur Evans excavated the economic and religious center of the Minoans some 5 km (3 mi) south-east of the island capital at Knossos: a building complex

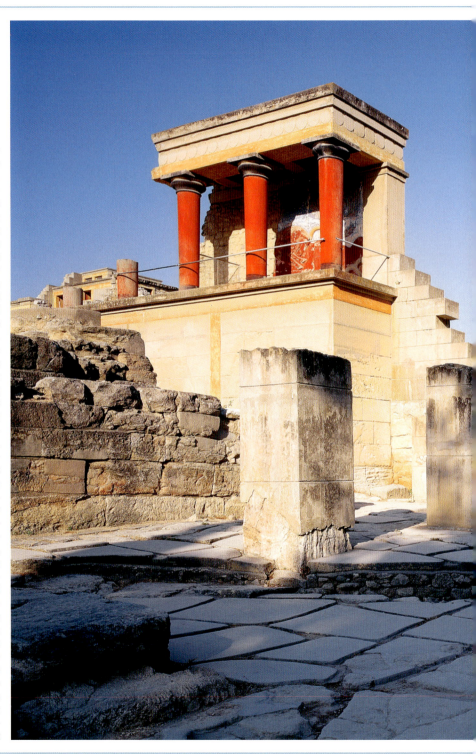

up to four stories high with 1,400 rooms and covering 20,000 sq m (215,200 sq ft). Many of the corridors and halls in Knossos were adorned with artistic frescoes. Drinking and sewage problems were solved with clever pipe systems. The Minoans also already had their own writing system. Western Crete is dwarfed by the 2,453-m (8,048-ft) summits of the Lefka Ori, the "White Mountains", which in winter form a snow-capped backdrop for Hania and Rethimno, the second- and third-largest towns on the island. There are four peninsulas here – the two lying furthest to the west are almost uninhabited – enclosing wide bays, with mountain slopes covered with olive groves and vineyards which gradually merge with the chestnut and coniferous forests higher up. The skyline of the Old Town of Rethimno is punctuated with the minarets of several mosques and the narrow streets of Hania radiate from palaces built by the Venetian aristocracy. Beaches that stretch as far as the eye can see can be found either side of Rethimno and to the west of Hania. The sandy shores near Falasarna on the west coast are lined with high dunes and the blue and turquoise hues of the shallow lagoon at Elafonisos are almost reminiscent of the South Pacific. Agios Nikolaos and Sitia in eastern Crete are the counterparts of Rethimno and Hania to the west. The coast further to the east is steep and rocky, and Sitia's only road connection to the west is less than 50 years old. The furthest eastern reaches feature rocky canyons, red sandstone, and the palm-fringed beaches at Vai.

Knossos (left) is considered the most important Minoan burial site. Detailed images of Cretan life in the late Bronze Age are provided on the walls of this palace. It was probably the ceremonial and political centre of the Minoan civilization and culture.

Turkey

ISTANBUL

Location: North-western Turkey
Best time to travel:
throughout the year
www.istanbul.com
www.istanbulcityguide.com

Its fairy-tale location would be enough to make Istanbul one of the most fascinating cities on earth. Situated on seven hills beside the straits of the Bosphorus, the meeting-place of Europe and Asia, this historic metropolis offers a wealth of sights lying between the Occident and Orient. A city of three names – Byzantium, Constantinople, and Istanbul – it is the legacy of two empires which led the fortunes of the Mediterranean for nigh on 2,000 years: the Eastern Roman or Byzantine Empire and its direct successor, the Ottoman Empire.

The Sultan Ahmed or Blue Mosque (right) has six minarets, an unusual number for a mosque. Legend has it that the minarets were initially intended to be covered with gold, but this would have exceeded the original budget, and so the builders intentionally misheard the Turkish word *alt'n* ("gold") as the number *alt* ("six"). Far right: another legend recalls how the population of Byzantium threw so much treasure into the harbor as they fled from the Ottomans that the water shone gold – and the "Golden Horn" (top, with the Galata Bridge and the Yeni Camii Mosque, completed in 1663) was born. The Hagia Sophia (middle), a masterpiece of Byzantine architecture, is no longer used as a place of worship but serves as a museum. The Hagia Sofia stood as the largest cathedral for more than a thousand years, until the completion of the Cathedral of Seville. The Great Bazaar (bottom) is the largest roofed bazaar in the world.

Turkey

PERGAMON

Location: Western Turkey
Best time to travel: March-October
www.tourismturkey.org
www.goturkey.com

Pergamon was an ancient Greek city in modern-day Turkey. The cliffs, soaring to heights of over 300 m (984 ft), were used by the rulers of Pergamon for their capital city's acropolis. The awe-inspiring Altar of Zeus is now actually housed in the Pergamon Museum in Berlin, but extensive remains of the royal city can also be seen on the original site and in the modern city of Bergama at the foot of the castle hill. The Temple of Emperor Trajan was completed by the emperor's successor, Hadrian, at the highest point of the ancient royal city.

The columns of the Trajaneum have been reconstructed on the acropolis at Pergamon.

MILETUS

Location: Western Turkey
Best time to travel:
March–October
www.kultur.gov.tr

Along with Ephesus and Priene, the ancient city of Miletus owes its wealth to sea trade, but had to be relocated several times due to the threat of silt buildup in the port. A field of ruins, with the mighty theater building, the agora, and the walls of the thermal baths has been preserved. Today, frogs and storks make their home in the compound, which was formerly the largest city in ancient Greece, a region that comprised some eighty daughter cities, where Thales, Anaximander and Anaximenes developed the basics of philosophy and mathematics.

The ancient and beautiful theater could accommodate up to 15,000 spectators.

EPHESUS

Location: Western Turkey
Best time to travel:
March–October
www.bodrumpages.com

This ancient city of ruins lies not far from the town of Selcuk. Long before Greek merchants and settlers arrived here, the Carians and Lydians considered it to be a holy place of the Goddess Kybele. In around AD 129, Ephesus became the capital of the Roman province of Asia and was home to an astounding 200,000 inhabitants. Archaeologists have been able to reconstruct more of this ancient city's temples, grand boulevards, baths, and residential dwellings than any other site in Turkey. Only the port has disappeared through centuries of silt deposits.

The majestic columns of the Celsus library.

PRIENE

Location: Western Turkey
Best time to travel: March–October
www.bodrumpages.com

Just like Miletus and Ephesus, the ancient city of Priene, located on the spectacular southern slope of the Mycale Mountain, was also a member of the mighty Ionian League, which was made up of 12 city-states and presumably founded sometime before the year 1000 BC. The city was created around 450 BC by master builder Hippodamus of Miletus. The Temple of Athena, built in the 4th century BC to honor the city's goddess, is considered a masterpiece of Ionian architecture, and Alexander the Great continued to fund the construction after capturing the city.

An authentic example of Hellenist city architecture: the ruins of Priene (left, the Temple of Athene).

BODRUM, TURKISH RIVIERA

Location: Western Turkey
Best time to travel:
March–October
www.bodrumpages.com
www.bodrumturkey.com

Lying in a bay on the Aegean Sea that resembles an amphitheater as it nestles between the foothills of the Taurus Mountains, Bodrum, stands on the site of the ancient Doric city of Halicarnassus – which once held the Mausoleum of Mausolos (375–353 BC), the ruler of ancient Caria. The ancient fortified city walls were destroyed in the 4th century BC as a result of Alexander the Great's devastating siege. Ancient Halicarnassus was also the birthplace of the "Father of History", Herodotus (c. 485–424 BC) and of Dionysus of Halicarnassus (c. 54– c. 8 AD), who has gone down in history as the greatest rhetorical speaker of the 1sr century BC. Herodotus' grandmother Artemisia I of Halicarnassus fought for the Persians in the sea battle at Salamis in 480 BC, outshining many of the men who stood alongside her, and her aggression and courage is said to have impressed even the great king Xerxes. The most important sight is the Castle of St Peter, built by the Hospitallers of St John in 1415. The Crusaders demolished the still impressive ruins of the Mausoleum to quarry stone for the castle, leading some archeologists to the conclusion that the mighty walls of the castle may well conceal complete friezes from the tomb, not unlike the Pergamon Altar. The castle is one of the last examples of Crusader architecture in the East. When Suleiman the Magnificent conquered Rhodes in 1523, Bodrum fell under Ottoman rule and the Knights of St John moved on to Malta. It is no great distance from the sun-kissed beaches of the Aegean to the Turkish Riviera, which is known as the Turquoise Coast because of the joy promised by the deep blue coloration of the water. Those who wish can hop aboard a gulet, one of the traditional local sailboats, and be ferried out for a picnic in one of the beautiful bays.

The castle (top) built by the Hospitallers of St John has become the iconic symbol of Bodrum, a white town set against a turquoise sea. The castle grounds includes a Museum of Underwater Archeology and hosts several cultural festivals throughout the year. The most popular holiday destination in the country is the Turkish Riviera (left, Olu Deniz bay near Fethiye is a perfect place for swimming). Fethiye is famous for its tomb monuments. The peninsula lying between Fethiye and Antalya was known as Lycia in earlier times.

Turkey

KAUNOS

Location: South-western Turkey
Best time to travel: March–October
www.kaunostours.com
www.marmaristown.com

The peculiar rock graves in the south-west of Turkey date back to the Lycians, an Indo-Germanic tribe who likely migrated here from Crete before the Greeks and settled between the modern cities of Fethiye and Antalya. Lycia's impressive funerary culture is still evidenced by the hundreds of tombs carved out of the local rocks and cliffs. The grave sites near the holiday resort of Dalyan on the river of the same name are particularly beautiful.

The monumental rows of graves on the eastern bank of the Dalyan were built in the 4th century BC for the citizens of the ancient city of Kaunos.

HIERAPOLIS

Location: South-western Turkey
Best time to travel: March–October
www.pamukkale.net

There have been settlements in the hot springs district of Pamukkale for thousands of years. The area was part of the Roman province of Asia in the 2nd century BC, and King Eumenes II of Pergamon had the city of Hierapolis built here in 190 BC. It was mainly planned as a fort complex. Along with the town came the construction of thermal baths, residential buildings, temples, a theater, as well as other Hellenic buildings.

The mountains above the modern-day resort of Pamukkale contain the ruins of the ancient Graeco-Roman settlement of Hierapolis with its city gates and paved main roads.

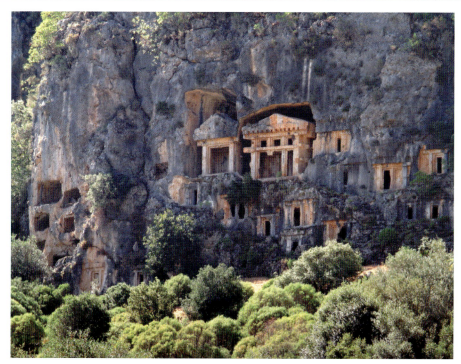

FETHIYE

Location: South-western Turkey
Best time to travel: March–October
www.fethiye.net

Modern Fethiye is a medium-sized agricultural town, with a large port on a sheltered bay, and a popular destination for boat and day trips. It was built on the ruins of the Lycian settlement of Telmessos, although little remains of of the old buildings. The Lycian rock graves, some of which date back to the 4th century BC, are certainly worth seeing. The Fethiye Museum, which is very rich in ancient and more recent artifacts, testifies to the successive chain of civilizations that existed in the area.

Fethiye is famous for its Lycian tombs hewn into the rock above the town. With their roofs, doors and protruding lintels, they are similar to Lycian homes.

Turkey

PAMUKKALE

Location: South-western Turkey
Best time to travel: March–October
www.pamukkale.net

and terrace-like basins, transforming Pamukkale into the surreal landscape you see today.

In addition to the remains of ancient buildings erected here until well into the 4th century, Pamukkale also has a magnificent and unusual natural spectacle to offer: hot springs which rise to a height of roughly 100 m (328 ft) from a ledge in the Cokelez Mountains and flow down into the valley. Over time, the sediments (sinter) of the water, which was very rich in minerals, have formed petrified waterfalls, forests of lime stalactites,

Pamukkale means "cotton fortress" or "cotton wool castle" and the name is a fitting description of the natural wonder that the limestone deposits from the hot springs have created here. The geothermally heated water, which also has healing properties, flows from one limestone basin to the next, at each stage giving rise to bizarre formations, which can be partly accessed by foot.

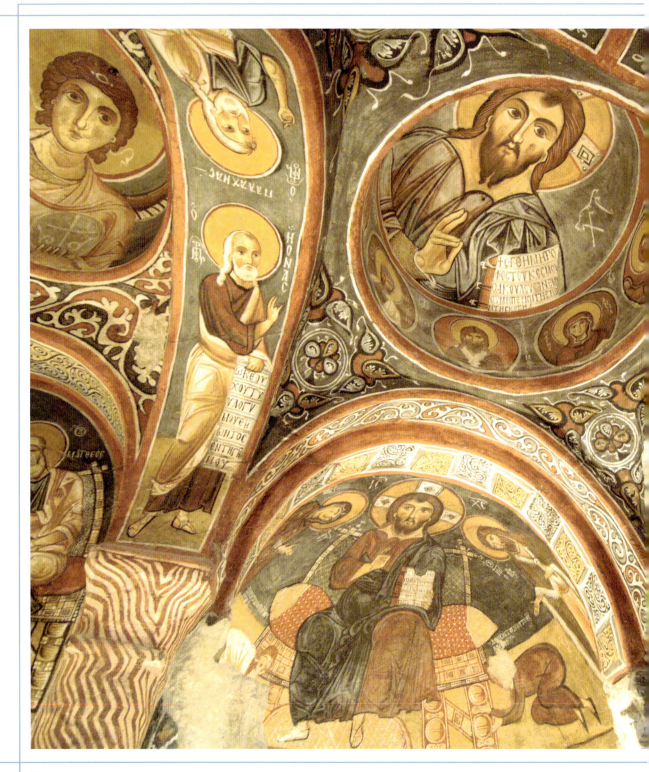

GOREME

Location: Central Turkey
Best time to travel:
March–October
www.fairychimney.com
www.goreme.org

The location of Goreme was first settled back in the Roman period. Christianity was then the prevailing religion in the region, which is evident from many rock churches that can still be seen today. Translated literally, Goreme means "thou shalt not go". This landscape of volcanic tuff rock stretches from the Kizilirmak ("red river") in the north to the underground cities of Kaymakli and Derinkuyu to the south. It seems incomprehensible to modern man that 1,000 years ago, people were able to excavate level after level of passageways and dwellings out of the sort rock here, to a depth of 85 m (280 ft), all to escape the attacking Muslims. Giant millstones closed the entrances to every level, air was admitted through narrow shafts, and water was drawn from cisterns. Ad-

vancing along the narrow corridors, visitors are able to explore Cappadocia's underworld here, but even the world above ground is not without its charms. The area comprises wide, verdant valleys and the abandoned stone chapels of early Christian hermits and monks, who copied the masons of their churches and painstakingly carved vaults and domes, arches and pillar capitals out of the local tuff – there are in excess of 150 examples.

The 11th-century Karanlik Kilise ("dark church", left) is famed for its frescos of Biblical scenes. The best artists of the late Byzantine period were brought from Constantinople to Cappadocia to paint this Greek cross plan church. Top: Cappadocia's scenery features bizarre tuff formations from which many cave dwellings and churches have been fashioned. These rocky spires are called "fairy chimneys" because of the caps of more resilient tuff stone that have formed.

Turkey

KONYA

Location: Central Turkey
Best time to travel:
March–October
www.konya.bel.tr

Medieval Crusaders were astonished to discover Konya was "as big as Cologne" as they entered the city. Its modern successor has wide boulevards and more green parks than all the other cities of inner Anatolia. The mosques and madrasas (teaching buildings) of this old Seljuk capital have enough beautiful carvings to satisfy any fan of historic architecture and sculpture. The Mevlana Tekkesi, a monastery of the Dervish order, has been a center of Mevlana worship for many centuries. The Hall of Huzuri Pir ("presence of the divine") is packed with visitors wishing to press their hands and lips to the sarcophagus of Jalal ad-Din Rumi and his closest followers. The founder of the order, who was born in Persia, taught for almost half a century in Konya and died there in 1273.

The Mevlana Monastery in Konya is now a museum but it has been the destination of pious pilgrims for centuries (left: the shrine of Jalal ad-Din Rumi, the founder of the order).
Far left: The Order of Whirling Dervishes, whose beliefs are based on the mystical and meditative teachings of Jalal ad-Din Rumi, was founded in Konya; his followers call him Mevlana ("Lord"), hence the name of the monastery. The striking bell-shaped white robes of the dervishes rise up as they whirl in their attempts to achieve ecstasy and draw closer to God. They dervishes hold their right hands in the air to receive God's blessing, and their left hands point downwards to pass this benefecence on to the world.

NEMRUT DAG

Location: Taurus Mountains, (South-eastern Turkey)
Best time to travel: March–September
www.nemrud.nl

After the collapse of the empire of Alexander the Great, Commagene, a small, independent empire which had arisen during the time of the Diadochi in the 3rd and 2nd centuries BC was ruled by King Antiochos I from 69 to 36 BC. During his lifetime, King Antiochos chose Nemrut Dag near the ancient city of Arsameia as his last resting place and, under his rule, he ordained that this little town in the south-east of modern-day Turkey's Taurus Mountains should be a religious site and the seat of the gods, as he considered himself to be a god incarnate. The ruins left by the Commagene culture were not rediscovered until the 19th century.

The monumental heads on Nemrut Dag unite the Greek and Persian roots of Commagene artistic thought. Greek influences were uppermost during the reign of Antiochos I, who was descended from Alexander the Great on his mother's side, as can be seen from the astonishingly naturalistic forms of the sculptures.

ISHAK PASA PALACE

Location: near Dogubeyazit (Eastern Turkey)
Best time to travel: March–September
www.goturkey.com

Situated in the remote mountains just a short distance to the south-east of Dogubeyazit, the giant complex of the Ishak Pasa Palace occupies a strategic location controlling the caravan traffic along the Silk Road. The palace was built between 1685 and 1784 at the orders of Çolak Abdi Pasa, the Kurdish emir of Dogubeyazit, and his son, Ishak Pasa II.

Built on a mountain slope 2,000 m (6,600 ft) above sea level, the complex had central heating, running water, and 366 rooms with a total floor area of 7,600 sq m (81,800 sq ft).

MT ARARAT

Location: Eastern Turkey
Best time to travel:
March–September
www.goturkey.com

At 5,165 m (16,950 ft) Mt Ararat is the highest mountain in Turkey. This extinct volcano actually has two summits – the smaller is 3,896 m (12,782 ft) high – and was first climbed by Friedrich Parrot in 1829. The expedition was led by Khachatur Abovian, the founder of modern Armenian literature. The ascent remains arduous to this day, and mountaineers need a permit from the ministry of tourism in Ankara.

"On the seventh day of the seventh month, the Ark settled in the mountains of Ararat", as the book of Genesis says of Noah's landfall after the devastating Flood.

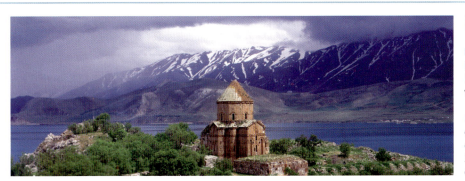

LAKE VAN

Location: Eastern Turkey
Best time to travel:
March–September
www.goturkey.com

Lake Van, which lies at an elevation of 1,600 m (5,250 ft) above sea level, has a total surface area of about 3,760 sq m (1,450 sq mi). The town of Van on its south-eastern shores was known as Tuspa 3,000 years ago and was the capital of the empire of Urartu, which was founded around 860 BC. The empire fought with Assyria and were known as skilled metalworkers and fortress-builders.

The little Armenian church built between 915 and 921 on the island of Akdamar is worth a visit. Peaks of up to 4,000 m (13,100 ft) surround the brackish waters of the lake, which can reach depths of up to 400 m (1,300 ft).

PAPHOS

Location: South-western Cyprus
Best time to travel:
March–September
www.zypern.org
www.visitpafos.com

This island state in the eastern Mediterranean has been thought of as the island of Aphrodite since she rose fully-formed from the waters here in ancient times, but Cyprus has far more to offer than love, fresh air, and long beaches. There is ancient art and culture in Paphos, or the barn-roofed churches and monasteries in the Troodos Mountains. Near the village of Kuklia to the southeast of the modern city of Paphos you will find the ruins of a town that was probably settled by the Phoenicians in the 12th or 13th century BC. A shrine to Aphrodite grew up here during Mycenean rule in the 12th century, and the ruins of the religious site in Old Paphos take the form of an oriental courtyard shrine constructed of giant blocks of limestone.

In the middle of the courtyard there was an oval stone symbolizing the goddess of love, beauty, and sensual desire. New Paphos was founded in the 4th century BC on the site of the modern city and here too there was a shrine to Aphrodite. The ruined city walls, burial sites, and several elaborate mosaics are evidence of the continuing importance of ancient Paphos as a trading center even into Roman times. Early Christianity and Byzantine culture also left major monuments here in the form of catacombs and churches, many of which have beautifully decorated interiors.

The Roman floor mosaic discovered in the House of Aion in 1962 illustrates the climax of the flute-playing competition between Apollo and Marsyas (left) as well as depicting a lyre-playing centaur paying court to a maenad (above). The mosaic floors of these elite villas are among the finest in the Eastern Mediterranean.

Cyprus

KYKKOS

Location: South-western Cyprus
Best time to travel:
March–September
www.kykkos-museum.cy.net

Kykkos Monastery is located near the town of Pedoulas. It is the most famous and also the mightiest monastery on Cyprus. It was founded by Alexios Komnenos toward the end of the 11th century, the Byzantine emperor who also donated his most precious treasure to the church: the fascinatiang and elaborate icon of St Mary painted by the Apostle Luke. Cyprus' first president, Archbishop Marakios III, who is buried in the nearby town of Throni, was a neophyte in the Kykkos Monastery during his younger years. The complex was completely burned down several times over the centuries. The ancient findings displayed in the monastery's museum are priceless antiques.

Kykkos is the oldest and most powerful monastery on the island.

ASINOU

Location: Northern Cyprus
Best time to travel:
March–September
www.visitcyprus.com

The Church of Our Lady of Asinou, or "Panagia Forviotissa", stands alone on a wooded hill near Nikitari. From the outside, it appears to be a simple facility, but inside it is home to what is probably the most amazing and beautiful Byzantine fresco treasure on the island. The *Last Supper*, *Annunciation* and *Nativity*, the *Vita Jesu* and dozens of pictures of martyrs illustrate the complete spectrum of exhilarating imagery from the Orthodox faith. Most of the murals date back to the 11th century. Some two-thirds of the frescos were painted between 1105 and 1106, just after the completion of the church; the monastery built at the same time has not survived the ages.

The beautiful frescos at Asinou have been painstakingly restored.

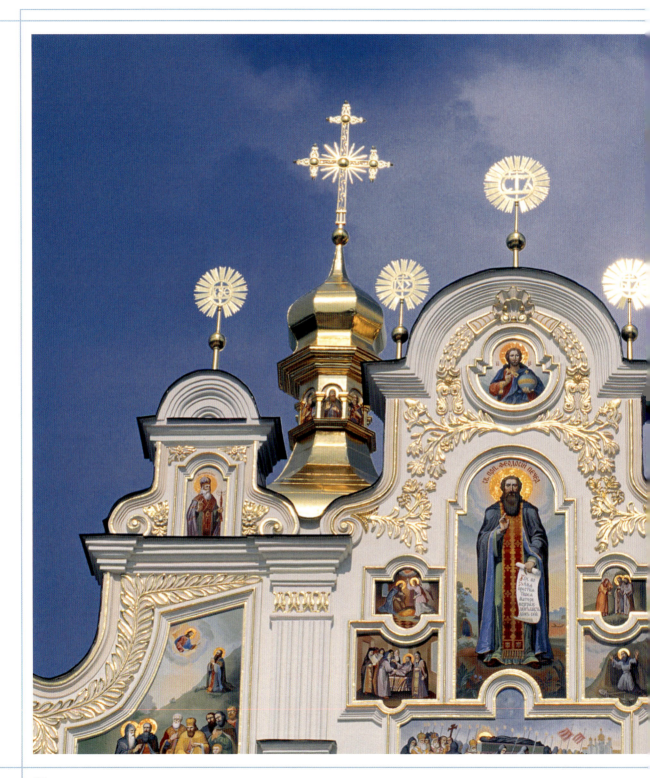

KIEV

Location: Northern Ukraine
Best time to travel:
throughout the year
www.kiev.info
www.traveltoukraine.org

Kiev was named after the city's alleged founder, Ki. The first official documented mention of the city dates back to 860. Yaroslav the Wise laid the foundation stone for the city's most important church, the St Sophia Cathedral, in 1037. The exterior of this, the oldest eastern Slavic church, is a highlight of Ukrainian baroque style, while the interior features a domed structure that exhibits Byzantine styles, with open galleries, gilded pillars, iconostases, as well as a number of wall paintings and frescoes. The church has 13 domes and originally comprised five naves with five adjoining apses. Extensive conversions over the course of time, however, have changed the cathedral's external appearance. With a width of 55 m (180 ft), a length of 37 m (121 ft) and a height of 29 m (95 ft), the interior has imposing dimensions and has retained its original Byzantine character. The 11th-century frescoes and mosaics depict scenes from the Gospel and portraits of the saints. The extensive gallery was once intended for the royal court. The Monastery of the Caves on the banks of the Dnieper was founded by hermits who submitted to a monastic regime in around 1050. Construction of permanent monastery buildings within the cave system began shortly thereafter. The caves subsequently served as tombs for these monks. While the damaged buildings above ground were redesigned and expanded in the 17th and 18th centuries, the caves have more or less remained in their original condition. Three of these 12th-century underground places of worship have survived to this day. The grandest effort in the monastery complex is the Dormition Cathedral, rebuilt after suffering war damage.

The St Sophia Cathedral (above) is the oldest eastern Slavic church of all. The hilly western banks of the Dnieper river are dominated by the domed towers of the Cave Monastery, and the Holy Dormition Cathedral (left).

Russia

MOSCOW

Location: Western Russia
Best time to travel:
throughout the year
http://mos.ru
www.moscow-city.ru

Russia's capital lies on the Moskva River, a tributary of the Volga. First mention was made of it in 1147, and by 1325 it had become a grand ducal residence. During the reign of Czar Peter the Great, Moscow lost its capital city status in 1713 to newly founded St Petersburg. It was the Bolsheviks who made Moscow the political center of Russia again in 1918. Over the course of its history the city has been plundered repeatedly as well as suffering devastating fires. At the beginning of the 20th century Moscow boasted 450 churches, 25 monasteries, and 800 charitable institutions. After the disintegration of the USSR, the metropolis still has an impressive cultural complement. For centuries, historical and political events in Russia have been inextricably linked to the Moscow Kremlin, seat of the czars and the metropolitan bishops since the 13th century. Architecturally speaking, the Kremlin had already attained its current size at the time of Grand Prince Ivan IV, known as Ivan the Terrible, who had himself crowned as czar in 1547. First mention of the city's defensive wall was documented in 1147; it was still a wooden construction until the 14th century. Ivan the Terrible gradually had the city walls and the numerous churches almost entirely rebuilt by the leading Italian and Russian master builders of the time, preferring to have more ostentatious and imposing buildings constructed in their place. These grand edifices were continuously expanded and remodeled until well into the 20th century. They now house priceless works of art. The Kremlin is still Russia's seat of government, for which the term

Russia

"Kremlin" is synonymous. Within its walls are magnificent palaces, armories, senate buildings, as well as cathedrals and churches with characteristic gilded domes. Red Square is roughly 500 by 150 m (1,640 by 492 ft) and was built at the end of the 15th century as a market and gathering place, in addition to its use as a place of execution. The famous St Basil's Cathedral was built by Ivan the Terrible after his victory over the Mongol Golden Horde. The cathedral, consecrated in 1561, is considered an outstanding masterpiece of Old Russian construction. The central, steepled church is surrounded by eight chapels on a single foundation and arranged in the shape of a cross. It was the addition of St Basil's Chapel that gave the whole complex its name. The central building with the pavilion roof is dominated by the nine differently designed chapels. At the time of its completion in 1893, GUM, which was designed as a marketplace and today houses one of the largest department stores in the world, was considered one of the most advanced buildings in Russia with its steel and glass roof. The architect Pomeranzev combined both Renaissance and traditional Russian architectural elements in the building, designing it as a shopping center.

The Kremlin in Moscow is composed of a whole collection of fortresses and church towers (opposite, top, the banks of the Moskva River).

The Church of the Deposition was built by Russian artisans between 1484 and 1485. Its ornate interior includes a beautiful 17th-century iconostasis (middle).

Red Square is surrounded by the Kremlin wall, St Basil's Cathedral (left) the GUM department store, and the Museum of History.

Russia / Lithuania

CURONIAN SPIT

Location: Western Russia/Southern Lithuania
Best time to travel: April–September
www.nerija.lt
www.welcome-to-lithuania.com

The Curonian Spit begins in Lesnoe, north of Kaliningrad, and ends shortly before the Lithuanian port of Klaipeda and the straits connecting the Baltic with the Curonian Lagoon behind the spit. The Russo-Lithuanian border runs down the middle of the peninsula. The Curonian Spit was created about 7,000 years ago as a sand bank, but man has since intervened and made drastic and far-reaching changes. The thick forests on the Spit were almost completely cut down in the 16th century, causing the sand on the seaward side to catch the wind and pile up on the lagoon side as dunes, which slowly advanced and engulfed whole villages. The dunes were only halted by a systematic program of tree-planting. The highest dunes are situated not far from the Russo-Lithuanian border. There are still traditional fishermen's cottages in the villages on the shores of the lagoon and many artists (such as Corinth, Pechstein, and Kirchner) have spent the summer in the principal town of Nida; Thomas Mann's summerhouse is now a museum.

The Curonian Spit, a narrow peninsula, 97 km (60 mi) long and surrounded by the Baltic to the west and the Curonian Lagoon to the east, has been nicknamed the "Sahara of the Baltic" for its 70-m (230-ft) high dunes. The cultural heritage of the Curonian Spit includes fishing villages of beautiful wooden cottages with roofs of thatch or red tiles (below, from left). The carvings decorating the gables are intended to ward off evil spirits.

Russia

ST PETERSBURG

Location: Western Russia
Best time to travel:
throughout the year
http://petersburgcity.com
www.saint-petersburg.com

After Czar Peter the Great had forced the Swedish King Charles XII to part with a strip of coastline along the Gulf of Finland, he finally gained his long-awaited access to the Baltic Sea, and thus to the West. He then built his new capital there, St Petersburg, which was intended to outmatch the splendor of other European cities. A great number of master architects and builders from Western and Central Europe such as Bartolomeo Rastrelli, Domenico Trezzini and Andreas Schlüter were involved in the construction of St Petersburg, a city that is particularly impressive with regard to the harmony created between its baroque and classical styles, grandiose squares, and numerous canals with more than 400 bridges. Nevsky Prospekt, St Petersburg's magnificent promenade, is lined with ostentatious buildings such as the Anitchkov and Stroganov Palaces. The Winter Palace is one of the most significant buildings in Russian baroque style. Begun in 1754 based on plans drawn up by Bartolomeo Rastrelli, it was intended as an imperial residence alongside the Neva River. The Winter Palace is the largest component of the Hermitage complex. The Hermitage is one of the most important art museums in the world. It comprises the Winter Palace, the Small, the New and the Old Hermitage, as well as the Hermitage Theater. The Hermitage art collection, which was started by Catherine the Great, is a museum of superlatives. The more than 1,000 magnificently designed rooms display around 60,000 exhibits, while the archive encompasses three million items. In addition to the archaeological section with ex-

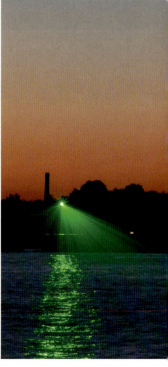

hibits dating back to antiquity, visitors can also enjoy a massive collection of classical European art. The Winter Palace owes its current design to Peter the Great's successor, Empress Elizabeth. In fact, the building where the Emperor died in 1725 – on the site that is now occupied by the Hermitage Theater – was torn down completely to make way for the new palace. The square in front of the Winter Palace with the Alexander Column has been the scene of key historical events. It was here that more than 1,000 demonstrators were murdered by czarist troops in 1905, and it was here that the October Revolution began in 1917, when the Bolsheviks stormed the grounds. The Peterhof residence was built in 1714. It has an ornately designed garden and is indubitably the most elegant of the imperial residences around St Petersburg. Particular attention was paid during its planning to sophisticated water features including decadent fountains for which special wells were built. The suburb of Lomonossov, once referred to as Oranienbaum, is home to an extensive complex of palaces and parks built for Prince Alexander Menshikov in the 18th century by Italian and German architects. It was later converted into a summer residence. The interior of this rococo palace boasts magnificent decor: furniture and parquet flooring of the finest wood, silk wall hangings, embroidery, porcelain vases and lacquer work as well as wall and ceiling paintings.

Left: the Winter Palace is one of the Russian baroque's finest creations. The Cathedral of St Peter and St Paul with its golden spire was built within the grounds of the fortress of the same name between 1712 and 1733. Opposite: middle, the Anichkov Bridge over the Fontanka; below, the Jordan Staircase in the Winter Palace; top, the interior of the Hermitage.

Russia

KIZHI POGOST

Location: Western Russia
Best time to travel:
April–September
http://kizhi.karelia.ru

The tiny island of Kizhi in Lake Onega provides an open-air museum of Russian architecture in wood: the two churches and a monumental bell tower here form a unique ensemble. The wooden Church of the Transfiguration, also known as the Preobrashensky Church, was built in 1714 without the use of a single nail and its 22 domes are proof of the immense skill of Russian joiners. The Church of the Intercession of the Virgin or Pokrov Church was built in the same manner in 1764, although its majestic octagonal bell tower only dates back to 1862. The churches share an impressively harmonious setting in the surrounding landscape. The historic buildings, which were completely dismantled and removed from their original sites and reassembled in the open-air museum, are a fascinating record of the development of Russian building techniques in wood over the centuries.

In both the Church of the Transfiguration (left) and the Church of the Intercession of the Virgin, an iconostasis, a wall adorned with many icons, and three doors separate the congregation from the altar, where the priests celebrate the mysteries of the sacraments.

THE GOLDEN RING

Location: Western Russia
Best time to travel:
April–September
www.visitrussia.com
www.vladimir-city.ru
www.museum.vladimir.ru
www.city-yar.ru
www.adm.yar.ru

The Golden Ring is the absolute zenith for fans of Old Russian art and architecture. The term Golden Ring, which was first coined in Russia at the start of the 1970s, refers to a ring of enchanting old towns north of Moscow. The main towns are Vladimir, Suzdal, Yaroslavl, Rostov Veliky, Sergiev Posad, Pereslavl-Za-lessky and Kostroma. What began in the Middle Ages as fortresses providing protection against the Mongolian hordes from Central Asia, have

since developed into a series of Old Russian towns with mighty kremlins, defensive monasteries and quaint churches whose magnificent mosaics, icons, and invaluable treasures stood in stark contrast to the misery of everyday life in these poor rural towns.

The term "golden" refers to the striking, gilded domes of the medieval churches (right, the Church of St Elias in Jaroslawl), and the word "ring" denotes the close cultural and historic ties that bind the individual towns. They stand as mute stone reminders of a bygone era – that of the "Old Russia" that existed up until the October Revolution of 1917, and until that time was a deeply religious nation.

Index

Index

Picture Credits

Abbreviations:
A = Alamy
Akg = akg Images
B = Bilderberg
C = Corbis
G =Getty Images
H =Bildagentur Huber
IB = The Image Bank
ifa = ifa-Bilderteam
JA = Jon Arnold Images Ltd
L = Laif
P = Premium
PC = Photographer's Choice
RH = Robert Harding
S = Schapowalow

p. 2/3 G/PC/Leanna Rathkelly, 4/5 A/Phil Degginger, 6/7 Zielske, 8/9 H/G.Simeone, 10/11 G/PC/Darrell Gulin, 12 t. a/JA, 12 b. C/Wolfgang Kaehler, 13 G/National Geographic/Paul Nicklen, 14/15 H/G. Simeone, 16/17 S, 18 t. A/Mikael Utterström, 18 b. G/IB/Harald Sund, 19 G/Arctic Images, 20/21 t. G/Panoramic Images, 20/21 b. G/Panoramic Images, 22 G/Nordic Photos/Thorsten Henn, 23 t. G/Nordic Photos/Johanes Long, 23 b. G/Photoica/Phillip Graybill, 24 Martin Schulte-Kellinghaus, 24/25 t. A/graficart.net, 24/25 b. H/Pinn, 25 L/Reiner Harscher, 26 Erich Spiegelhalter, 26/27 G/Taxi/Walter Bibikow, 27 H/Günther Gräfenhain, 28/29 alimdi.net/Christian Handl, 30 Erich Spiegelhalter, 30/31 t. S/Huber, 30/31 b. C/Carmen Redondo, 32 ifa/JA, 33 Reiner Harscher, 34 G/Stone/Arnulf Husmo, 34/35 Erich Spiegelhalter, 35 Erich Spiegelhalter, 36 Erich Spiegelhalter, 37 A/OJ_Photos, 38/39 A/Oyvind Martinsen, 39 t. A/Oyvind Martinsen, 39 M. A/Oyvind Martinsen, 39 b. A/Arco Images, 40 Fan/Achterberg, 41 Vario Images, 42 F1 online/Jan Byra, 43 G/Hans Strand, 44/45 t. G/PC/Warwick Sweeney, 44/45 b. ifa/IB/Jan Tove Johannson, 46/47 t. ifa/F. Chmura, 46/47 b. H/Günther Gräfenhain, 48/49 L/Riehle, 50 G/Johner, 51 A/JA, 52/53 t. B, 52/53 b. F1online/Johnér RF, 54/55 t. G/Altrendo Panoramic, 54/55 b. alimdi.net/Karsten Koch, 56 t. G/Riser/Hans Strand, 56 b. A/Blickwinkel, 57 t. A/Nigel Hicks, 57 b. A/blickwinkel, 58/59 L/Glaescher, 60 t. L/Kreuels, 60 b. G/Lonely Planet images/John Elk III, 61 t. G/PC/Greg Pease, 61 b. C/Phillip Gould, 62 mauritius images/ Jose Fuste Raga, 63 t. L/Raach, 63 b. L/Raach, 64/65 C/Jon Hicks, 66 G/IB/Guy Edwardes, 67 t. l. A/Blickwinkel, 67 t. r. A/Jef Maion/Nomads Land, 67 b. l. A/Interfoto pressebildagentur, 67 b. r. G/IB/Andy Rouse, 68

L/Galli, 68/69 A/imagebroker, 69 G/RH World Imagery/Jenny Pate, 70/71 G/RH World Imagery/Real Clark, 72/73 alimdi.net/White Star/Monica Gumm, 74/75 H/R Schmid, 76/77 Zielske, 78 H/Ripani Massimo, 78/79 A/Oleksandra Ivanchenko, 79 G/Panoramic Images, 80 t. S/RH, 80 b. A/David Noton Photography, 81 t. B/artur, 81 M. Zielske, 81 b. L/Kuerschner, 82 t. G/National Geographic/Richard Nowitz, 82 b. A/Guy Edwardes Photography, 83 t. B/Till Leesner, 83 b. A/Trevor Smithers ARPS, 84 Zielske, 84/85 Look/Holger Leue, 85 C/Massimo Listri, 86 t. A/David Chapman, 86 b. A/ImageState, 87 t. L/RAPHO, 87 b. L/Zielske, 88 G/IB/Guy Edwards, 88/89 A/Zuckermann, 89 Arco Images/ NPL, 90/91 G/Andrew Ward/Life File, 92 G/Stone/Travelpix Ltd, 93 Zielske, 94 Visum/Rezac, 94/95 A/AA World travel Library, 95 t. C/Michael Freeman, 95 b. Visum/rezac, 96 t. A/JA, 96 b. Mauritius images, 97 t. A/David Noble Photography, 97 b. l. Bildarchiv Monheim/Florian Monheim, 97 b. r. Look/Ingolf Pompe, 98 t. A/nagelestock.com, 98 b. L/Babovic, 98/99 A/Jon Gibbs, 99 A/PINK, 100/101 t. A/John Potter, 100/101 b. G/Panoramic Images, 102 G/Stone/ Mike Caldwell, 103 t. G/IB/Chris Simpson, 103 M. G/Iconica/Macduff Everton, 103 b. G/Stone/Chris Simpson, 104 t. G/Stone/Guy Edwardes, 104 b. A/RH Picture library Ltd, 105 t. G/digital Vision/Joe Cornish, 105 b. G/RH World Imagery/Lee Frost, 106 t. CW Images, 106 b. A/Ben Plewes, 107 t. A/Matt Bodwood, 107 b. A/Manor Photography, 108 A/Barrie Watts, 108/109 G/Panoramic Images, 109 l. A/David Noton Photography, 109 r. G/IB/Peter Adams, 110 t. A/The photolibrary Wales, 110 b. A/BL Images Ltd, 111 G/RH World Imagery/Roy Rainford, 112/113 L/Hartmut Krinitz, 114 t. Karl-Heinz Raach, 114 b. A/David Gowans, 115 A/Arco Images, 116/117 P, 118/119 Karl-Heinz Raach, 120/121 t. P, 120/121 b. P/ImageState, 122 t. L/Jörg Modrow, 122 b. ifa/Panstock, 123 Hartmut Krinitz, 124/125 P/Nägele, 126/127 P/ImageState, 128/129 L/Jörg Modrow, 130/131 t. A/Stephen Emerson, 130/131 b. P, 132/133 G/IB/Dennis Flaherty, 134/135 H/Massimo Ripani, 136/137 t. Zielske, 136/137 b. L/Zielske, 138 A/Christopher Hill Photographic/scenicireland. com, 139 G/PC/Tim Thompson, 140 t. P, 140 b. A/JA, 141 t. G/PC/Dennis Flaherty, 141 b. C/Richard Cummins, 142 t. Ernst Wrba, 142 b. ifa, 142/143 P, 143 t. P,

143 b. C/Richard Cummins, 144 t. ifa/JA, 144 b. C/Grehan, 145 B/Klaus D. Francke, 146/147 G/Digital Vision/ RH, 148 C/Dave Bartuff, 148/149 P/Pan.Images/Vladpans, 149 G/PC/ Frans Lemmens, 150 A/Bildarchiv Monheim, 150/151 S/RH, 151 C/Bill Ross, 152/153 t. P, 152/153 b. P, 154/ 155 A/nagelestock.com, 156 A/Imagina Photography, 157 L/hemis, 158/159 L/Zenit/Boening, 160/161 L/Meyer, 162 t. L/hemis, 162 b. l. L/hemis, 162 b. r. akg-images/Joseph Martin, 163 A/JA, 164 t. L/hemis, 164 b. B/Andrej Reiser, 165 L/hemis, 166 ifa/Panstock, 167 H/Simeone Huber, 168/169 A/David giral, 170/171 Bildarchiv Monheim, 172 t. A/JA, 172 b. P/Buss, 173 t. ifa/JA, 173 b. B/Thomas Ernsting, 174 L/Jonkmanns, 174/175 ifa/Panstock, 175 B/Thomas Ernsting, 176 L/hemis, 176/177 C/Vanni Archive, 177 L/hemis, 178/179 A/Peter Huggins, 180 t. Focus/Harf Zimmermann, 180 b. l. B/Berthold Steinhilber, 180 b. M. L/Kirchner, 180 b. r. L/hemis, 181 L/Kirchner, 182 L/Le Figaro Magazine, 183 t. l. L/hemis, 183 t. r. L/hemis, 183 b. l. L/hemis, 183 b. r. A/Jupiterimages/Agence Images, 184 Taxi/Bryan Peterson, 185 L/hemis, 186 t. L/Kürschner, 186 b. Biosphoto/Bousseaud Philippe, 187 t. Iris Kürschner, 187 b. A/Rod Edwards, 188 ifa/Panstock, 189 LOOK/Karl Johaentges, 190 t. ifa/Panstock, 190 b. G/IB/Jeremy Walker, 191 G/Time & Life Pictures/Denis Waugh, 192 t. l. B/Wolfgang Kunz, 192 t. r. B/Berthold Steinhilber, 192 b. L/Heeb, 193 t. Look/Jürgen Richter, 193 b. L/hemis, 194 G/Gallo Images/ travel Ink, 194/195 ifa/Panstock, 195 G/IB/Scott R. Barbour, 196 G/Riser/Art Wolf, 197 Visum/Cooperphotos, 198 G/IB/Werner Dieterich, 199 A/Images Etc Ltd, 200/201 t. L/hemis, 200/201 b. A/David Noton Photography, 202 t. L/hemis, 202 b. A/Andre Jenny, 203 t. L/Heeb, 203 b. A/dfwalls, 204 L/hemis, 205 P, 206 Visum/ASK, 207 L/hemis, 208/209 G/IB/David Madison, 210/ 211 G/PC/Peter Adams, 212 t. Jürgen Richter, 212 b. Jürgen Richter, 213 t. Jürgen Richter, 213 b. Jürgen Richter, 214/215 Bridgemanart, 216/217 G/IB/Allan Baxter, 218 G/IB/Luis Castaneda, 218/219 C/Jon Hicks, 220/221 C/Jon Hicks, 222 L/Piepenburg, 223 t. G/PC/David C. Tomlinson, 223 b. A/Cephas Picture Library, 224/225 Jürgen Richter, 226/227 H/Gräfenhain, 227 t. L/hemis, 227 b. G/Riser/Allan McPhall, 228 G/PC/Peter Adams, 228/229 White Star/Monica Gumm, 229 t. B/Frieder Blickle, 229 b. L/Raach, 230 L/Agence

VU/Navia, 230/231 t. A/David Zanzinger, 230/231 b. A/Ken Welsh, 231 L/hemis, 232 t. Visum/Bjoern Goettlicher, 232 b. A/Jordi Cami, 233 t. H/Dutton Colin, 233 b. Visum, 234/235 t. P, 234/235 b. Jürgen Richter, 236 A/look, 237 B/Felipe J. Alcoceba, 238/239 ifa/K. Welsh, 240 t. C/Abilio Lope, 240 b. G/PC/Marco Cristofori, 241 t. P/ImageState, 241 b. White Star/Jörg Steinert, 242 A/Jam World Images, 242/243 A/Alberto Paredes, 243 Visum/Bjoern Goettlicher, 244/245 P, 245 t. G/PC/Allan Baxter, 245 M. B/Ernsting Thomas, 245 b. Look/Sabine Lubenow, 246/247 G/IB/Allan Baxter, 247 L/hemis, 248/249 Look/Jürgen Richter, 250/251 ifa/Kanzler, 251 t. P, 251 b. ifa/Lescourret, 252 A/JA, 252/253 G/PC/Guy Vanderelst, 253 G/Stone/Robert Frerck, 254 t. P, 254 M. Martin Siepmann, 254 b. G/Stone/Manfred Mehlig, 254/255 G/IB/ Hans Strand, 256/257 Argus/Schwarzbach, 257 t. G/IB/Bruno Morandi, 257 M. H/Schmid, 257 b. A/Alandawsonphotography, 258 G/Taxi/Guy Vanderelst, 259 t. G/PC/Guy Vanderelst, 259 b. G/PC/Guy Vanderelst, 260 t. L/hemis, 260 b. C/Hans Georg Roth, 261 t. C/Godong/Fred de Noyelle, 261 b. B/Felipe J. Alcoceba, 262 L/Jonkmanns, 263 ifa/JA, 264/265 t. L/Zanettini, 264/265 b. L/hemis, 266 t. G/Riser/Ed Freeman, 266 b. G/IB/Davis McCardle, 267 t. G/Panoramic Images/Frerck, 267 b. B/Felipe J. Alcoceba, 268/269 C/Jose Fuste Raga, 270 l. Biosphoto/Borrero Juan, 270 r. Biosphoto/Borrero Juan, 270/271 A/photolocation 2, 272/273 A/Peter Mc Cabe, 274/275 t. G/PC/Guy Vanderelst, 274/275 b. G/PC/Siegfried Layda, 276 t. B/ Puschmann, 276 M. G/LOOK/Konrad Wothe, 276 b. P, 277 G/LOOK/Karl Johaentges, 278/279 Zielske, 280 G/IB/Siegfried Layda, 281 t. Wandmacher, 282/283 Klammet, 283 t. Zielske, 283 M. Bieker, 283 b. Böttcher, 284 t. Zielske, 284 b. F1 online/Steiner, 285 t. Zielske, 285 b. L/Zielske, 286 t. l. Wildlife, 286 t. r. Wildlife, 286 b. l. Wildlife, 286 b. r. Wildlife, 287 Zahn, 288/289 Zielske, 289 t. Zielske, 289 M. S, 289 b. Zielske, 290/291 L/Zenit/Boening, 292 l. Zielske, 292 r. L/Zielske, 293 L/Zielske, 294 L/Hahn, 295 t. G/Panoramic Images, 295 M. G/IB/Siegfried Layda, 295 b. G/IB/Wilfried Krecichwost, 296 L/Kirchner, 297 l. Zielske, 297 r. t. Zielske, 297 r. b. Zielske, 298 t. Zielske, 298 b. Westend 61/Mel Stuart, 298 b. L/Babovic, 299 L/Zielske, 300/301 B, 302 Zielske, 303 Zielske, 304/305 G, 305 t. G, 305 M.

Picture Credits

ifa, 305 b. L/Zenit/ Boening, 306/307 Zielske, 308 t. H, 308 b. H, 309 t. H/Schmid/Radelt, 309 b. H, 310 t. H, 310 M. H, 310 b. H, 310/311 H, 312 t. Bieker, 312 b. Bildarchiv Monheim/Florian Monheim, 313 t. Bieker, 313 b. Blickwinkel/N. Dautel, 314/315 C, 315 t. Bieker, 315 M. A/Rolf Richardson, 315 b. L/A. Hub, 316 t. Freyer, 316 b. transit/Thomas Haertrich, 317 t. Zielske, 317 b. Zielske, 318 t. B/Jörg Heimann, 318/319 L/Bialobrzeski, 319 B/Thomas Ernsting, 320 t. Klammet, 320 b. ifa/Stadler, 321 t. C/Richard T. Nowitz, 321 b. Zielske, 322/323 LOOK/Ingrid Firmhofer, 324 Klaes, 325 t. C/Zefa/Svenja-Foto, 325 b. G/LOOK/Ulli Seer, 326 Visum/Alfred Buellesbach, 327 t. A/mediacolors, 327 b. L/Kirchgessner, 328 Visum/Alfred Buellesbach, 328/ 329 G/Panoramic Images, 329 Visum/Alfred Buellesbach, 330 G/PC/ Dan Tucker, 331 t. A/mediacolors, 331 b. L/Specht, 332/333 L/Heeb, 333 t. F1 online/Prisma, 333 M. A/nagelestock. com, 333 b. A/JA, 334/335 mediacolors, 336/337 G/RH, 338/338 S/H, 339 t. G/IB/Hans Wolf, 339 M. A/Interfoto Pressebildagentur, 339 b. A/Wilmar Photography, 340 L/Kirchgessner, 340/341 t. L/Kirchner, 340/341 b. Iris Kürschner, 341 G/LOOK/Ingolf Pompe, 342/343 C/Zefa/Fridmar Damm, 343 t. Anzenberger/Yadid Levy, 343 b. Bildarchiv Monheim/Florian Monheim, 344 Bernd Ritschel, 345 Bernd Ritschel, 346 A/JA, 347 t. A/WoodyStock, 347 b. Mauritius images/photononstop, 348 t. S/H, 349 t. G/LOOK/Andreas Strauss, 349 b. G/Riser/Hans Peter Merten, 350 t. l. Arco Images/ Rolfes, 350 t. r. A/WoodyStock, 350 b. l. Arco Images/ Usher, 350 u .r. P/Schuyl/FLPA, 351 t. G/Altrende Panoramic, 351 b. L/hemis, 352 ifa/Lecom, 352/353 t. Das Fotoarchiv/Riedmiller, 352/353 b. ifa/JA, 353 A/ Bildarchiv Monheim, 354/355 t. H, 354/355 b. G/IB/Darryl Leniuk, 355 t. l. alimdi.net/C. Kosantezky, 355 t. r. Okapia, 355 b. G/IB/Walter Bibikow, 356 A/imagebroker, 357 t. F1 online/ Prisma, 357 b. H, 358 t. L/Kristensen, 358 b. G/PC/Guy Edwardes, 359 t. Vario Images, 359 b. A/Simon Reddy, 360 t. L/Bialobrzeski, 360 b. L/hemis, 361 t. L/hemis, 361 b. l. P, 361 b. r. G/Taxi/Peter Adams, 362 t. ifa/Alastor Photo, 362 b. L/Galli, 362/363 L/Galli, 363 t. akg/Erich Lessing, 363 b. B, 364 A/RH, 364/365 A/Blickwinkel, 366/367 t. G/PC/Elliott, 366/367 b. G/IB/ Macduff Everton, 368 t. Udo Bernhart, 368 b. l. L/Kuerschner, 368 b. r. L/Krinitz, 369 t. L/Galli, 369 M. L/Kreuels, 369 b. L/Standl, 370/371 t. G/LOOK/Jan Greune, 370/371 b. G/Panoramic Images, 372/373 t. NN, 372/373 b. G/IB/Andrea Pistolesi, 374 t. S, 374 b. Mauritius images/Rene Truffy, 375 l. L/Eid, 375 r. ifa/Aigner, 376 t. ifa/JA, 376 M. P, 376 b. G/Stone/travelpix Ltd., 377 L/Le Figaro Magazine, 378/379 P, 379 t. L/Zanettini, 379 M. P, 379 b. G/The Bridgeman Art Library/Leonardo da Vinci, 380 L/Eid, 380/381 L/Galli, 382/383 Axel M. Mosler, 384 t. G/IB/David Noton, 384 b. L/Kirchner, 385 t. L/Galli, 385 b. L/Zenit/Jan Peter Boening, 386 t. G/PC/Adrian Pope, 386 b. Ernst Wrba, 386/387 L/Celentano, 388 L/Amme, 388/389 t. L/Celentano, 388/389 b. L/Galli, 389 C/David Lees, 390 t. G/National Geographic/t. Louis Mazzatenta, 390 b. L/Celentano, 391 t. B, 391 M. G/RH World Imagery/Bruno Morandi, 391 b. Josef H. Neumann, Dortmund, 392/393 ifa/Aberham, 393 t. Gerhard P. Müller, 393 b. B, 394 t. G/IB/David Noton, 394 b. P/ImageState, 395 t. G/Taxi/David Noton, 395 M. Hubert Stadler, 395 b. P, 396 t. A/JA, 396 b. G/De Agostini, 397 t. G/PC/Peter Adams, 397 b. G/Photodisc/Stefano Stefani, 398 Bridgemanart, 398/399 C/Archivo Iconografico, 399 C/Araldo de Luca, 400 L/Zanettini, 400/401 L/Zanettini, 401 t. L/Eligio Paon, 401 b. L/Celentano, 402 L/Celentano, 402/403 C/Roger Ressmeyer, 402/403 b. L/Celentano, 403 C/Jodice, 404/405 P, 405 t. L/Celentano, 405 M. ifa/Harris, 405 b. A/LOOK/Hauke Dressler, 406 t. G/PC/Lorentz Guilachsen, 406 b. L/Galli, 407 L/Martin Sasse, 408/409 G/Massimo Sestini, 409 t. C/Jay Dickmann, 409 M. C/Jay Dickmann, 409 b. L/Heuer, 410 G/Stone/Duane Rieder, 410/411 L/Top, 411 t. L/Galli, 411 b. L/Harscher, 412/413 t. C/Everton, 412/413 b. A/Cubolmages srl, 413 Rainer Hackenberg, 414 t. L/Celentano, 414 M. L/hemis, 414 b. L/Galli, 414/415 G/IB/David Trood, 416/417 t. G/IB/Andrea Pistolesi, 416/417 b. L/Galli, 417 l. A/PCL, 417 r. A/Banana Pancake, 418/419 ifa, 420/421 L/Kirchner, 421 L/hemis, 422 L/Martin Kirchner, 423 L/Kirchgessner, 424 t. Jahreszeiten Verlag/Florian Bolk, 424 b. l. FAN/R. Hackenberg, 424 b. r. C/Jon Hicks, 425 H/Schmid, 426 Das Fotoarchiv/ Müller, 426/427 P, 427 A/David Sutherland, 428 LOOK/Florian Werner, 429 P/Buss, 430/431 Voller Ernst/Roland Marske, 431 Bildarchiv Monheim/Markus Hilbich, 432 akg/Erich Lessing, 432/433 G/IB/Siegfried Layda, 434 L/hemis, 435 mauritius images/Peter Widmann, 436/437 ifa/JA, 437 t. G/Taxi/Guy Vanderelst, 437 M. akg-images, 437 b. B/Madej, 438 t. A/Steven Minle, 438 b. alimdi.net/Egmont Strigl, 439 t. L/Henseler, 439 b. L/Henseler, 440 t. L/Westrich, 440 b. vario images, 441 t. C/Atlantide Phototravel, 441 M. C/Atlantide Phototravel, 441 b. C/Atlantide Phototravel, 442 t. l. S/Heaton, 442 t. r. S/Heaton, 442 b. C/Atlantide Phototravel, 443 t. S/Heaton, 443 b. B/Berthold Steinhilber, 444 A/Magdalena Rehova, 444/445 ifa/Strobl, 445 t. ifa/Strobl, 445 b. B/Karol Kallay, 446/447 H, 447 L/Kristensen, 448 t. A/imagebroker, 448 b. A/imagebroker, 449 l. A/Peter M. Wilson, 449 r. Bildarchiv Monheim, 450 t. H/Bäck, 450 b. l. Okapia, 450 b. r. Blickwinkel/M. Woike, 451 A/Cephas Picture Library, 452 S, 452/453 C/Jose Fuste Raga, 453 A/Peter Adams Photography, 454/455 Bildagentur Geduldig, 455 L/Kuerschner, 456 L/Zanettini, 456/457 L/hemis, 457 S/Sime, 458 L/Zanettini, 458/459 H/Johanna Huber, 459 L/Heuer, 460 t. L/hemis, 460 b. C/Rudy Sulgan, 461 t. Visum/Ilja C. Hendel, 461 b. Visum, 462 t. L/hemis, 462 b. H, 463 t. G/PC/Simeone Huber, 463 b. L/hemis, 464 l. A/Danita Delimont, 464 r. t. A/Diomedia, 464 r. b. A/Diomedia, 465 l. A/Sean Sprague, 465 r. A/JA, 466/467 Naturbildportal/Martin Zwick, 468 t. B/Angelika Jakob, 468 b. L/Kirchgessner, 469 Lonely Planet Images/Tim Hughes, 470 A/Nikreates, 470/471 mauritius images/age, 472/ 473 A/Miha Krofel, 473 t. A/Vladimir Alexeev, 473 b. Blickwinkel/M. Walch, 474 t. H/R. Schmid, 474 b. Transit/Tom Schulze, 474/475 FAN/R. Hackenberg, 476 l. akg, 476 r. G/AFP/Johannes Eisele, 476/477 C/P. Saloutos, 477 L/GAFF/ Adenis, 478 t. L/IML, 478 M. mauritius images/imagebroker, 478 b. L/IML, 478/479 L/IML, 480/481 L/Galli, 481 t. C/Reuters, 481 M. L/Zanettini, 481 b. L/Zanettini, 482/483 C/J. Hicks, 484/485 ifa/JA, 486 B, 487 G/DEA/A. Garozzo, 488 C/ A., 488/489 t. A/David Crossland, 488/489 b. B, 489 B/Angelika Jakob, 490/491 t. P/ Bunka, 490/491 b. L/Hilger, 491 L/IML, 492 P/imageState, 493 L/IML, 494 akg/ Erich Lessing, 495 l. A/terry harris just greece photo library, 495 r. A/terry harris just greece photo library, 496/497 L/hemis, 498 t. B, 498 b. L/IML, 498/499 A/JA, 500 L/IML, 500/ 501 G/Taxi/Maremagnum, 501 L/Harscher, 502 t. L/IML, 502 b. G/National Geographic/James L. Stanfield, 503 t. G/IB/Walter Bibikow, 503 b. L/Huber, 504/505 S, 506/507 P, 507 t. A/Paul Carstairs, 507 M. C/Atlantide, 507 b. B/Klaus Bossenmeyer, 508 t. A/John Farnham, 508 b. LOOK/Konrad Wothe, 509 t. A/Blaine Harrington III, 509 b. A/Images&Stories, 510/511 H/R. Schmid, 511 A/ImaesGap, 512 L/Müller, 512/513 S/RH, 513 A/Alan Novelli, 514 t. G/IB/Dario Mitidieri, 514 M. Caro/Riedmiller, 514 b. P, 514/515 G/RH World Imagery/Bruno Morandi, 516/517 Das Fotoarchiv/Manfred Vollmer, 517 Pictor, 518/519 G/AFP, 519 t. H/R. Schmid, 519 b. G/National Geographic/Martin Gray, 520 A/Paul Carstairs, 520/521 ifa/JA, 522 t. A1Pix/ SIP, 522 b. L/hemis, 523 t. B/Wolfgang Kunz, 523 M. A/Images&Stories, 523 b. L/Harscher, 524/525 B/Berthold Steinhilber, 525 B/Berthold Steinhilber, 526 L/Raach, 527 L, 528/529 ifa/JA, 529 mauritius images/Ferdinand Hollweck, 530 t. A/JA, 530 M. L/hemis, 530 b. L/Babovic, 530/531 ifa/JA, 532 S/H, 532/533 t. Voller Ernst/Roland Marske, 532/533 b. transit/Peter Hirth, 533 L/Babovic, 534 t. mauritius images/Ferdinand Hollweck, 534 M. L/Galli, 534 b. G/PC/Fotoworld, 534/ 535 t. G/National Geographic/Richard Durrance, 534/535 b. A/David Crossland, 536/537 H/Günter Gräfenhain, 537 C/Diego Lezama Orezzoli, 538 t. G/National Geographic/Dean Conger, 538 b. C/P. Turnley, 538/539 mauritius images.

Cover: M/Alamy

The publisher made every effort to find all of the copyright holders for the images herein. In some cases this was not possible. Any copyright holders are kindly asked to contact the publisher.

Imprint

MONACO BOOKS is an imprint of Verlag Wolfgang Kunth
© Verlag Wolfgang Kunth GmbH & Co.KG, Munich, 2010

For distribution please contact:

Monaco Books
c/o Verlag Wolfgang Kunth, Königinstr. 11
80539 München, Germany
Tel: (+49) 89 45 80 20 23
Fax: (+49) 89 45 80 20 21
info@kunth-verlag.de
www.monacobooks.com
www.kunth-verlag.de

Translation: Silva Editions Ltd., UK; Emily Plank; Katherine Taylor
Dtp: Robert Fischer (www.vrb-muenchen.de)

Printed in Slovakia

All facts have been researched to the best of our knowledge and with the outmost care. The editors and publishers are, however, unable to guarantee the absolute correctness and completeness of the information contained herein. The publisher is always grateful for any information and suggestions for improvement.